D0020925

The Silver King

Tangled Destinies: Latin America and the United States
— Don Coerver, TCU, and Linda Hall, University of New Mexico

Everyday Life and Politics in Nineteenth Century Mexico:
Men, Women, and War
—Mark Wasserman, Rutgers, The State University of New Jersey

Lives of the Bigamists:
Marriage, Family, and Community in Colonial Mexico
—Richard Boyer, Simon Fraser University

Andean Worlds: Indigenous History, Culture, and
Consciousness Under Spanish Rule, 1532–1825
—Kenneth J. Andrien, Ohio State University

The Mexican Revolution, 1910–1940
—Michael J. Gonzales, Northern Illinois University

Quito 1599: City and Colony in Transition
—Kris Lane, College of William and Mary

A Pest in the Land: New World Epidemics in a Global Perspective
— Suzanne Austin Alchon, University of Delaware

Argentina on the Couch: Psychiatry, State, and Society, 1880 to the Present
—Edited by Mariano Plotkin, University of Tres de Febrero, Argentina

SERIES ADVISORY EDITOR:
Lyman L. Johnson,
University of North Carolina at Charlotte

Frontispiece. Portrait of Pedro Romero de Terreros, first Count of Regla (1710–1781). Courtesy of Escuela de Estudios Hispanos Americanos, Sevilla.

The SILVER KING

The Remarkable Life of the Count of Regla in Colonial Mexico

EDITH BOORSTEIN COUTURIER

UNIVERSITY OF NEW MEXICO PRESS
ALBUQUERQUE

To Andy, Lance, Denise, John, Michelle,
and Anna Lisa Couturier,
who came together as a family shortly before
I decided to write about Pedro Romero Terreros
and the family he founded.

The University of New Mexico Press gratefully acknowledges
funding provided as a grant by the Program for the
Cultural Cooperation between the Spanish Ministry of Education,
Culture and Sports and the United States Universities.

© 2003 by the University of New Mexico Press
First edition
All rights reserved.

LIBRARY OF CONGRESS CATALOGING-IN-PUBLICATION DATA

Couturier, Edith Boorstein, 1929–
The silver king : the remarkable life of the Count of Regla
in colonial Mexico / Edith Boorstein Couturier.— 1st ed.
p. cm. — (Díalogos)
Includes bibliographical references and index.
ISBN 0-8263-2873-3 (cloth : alk. paper) — ISBN 0-8263-2874-1 (pbk. : alk. paper)
1. Romero de Terreros, Pedro, conde de Regla, 1710–1781.
2. Mexico—History—Spanish colony, 1540–1810.
3. Silver mines and mining—Mexico—Hidalgo (State)—History—18th century.
4. Charities—Mexico—History—18th century.
5. Businessmen—Mexico—Biography. 6. Philanthropists—Mexico—Biography.
7. Hidalgo (Mexico : State)—Biography. I. Title.
II. Díalogos (Albuquerque, N.M.)
F1231.R72C68 2003
972'.02'092—dc21
2003007853

DESIGN: Mina Yamashita

Table of Contents

LIST OF ILLUSTRATIONS

Acknowledgments

I have incurred many debts in the years of researching and writing this book, and I am grateful to those historians, archivists, friends, and family members whose assistance has made this enterprise possible. Various institutions and foundations have aided me. At the beginning of this project a year-long fellowship from the National Endowment for the Humanities permitted me to carry out research in Spain and Mexico. John Russell-Wood of the History Department at Johns Hopkins University made possible a visiting appointment in 1988–89. A teaching grant from the Fulbright Program facilitated continued research in Mexico, and grants from the Program for Cultural Cooperation between Spain's Ministry of Culture and United States' Universities and from the American Philosophical Society in 1995 allowed further research in Spain. During my time in Mexico under the Fulbright Program, I taught at the Universidad Ibero-Americana; I am grateful to students and colleagues there who showed interest in the lives of Mexican families in the past. While in Mexico, I delivered papers or taught courses at CIESA in Guadalajara, the School of Anthropology in Toluca, and the Colegio de México. I am grateful for help from Professors Leonor Correa, Cristina Torrales, Carmen Castañeda, and Guadalupe Jiménez Codinach, whose ideas during our times together in both Mexico and Washington, D.C. have been exceptionally stimulating.

A colleague and friend of particular note is Asunción Lavrin, who has been present almost from the beginning; she has been a source of companionship, encouragement, fun, and passion for history. She has patiently read almost everything I have written, including parts of this manuscript in its various permutations. Our work together on women's dowries and wills in colonial Puebla and Guadalajara provided me with essential knowledge about several hundred other families and gave a comparative perspective to this work. Dauril Alden lent support and encouragement to this project. Anna Macias's career as a historian began almost at the same time as mine, and her friendship, inquiring mind, and exacting historical standards have been a constant inspiration and challenge.

Joan Cunningham Zamora and Dr. Carlos Zamora frequently housed me in Mexico City and assisted in countless ways with this project, including arranging access to archives that usually did not accept researchers. Luba Eleen, Marcia Osofsky, and Joan Poole have read chapters of this book and provided valuable commentary. Jane Shumate and Anne Himmelfarb edited parts of this book; Linda Martz edited several versions; and the final version was examined by Marsha Orgeron. Beatrice Patt, William Willcox, Andy Couturier, Richard Ahlborn and Mary Karasch offered painstaking editorial and historical advice. David

Lavrin provided his knowledge and advice about computers. These individuals are among a special group of friends who have provided support throughout many years and across considerable distances. Others include Fred Bronner, Anne Chapman, Sally Hastings, James Riley, Harriet Tyson, Vicenta Cortés, Enriqueta Vila Villar, Anita Aguilar, Peggy Liss, and the late Dorothy Bilik.

I am grateful to members of the Romero de Terreros family, especially to Luis Romero de Terreros, who has continued the preservation of his family's archive and who permitted it to be preserved on microfiche. Juan Romero de Terreros and Carmen Fuente, a couple from Spain whose acquaintance I made in Washington, D.C. in 1998, visited sites of importance with me, and their interest and knowledge of the history of the Regla family have been unfailingly helpful.

I owe a great debt to archivists and librarians. The possibility of turning this family history into a biography of the founding father occurred when Belem Oviedo, the director of the Archivo Histórico de la Compañía Real del Monte y Pachuca, carried through the project of making microfiche copies of the archive of Manuel Romero de Terreros. I would like to thank the archivists of Archivo General de Indias, Archivo Histórico Nacional, Archivo General de Simancas, Museo Naval, and Archivo de Notarias in Cádiz and in Aracena, all of which are in Spain. I especially want to thank Antonio Fernández of Aracena for his special assistance in facilitating research. At the Hispanic Division of the Library of Congress, Georgette Dorn, Everette Larson, Dolores Martin, and Barbara Tenenbaum and the staff of the Handbook of Latin American Studies provided invaluable research help. I am indebted to Marisa Vargas, who searched through Archivo General de Indias documents in pursuit of material about later generations of the family, and Silvia Bravo, who undertook research in the Mexican notarial archives.

Various portions of this manuscript have been read at professional meetings. I am grateful to John TePaske and the Virginia Carolinas Georgia Colonial Latin American History Seminar, the Middle Atlantic Council of Latin American Studies, and the Washington Area Symposium on Latin American History, as well as the organizers of several meetings of the International Congresse of Mexican History for providing opportunities to read chapters and receive insightful comments. Marc Pachter and the Washington Biography Group have been a source of excellent ideas and cautions.

My family has offered encouragement and criticism over these many years. My parents made possible my career as a historian, and my brother, Allen Boorstein, often offered supportive counsel. My former husband, Jean Jacques Couturier, suffered through and delighted in our many family trips to Mexico, and his faith in my various projects continues to be a source of strength and sustenance. For those who have been important in the development of this project, and whose names I have neglected to mention, I hope you will forgive my faulty memory. All errors are mine.

Prologue: Ceremonies and Celebrations

In the last days of June 1756, Pedro Romero de Terreros, at the age of forty-six already a successful silver miner in Real del Monte, a mining center not far from Mexico City, celebrated his marriage to María Antonia Trebuestos, the youngest daughter of the countess of Miravalle. The wedding ceremonies lasted two days and included four processions through the streets of Mexico City. The groom and the bride's mother spent more than 50,000 pesos on clothing, jewelry, carriages, mules, household effects, and more ephemeral things such as elaborate decoration and food and drink.

The celebration of this joyous and extravagant wedding was very close chronologically to the pauper's burial of Isidro Rodríguez de Madrid, who had once walked among the powerful nobility of Mexico City. Don Isidro, Pedro Romero de Terreros's predecessor as the owner of mines in Real del Monte, was "buried by charity at the church of San Bernardo, having been only a few years ago the richest man in these kingdoms."[1] But mining was an unpredictable business in which men rarely both accumulated and retained wealth. The subsequent career of Pedro Romero de Terreros sometimes demonstrated the fragile line between success and failure that threatened those who sought great wealth from silver mines.

Individual rites of passage such as weddings and funerals were significant in the social and personal life of eighteenth-century Hispanic peoples. These rites—baptism, marriage, and death—represented only one aspect of a rich ceremonial life that also included celebrations such as processions, masquerades, jousting, and plays. The architectural design of Mexico's cities presented an ideal backdrop for these celebrations, with large public plazas and the elaborate decorated facades of churches providing space and setting for community life.[2] All social classes mingled at these events, but those with the greatest wealth, those wearing the most ornate clothing, occupied the principal places, commonly elevated above and separated from the masses.

Many years before his own wedding, Pedro Terreros probably witnessed one of the most impressive ceremonies in eighteenth-century Mexican history. For fifteen days in October 1738 the city of Querétaro, north of Mexico City, celebrated the completion of an aqueduct, one of the great public works of eighteenth-century America. The aqueduct provided much-needed water to institutions and individuals in the city of Querétaro, making it possible for the city to expand. At this defining point of Terreros's early life, when he was twenty-eight years old and already the administrator of a substantial mercantile business in this prosperous provincial city, such events offered a vision of potential future achievement and distinction

The desire to equal the works of other notable men drove the ambition of Terreros, the future count of Regla. One man he would have been anxious to emulate has sponsored the construction of the aqueduct and had been lauded in the celebration. This was the marqués de Villa Villar de Aguila, who, at the entreaties of the Capuchin nuns, led the city's effort to raise funds for an aqueduct.[3] The marqués organized the populace, personally pledged his fortune to the task, and obtained a bondsman to underwrite his agreement with the city to raise the additional funds needed to build the aqueduct. The nuns' desire for a secure source of potable water meshed with the needs of a city frustrated by frequent shortages and the necessity of bringing water by wagon and mule from a long distance to supply the demands of a growing city. The completion of this impressive task led to the fifteen-day ceremony that honored the marqués and his wife.

The eight-mile-long aqueduct, with its sixty-four stone arches, is as admirable and graceful today as when it was completed nearly three centuries ago. One of the orators in the 1738 celebrations boasted, "Querétaro does not need to envy Rome her fountains, needles, and obelisks, nor Memphis her pyramids so marvelous was the construction of the aqueduct."[4] This expression of civic pride was echoed by a friar who preached that "a city without water was like a soul without grace." Classical allusions to water, and particularly to Neptune, abound in the descriptions of these fifteen days, in the backdrops constructed for the production of plays, and in the fountains and basins used to collect the water that came from the aqueduct. Neither was the Old Testament neglected. Juan Caballero y Ocio, one of the men responsible with the marqués for the completion of the aqueduct, was compared with Moses, who struck a rock to supply his people with water.

The 1738 festivities presaged the importance of water in Terreros's life. Like so many mine owners before him, Terreros moved silver ore from his mines to an area some 20 miles east where water—an important component of the silver ore-refining process—was more plentiful. So significant did he consider his solution to the provisioning of water that when he first chose the noble title by which he would be known, the count of Regla, he added to it "en el Salto" (of the waterfall), after the original name of his hacienda where the silver ore was refined. Although water used in refining was essential to the success of Terreros's mining enterprise, its excess, in the form of underground water, threatened his mines through flooding of shafts. It was only as a result of enormous efforts that the mines were saved by the construction of drainage devices.

In selecting the profession of a silver miner, Terreros chose a labor-intensive industry, and he faced lifelong challenges in his treatment of labor. Terreros might have learned a valuable lesson about labor from one of the multitude of plays and floats executed by the various trades in 1738 for this festival of the aqueduct, if he had only heeded its message. The poet argued for the central importance of labor, reminding the audience in poetic form that

The Indians sow the fields;/ the Indians reap the wheat;/ the Indians make the bread./ Everything is done by the Indians./ In truth, if there were no Indians/ in these dominions, then/ there would be nothing at all,/ for they are the fifth element./ And so the world may know/ the great service they have performed/ in distributing the water,/ let this now be proclaimed for all to hear./ From beginning to end,/ they alone have been/ the ones who, with much travail,/ have brought water to the residents./ They dug the reservoir/ and, despite dire danger,/ they built the columns and arches,/ the wells, masonry and brickwork./ And though their work has been/ well paid, we must conclude that/ the cost would have been far greater/ had they not so faithfully labored.[5]

This narrative of the often cruel history of progress was the reality that most members of the elite paid little attention to, Terreros included. Pedro Terreros himself sometimes appeared to value laborers in the same way he valued mules, the chemicals for refining, the wood used to shore up the mines, and all the other elements on which he depended to produce silver. This poem offered an unusual, if fleeting, reminder of colonial Mexico's exploitation of native labor, but the festival was otherwise focused on the community's forward-moving prosperity.

As soon as Terreros had accumulated sufficient wealth, he began to organize public ceremonies himself. While a bachelor, he supplied dowries to young women entering convents and organized their entrance celebrations. We do not know with certainty that Terreros paid for the elaborate ceremonies and the expensive clothing and jewelry that sometimes accompanied a nun's entry into the convent, or if the ceremonies were more modest. However, the fact that Terreros's name was mentioned in the press as having sponsored and paid the dowry of nuns would indicate that some ceremony accompanied this charitable act.[6]

Legend has it that after the birth of his first son in 1761, Terreros paved the streets of Pachuca with silver in celebration. Certainly the baptismal ceremony, which was attended by high officials from Mexico City, would have been an elaborate one. In 1763 he sponsored and paid for yet another enormous celebration, this one in Pachuca for the coronation of Spain's Charles III. This event included bull fights as well as the consumption of vast quantities of food and wine. In 1775, Terreros sponsored a large ceremony held to open the Monte de Piedad, the large charitable lending institution that Terreros founded in Mexico City for pawning furniture, jewelry, and clothing.

It could hardly be imagined that a poor young man from an impoverished region of southern Spain would achieve such renown. But for his sponsorship of such festive events Terreros earned the frequent praise of Spanish officials, including the king and the high officials of the Council of the Indies. Ceremonies, such as that held in 1738 in Querétaro, gave Terreros a foretaste of the glory that he might encounter as he pursued his ambitions, which put ever-increasing distance from the relative poverty of his early years in Cortegana, Spain.

Introduction

*The web of our life is a mingled yarn, good and ill together; our
virtues would be proud, if our faults whipt them not, and our crimes
would despair, if they were not cherished by our virtues.*
—Shakespeare, "All's Well that Ends Well"

Around the figure of Pedro Romero de Terreros, the first count of Regla, who
lived in Mexico between 1728 and 1781, circle the issues of eighteenth-century
Mexican history, including some that persist to this day. Any student of his life is
brought face to face with the vast inequalities between rich and poor; the dis-
junction between the paltry rewards of the laboring masses and the wealth enjoyed
by the upper class; the relationship between individuals and the crown; and the
degree to which the exploitation of natural resources benefited the colony. Pedro
Terreros's life illustrates the complex rhythms of conflict and cooperation that
connected immigrant Spaniards and local-born elites. His life illuminates many
of the dilemmas of colonial history, providing a window on family life, business
practices, labor relations, and, therefore, the nature of colonial entrepreneurship.
His career demonstrates the growing social tensions of the eighteenth century
by dramatizing how Spanish immigrants could acquire fortunes and ascend to
the top of society. Terreros's life exemplifies the nature of entrepreneurship that
permitted such social climbing, while also shedding light on the rise and fall of
elite families in New Spain.

A contradictory and sometimes controversial figure, Pedro Terreros was a
mining entrepreneur, merchant, philanthropist, and founder of one of the great
fortunes of his day.[1] On the one hand, Terreros was hated by some workers, one
of whom called him a man of "terrible disposition and cruelty." On the other
hand, he won the title "Father of Orphans and the Destitute" and the admiration
of many for his philanthropies.[2]

Given Terreros's fame, fortune, and difficult nature, he has inspired many
biographers, who are divided in their opinions of him. The orator at his funeral
in 1782, Friar José Ruiz Cárdenas de Villafranco, suggested making a map of
his virtues, finding him to be both "simple and magnificent, humble and
pious."[3] He could often be found in a simple black suit working around his
mines, refining mills, and counting house. But he also possessed an enormous
wardrobe of rich clothing made from the most expensive fabrics by the finest
tailors. The juxtaposition of piety and generosity, aristocratic extravagance and
penny-pinching business practices, reveals much about him and also about
the conditions under which a successful entrepreneurial personality could
flourish in the eighteenth century.

In 1858 Terreros's great-grandson, Juan Ramón Romero de Terreros, published the first biography of the count of Regla. In it he praised his ancestor's "inexhaustible generosity," noting that it provided a "heroic contrast" to the "pernicious tendencies" of the nineteenth century, an age that might have viewed Pedro Romero de Terreros as "fabulous and even ridiculous."[4] An early twentieth-century commentator, José María Marroquí, in a slightly more thoughtful yet still celebratory description, suggested

> His greatness did not depend upon the size of his fortune, doubtless the greatest in New Spain since that of Hernán Cortés, nor on the munificence with which he assisted various pious establishments, of which there are many examples, . . .; what made the count of Regla a unique and extraordinary person, without equal before nor imitator since, the motive that impelled all his actions, was the limitless confidence that he had in Providence and the rapidity with which he executed the Divine Will without hesitation and even, we may say, without reflection.[5]

Two twentieth-century biographies continued the adulatory school. In 1943, Manuel Romero de Terreros, the sixth-generation of the family, wrote the first modern biography of his ancestor, calling him the Croesus of New Spain. His was a hagiographic and uncritical account, but it contains much material of great interest that renewed interest in the count's life.[6] Although writing in the middle of the twentieth-century, Don Manuel reflected some of the values of his illustrious predecessor, acquiring and using the title of marqués de San Francisco, one of the titles chosen by Pedro Terreros for one of his sons.

Alan Probert, a mining engineer and an administrator of the Compañía Real del Monte y Pachuca, the successor organization to Regla's mining properties, was the first and still the only professional miner to write about Regla. When the Mexican government nationalized the silver mines in 1948, Probert began to write history and genealogy. He collected documents in Mexico and Spain about the Terreros family and contributed this archive to the University of Texas at Austin.[7]

The birth of the field of labor history in Mexico in the mid-twentieth century also witnessed the emergence of a more critical perspective of Pedro Romero de Terreros's relations with his workers. In many respects his behavior was typical of the mine owners of his period, but Terreros seemed to have the capacity to provoke conflicts, and these conflicts led to strikes, violence, law suits, and complaints from workers. The stream of critical works, which questioned aspects of his personality and condemned his treatment of his workers, began with historian Luis Chávez Orozco's study. Chávez Orozco published a collection of documents called *Conflicto de Trabajo,* dealing with the work stoppages against Pedro Romero de Terreros in 1766 and 1767. The author describes Terreros as a greedy boss who operated his mines unjustly and possessed a "profound evil spirit that penetrated to the core of his being." He excoriated Terreros's "disgraceful pretensions" as well as his "avariciousness accompanied by vengeance."[8] Recently, historian Doris Ladd followed these judgments in a major work, *The Making of a Strike*, characterizing Terreros as "perhaps the greatest entrepreneur in Mexican colonial history" and concluding that he was a "great man and a dedicated and brave, if bad, boss." She also identified him as a "man of cold vengeance."[9] The most recent writer to assess negatively Regla is Agustín Ramos, an archivist and novelist who has written several accounts of the count of Regla after finding important archival materials that had eluded others.[10]

In the 1970s, several historians initiated a more neutral strand of commentary about the count of Regla. David Brading addresses Terreros's work and personality within a larger study of miners and merchants in eighteenth-century Mexico. He follows those scholars who see Regla as a successful entrepreneur, viewing him in a positive light as representative of eighteenth-century Spanish-born entrepreneurs. He seems to accept the judgment of a royal official who praised Regla for "undertaking and concluding a magnificent work at extraordinary cost because of his tenacity, vigor, constancy," and he also quotes José de Gálvez, the famous Spanish reformer, who called Regla the "restorer of his profession."[11] Robert Randall, in a history of the nineteenth-century British mining enterprise based on the company founded by Pedro Romero de Terreros, recounts some of the legendary tales about the amount of wealth drawn from the mines of Real del Monte and the flamboyant way in which Regla chose to spend it. Randall depicts Regla as an accomplished and masterful entrepreneur, whose labor troubles stemmed from the militancy of the workforce in Real del Monte.[12] Historian Doris Ladd's first book focuses on the Mexican nobility before independence. In this she characterizes Pedro Terreros as a "spectacularly successful business-man...[who] made one fortune in trade, another in mining, another in agriculture."[13] All these characterizations of the count of Regla underline his forceful personality and his significance for Mexican history.

The mythology of the count of Regla has been enlarged and expanded in part because his family has maintained its identity in Mexico until the present day. The family's longevity, and with it the renown of its founding father, derives from a succession of fortunate genealogical accidents that provided an adequate number of sons and daughters in each generation. The family's reputation also benefited from their inherited position on the governing board of the philanthropic organization founded by the count of Regla and, above all, from the conservation of an extraordinary archive that preserves the count of Regla's memory. Our knowledge of the count of Regla differs from our knowledge of other miners and merchants of his time because of the existence of this unique archive, which now constitutes one of the documentary treasures of colonial and early national

Mexico, and because of the family's strong sense of their place in Mexican history. Terreros himself began preserving the records of his mining company in 1750.

Pedro Terreros was also an indefatigable letter writer. The family archive includes account books and records of business affairs—purchases of slaves, land, titles to mines and real estate or land, and accounts of litigation. In about 1752, Terreros began to save letters that were written to him. A number of these letters have survived, as do some that predate his conscious attempts to preserve his own legacy. At various points, family members or employees organized these letters by correspondent into distinct volumes. One volume includes all the surviving letters from nuns; another the letters written to him by his wife and mother-in-law. Other documents considered of special importance to family history have been bound into hard leather bindings and bear the title of *First Count of Regla*. The second and third counts of Regla continued the collection, and the letters written to them are even more abundant.

This entire archive came to be stored in one of the haciendas belonging to a member of the fourth generation of the family. Sometime before 1918 Manuel Romero de Terreros retrieved and organized the documents in his Mexico City house. In 1939, a part of this collection was sold to Washington State University Library in Pullman, Washington, and entered the historical literature under the title *Papers of the Count of Regla*. However, much of this documentation concerns the families that intermarried with the Reglas, while only a small portion of it sheds light on the life of the count himself.

In the early 1990s, Luis Romero de Terreros, the son of Don Manuel, the preserver of the original archive, allowed the successor company that owns Regla's former mines—Compañía Real del Monte in Pachuca, Hidalgo—to make microfiche copies of the documents. It is regrettable that this archive contains only letters written to Regla and that few letters written by him remain in the collection, but reading even one side of the correspondence does illuminate much about the first count of Regla. No equivalent archives exist for other important eighteenth-century figures. The archive of a less politically important family, the Ireatas, is located at the Universidad Iberoamericana in Mexico City. This collection focuses on the end of the century and appears to be more limited in scope.[14] Another collection of letters written by Roque Yáñez, a Spanish bureaucrat residing in Mexico in the latter part of the eighteenth century, illustrates attitudes and experiences but lacks the dimensions of family and business that emerge so richly in the archives of Manuel Romero de Terreros.[15]

The Terreros legacy continues in contemporary Mexico. Mexicans who pawn their goods at the Monte de Piedad—a government-sponsored institution that lends money in exchange for objects of value such as jewelry and clothing—receive a pawn ticket that carries a portrait of Regla, which they retain until they redeem their property. (See Figure 1.) Both a street name in Mexico City and a

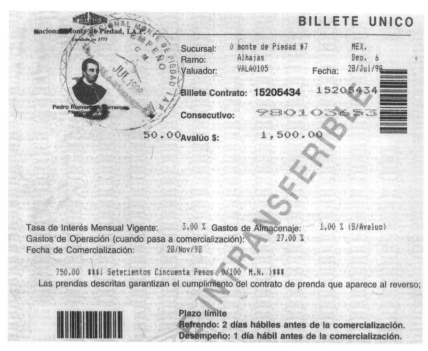

Fig. 1. Pawn ticket from the Monte de Piedad with portrait of the count of Regla, 1998.

colonia (a term used to denote a geographical subdivision) in the south of the city are called "Pedro Romero de Terreros," the name that he used until he became the count of Regla in 1769.

In this biography, I trace Pedro Romero de Terreros's family back to its origins in western Andalucía and to the city of Querétaro in Mexico. The cultural and political conditions of both early eighteenth-century Spain and Mexico, I argue, facilitated his career as a successful merchant and miner. I also examine how Regla began the daunting task of accumulating capital for investment in the silver mines, a step that allowed him to inch toward dominating the communities of Pachuca and Real del Monte. In telling the story of Terreros's remarkable life, this biography charts the ways in which he provoked strife even as he produced great wealth for the crown and rejuvenated the mining communities of Real del Monte and Pachuca.

The best documented section of Terreros life concerns his troubled relationships with mine workers. Traditionally, Mexican mine owners paid free workers with both currency and a portion of the ore-bearing rock that they took from the mines. Each laborer then sold his earned ore to independent refiners. In the count of Regla's efforts to dominate the mining industry, he attempted to change this custom as well as to reduce the wages of workers. He also made abundant use of his legal right to demand forced labor from surrounding

Indian communities. The law gave certain miners the right to demand that surrounding Indian communities supply workers who were paid at a lower rate than free workers and who could not leave the mines during their tour of duty. These tactics led to work stoppages and rebellions. The colonial government's policies in adjudicating these issues illustrate the crown's increasing tendency to repress labor rather than to mediate between conflicting interests.

The silver mines of Regla and other entrepreneurs enabled Spain to again play a role on the international scene, to expand its effective territorial control farther into the north (in the present United States), and to build impressive secular and religious buildings in Mexico. These achievements account in part for the modern view of the eighteenth century as a period of prosperity in Mexican history. However, this vision, as well as the contribution to economic development in Mexico made by these mining entrepreneurs, has been called into question by modern historians. Some historians argue that effects of the mining booms of the eighteenth century were injurious. These historians also point out that epidemics and famines dramatically affected the colony's population. Terreros's exploitation of labor occurred amid a rapidly growing population, resulting in a lowered standard of living.[16] The proximity between the rich owners of the mines and the poor laborers who made their profitability possible was an inescapable fact for Regla and those who worked for him. Regla, however, saw only the prosperity and good deeds deriving from his entrepreneurship. Through his work and "sleepless nights," frequently referred to in his correspondence, he believed that he had developed vast opportunities for the people of the mining region, contributed significantly to the spiritual life of his time, and fulfilled his religious obligation for charitable works.

The events of Regla's life touch on major issues in Mexican history, from the general use and abuse of labor in the mines throughout the eighteenth century to the 1767 expulsion of the Jesuits, who had been the wealthiest religious order in Mexico. Regla's life details the important functions of charity and religiosity in colonial Mexico, which helped to facilitate the colony's aggressive expansion to the north. Regla's career also sheds light on the relationship of *peninsulares* (those born in Spain) to creoles (local elites), which later developed into a deeper conflict during the protracted War of Independence between Spain and its colony, Mexico.

Regla's ideas and actions affected the decisions of eight different viceregal administrations spanning 1742 to 1782. His labor relations epitomized the conflict between those who produced and those who organized and supplied the capital for production, between the needs of different groups of local people and the demands of the Spanish government. His life also demonstrated how this member of the colony's wealthy elite elected to spend his fortune. His philanthropies ranged from interest-free loans to the Spanish government, dowries for nuns, and funds for missions and missionaries on the frontier, to the establishment of a philanthropic banking institution that enabled both the rich and poor to pawn their goods when in need of cash. He also spent lavishly on official and private celebrations, as well as on luxury objects for himself and his family.

There were four great international wars during Regla's lifetime, and each of these wars affected him. The first was the War of the Spanish Succession (1700–13), which ushered in a limited period of prosperity for his ancestral region in Spain thanks to the revival of the mercury and tin mines and to increased opportunities to trade with the colonies. The War of the Austrian Succession (1740–48), occurring when Regla was already established as a merchant in Mexico, aided the expansion of his mercantile business in Querétaro. The Seven Years War (1756–63) coincided with a period of prosperity for Regla and influenced events both in his own life and in colonial Mexico. Shortly after the onset of the American Revolution, 1776–83, in which Spain would ally with the American colonists, he contributed an eighty-cannon battleship, the *Count of Regla*, to the Spanish fleet.

This biography is also concerned with family history. Letters written to Regla by his wife and mother-in-law constitute a unique record about the life of an upper-class family. Health, childbirth, travel, luxury spending, and relations between husband and wife are all discussed. Other sources enlighten us about Regla's decisions on how to educate his sons and daughters, the kinds of property to leave to his children, and how to preserve the family fortune into the future. While most other wealthy Mexican families of the era requested one noble title and one entail, Regla requested and received three noble titles and the entails to accompany them. His decisions to not arrange the marriage of any of his daughters or to not place any of them in convents was unusual among members of the nobility. Exploring the reasons for these decisions illuminates crucial aspects of elite family history.

The field of family history emerged in early 1970s as a branch of social history. Historians began to examine a whole range of questions, including the duration and longevity of families and individuals, matrimonial strategies, the ways in which the family transmits culture, inheritance laws and customs, the organization of households, and the nature of business enterprises. These issues both inspired me and, as I found, constituted the experience of the Regla family. Given the Regla family's importance and the richness of the material that has surfaced in public archives, a detailed history of their family seems tenable.

The count of Regla's life kept intruding on my academic interests. When I began to do research for my dissertation on the history of debt peonage and labor systems in nineteenth-century Mexico, I saw a collection of papers that had originated from the haciendas of the Regla family. The hacienda on which I focused my dissertation had been owned by the Regla family for nearly a century. While the bulk of my dissertation concerned the agricultural changes of the late nineteenth century and agrarian reform, the notion of further exploring the history of the families that had possessed haciendas occurred to me as a project of special interest.

The Regla family seemed an especially important case study as material about them surfaced in easily accessible public archives. My expectations were not disappointed, and except for the count of Regla's propensity to scatter his business records in the files of many different notaries in Mexico City, the archival materials proved to be abundant. Through the fortunate intervention of a friend, I received permission to use the archive of the family in Mexico City and many of my future academic and personal concerns in the intervening years stemmed from my expanding knowledge about the count of Regla and his family. My research in the history of family, women, and philanthropy continued to touch on his life. During my years as a program officer at the National Endowment for the Humanities, I often had cause to speculate about both bureaucracy and philanthropy–issues that also dogged one aspect of the life of the count of Regla.

Biographers lament how difficult it is to make another human being come alive on pages that depend on necessarily limited sources. There was much about Regla's personality that was difficult to understand, such as his faithful Franciscan religiosity—which emphasized love, charity, and conversion—combined with his cutthroat ambition; his parsimoniousness and his generosity; his bravery coupled with his fears of assassination; his pertinacity and his flexibility; his grandiosity and his modesty. Regla was a complex man who was both much-loved and much-hated. His tremendous aspirations, ceaseless work, exceptional talents, and great good fortune render him a towering figure in his own time. I have often wondered how I, a middle-class academic woman, could possibly understand the life of an ambitious, power-hungry, strong-minded man such as Pedro Romero de Terreros. It seemed as though the archive that he established formed our chief tie. But because his life had for so long provided a path for my academic interests, I decided to try to find the wisdom to understand and represent his life with both a critical and sympathetic eye. How successful this portrait in words will be, only my readers can determine.

CHAPTER 1

Spain in the Life of Pedro Terreros: 1710–1730

Stretched out like 'an ox-hide'. . . . Iberia appeared . . . as a poor, mountainous land, 'whose soil is thin—and even that not uniformly well watered.'

—FIRST-CENTURY GEOGRAPHER STRABO,
QUOTED IN CASEY, *Early Modern Spain*

Consider the situation of a relatively poor but ambitious young man living in early-eighteenth-century Spain. In the barren and impoverished province he grew up in he sees for himself no future as a fourth son and fifth child of a family poor in both land and material possessions. From afar, the success of Spain's colonies in the New World beckons as donations of silver trickle into the villages and towns all around him.

These were the options that lay before the main character of this story, Pedro Terreros, who eventually became one of the wealthiest men in the eighteenth-century world. He became famous enough to inspire a special annotation in his baptismal register in the parish church, which noted that at the time of his death he was "one of the great noblemen of Spain." Terreros followed the route of emigration of an average of 4,000 Spaniards annually who left their homes to migrate to the Indies.[1] But, unlike most of them, Terreros was tremendously successful.

Pedro, later called Romero de Terreros, or simply Terreros, was born on June 28, 1710, and baptized a week later on July 6, in the parish church of San Salvador in Cortegana.[2] He was the child of a couple registered at the time of his birth as Ana Gómez and Joseph Romero. The baptismal name of Pedro may have been chosen because the day of celebration for San Pedro, June 29, was the day after his actual birthday, but Pedro was also a common name both in the town and his family. There were, in fact, two other men named Pedro, perhaps relatives, who were active purchasers of land in Cortegana in the early 1730s.

His memory of his ancestor's names changed as his ambitions and accomplishments grew. He drew on the most distinguished of his ancestral names—Terreros, Ochoa, and Castilla—to embellish the name of Romero, his father's first last name. He may have selected the name of Romero not only because his father had chosen it, but because it derived from the notion of pilgrimage (*romería*). Years later, when he came to decorate the outside walls of two of his silver-refining haciendas, he again made reference to pilgrims by using shells,

Fig. 2. One of many shell designs in Pedro Romero de Terreros's haciendas, this one from San Miguel Regla. Photograph by Marco Hernández.

the symbol of Spanish pilgrims (see Figure 2). His choice of names also reflected the path he chose in life: a *terrero* was a place where miners stored the rubble left over from the refining of silver ore.

A modern descendant of the Cortegana Terreros family, Juan Romero de Terreros, writes that family tradition suggests that the Terreros family name comes originally from Vizcaya in northern Spain from the middle of the tenth century. Relatives from Vizcaya maintained connections with the Cortegana Terreros family, for example, Pedro Ochoa, who became an important assistant to Pedro Terreros in Querétaro.[3] In fact, Pedro Terreros selected two wolves, a common Basque symbol in heraldry, as part of his coat of arms when he became the count of Regla and also chose this symbol for the coats of arms for two other noble titles that he purchased for his two younger sons.[4] These efforts by Pedro Terreros and his family to utilize the names of the most prestigious branches of their family failed to convince the genealogical investigators of the family's nobility when he sought to become a member of a military order. On the contrary, they concluded that no members of the family had possessed noble status or had used the honorific "don" in front of their names. In this region, Pedro Terreros's family was not alone in lacking nobility. Few residents of Cortegana had the right to noble status and *hidalguía*, and petty nobleman were more common in the north of Spain than in Andalucía.

Of Pedro Terreros's education we know only that he and his brothers were all literate. His father signed documents in a labored hand, and his mother was unable to sign her name. We know from a survey of the town carried out in 1761 that Cortegana had two schoolteachers (*maestros de primeras letras*), so it is possible that Pedro did receive his early education in the town.[5] Given his later passion for maintaining his accounts with unflagging attention, he must have been good at figures. A man of his business acuity would keep a very close watch on details, especially details having to do with numbers.

The notarial archive of Cortegana contains no records of land transfers or commercial transactions for any Romero de Terreros family members before 1735. The family did, however, have access to wealth through their connections to two men who were the principal landowners in Cortegana: Diego Terreros and José Martínez Romero, local priests who purchased vineyards and other property during the 1730s. José Martínez Romero, the parish priest of San Salvador, the principal church in Cortegana, was a nephew of Juan Vázquez Terreros, Pedro Terreros's maternal uncle who owned a large mercantile business in New Spain. When this Mexican uncle funded a chaplaincy in 1735, the priest from Cortegana was appointed patron.[6]

Connections with these two local priests were considerably less important to the family than were connections with this prosperous maternal uncle, Juan Vázquez Terreros. This uncle and a great-uncle, Bartolomé Terreros y Ochoa, had both left Cortegana on separate occasions before Pedro's birth; Vázquez made his way in Querétaro and Terreros y Ochoa ended up in Mexico City and Veracruz. The Cortegana Terreros family fortunes took a sudden upswing in 1735 with the death of Juan Vázquez Terreros in Querétaro. By this time Pedro had been working for his uncle in Mexico for at least five years and served as one of the two executors of his estate. Improved economic circumstances after the inheritance led to the family name appearing with some frequency in the notarial transactions of Cortegana.

By 1736, Pedro's father had become administrator (*mayordomo*) of the local confraternity dedicated to the worship of the Virgin de la Piedad. He was also able to outbid all others for the purchase of a prosperous vineyard and lands that were to be planted with chestnut trees, which would be used to feed hogs. The income that the Terreros family received from the sale of hogs could be used to build a new sanctuary for the Virgin de la Piedad that would abut the old castle guarding the town.[7] By October 1738, the family also paid for a chaplaincy for one of the sons. The changing of 4,000 Mexican pesos into 60,000 Spanish reales produced more cash, in one transaction, than had been traded in the town of Cortegana during the period 1720–60. During this time, Pedro's father purchased property belonging to a Jesuit college in one of the more distant hill towns. An older brother, José Romero Felipe de Castilla, administered this land and became a resident of Higuera de Vargas.[8]

Pedro Terreros's youngest brother, Manuel Romero de Terreros or Castilla (his name appears in different forms at different times; sometimes he is Don

Manuel and sometimes he does not use the "don"), also profited from his uncle's Mexican estate. Selected to be the holder of the chaplaincy, he was to study for the position of presbyter (*presbítero*) so that he could take minor religious orders. In addition, he later became a town councilman (*regidor*) in Cortegana in 1750 and also entered commerce in various commodities, especially mules. Despite the gift of the chaplaincy, Manuel had only modest possessions in 1762, although he was apparently better off than his brother Diego, the second brother who remained in Cortegana. While Manuel Romero de Terreros (or Castilla) was not an immensely wealthy man, he did own some vineyards, 130 goats, two milk cows, and a couple of mules.[9]

Income from Juan Vázquez's estate in Querétaro, now administered by Pedro Terreros, certainly improved the lives and prospects of his Spanish relatives. Money from Vázquez's estate made it possible for Pedro's father to give each of his offspring 3,500 reales (or 166 Mexican pesos) when his wife died in 1741. Judged by local prices, 3,500 reales was a tidy sum that represented more than half the value of their house on the Calle de Cano. In the mother's will she asked that certain rather modest goods be given to a woman who had served her. In her husband's will, signed in 1743 in Aroche, a community to the west of Cortegana, close to the Portuguese border, he asked that some land which had originally belonged to his brother be returned to his nieces on his death.[10] As was customary, both parents took the opportunity of their last will and testament either to repay a debt or to remember through a bequest those who had been important to them. Both chose to remember women. Their wealthy son, Pedro Terreros, in his various benefactions also donated to charities devoted to women. He provided dowries for the daughters of one of his former partners and a dowry for his sister's daughter. He further sought to establish a convent for women and sent 500 pesos to assist needy girls in a village in Extremadura, the province just north of the Province of Huelva.[11]

In 1762 or perhaps early 1763, Pedro Terreros proposed that an entail be established for his father's lineage, and his friend and agent observed that this would "redound to the honor, credit, and luster" of the founder even though the entail was small. The agent had warned earlier, however, that setting up this particular entail would lead to "a thousand jealousies" among his brothers. He reminded Terreros that in the past, when Pedro had altered a contribution to his brothers, "instead of being happy with the division that you [Terreros] had made there had been envy because one had more than another."[12] This prediction that the brothers would fight over the gift failed to deter Pedro Terreros. In 1767, Domingo López de Carvajal mentions again the foundation of a small entail for a family member in Cortegana.[13]

Clearly, money from Mexico did not promote family harmony; on the contrary, it caused envy among Pedro's brothers. It is, however, well-known that an unequal distribution of money from a relative might strain bonds among the siblings of any family. Nonetheless, Pedro's Mexican wealth boosted the extended family's social status. It allowed one brother to take minor orders and to receive income from a chaplaincy, a second brother to enjoy the fruits of lands purchased in another town, a nephew to enter the priesthood, a niece to make a "better" marriage than she might have enjoyed without Mexican silver, and cousins to find positions in Pedro Terreros's enterprises in Mexico. This suggests a modest, but not dramatic, improvement in the family's material conditions resulted from Pedro Terreros's success in Mexico.

PLACE

Cortegana, one of the "hill towns" of western Andalucía, is located in the southwestern section of Spain. This is where Pedro Romero de Terreros was born in 1710. An area of mountains, forests, and thin, desiccated soil, it was described in the seventeenth century as "rough and rugged...but abounding in honey, game, livestock, wine, and bread."[14] More than one hundred years later, a British traveler portrayed the region "as more savage and more desert-like" than any region he had seen in his extensive travels in Spain.[15] Cortegana and the other hill towns lie in the frontier between Spain and Portugal, a kind of transitional zone between the low, rich country of the Guadalquivir River basin of lowland Andalucía, and the high, arid plains that form the modern-day Province of Extremadura, for many centuries given over to sheep breeding and grazing. The present-day Province of Huelva, where these hill towns are located, forms the western part of Andalucía. Two mountain ranges, the Sierra de Aracena and the Sierra de Aroche, form the western extension of the Sierra Morena, which divides Andalucía from the central Spanish tableland and from the sheep-grazing regions of Extremadura. (See Map 1.)

Green hills and meadows mask the agricultural poverty of the hill towns where neither wheat farming nor sheep breeding provided adequate sustenance for the region's inhabitants in the eighteenth century. The mountainous, rocky landscape had significant effects on the local society. It limited the growth of large estates that dominated other parts of Spain. Residents of Cortegana tended to own some of the land that they worked at a higher rate than those who lived in the flat river valleys or those inhabiting the sheep-breeding regions in the northern part of the Sierra Morena. This distribution of land ownership created a much less hierarchical society.

The rocky soil and the steep slopes also limited cereal production, forcing inhabitants to produce a variety of crops (including a small amount of wheat that could be grown on the limited good land) and other goods to be exchanged for bread. The most active trade in land in Cortegana during the 1730s and 1740s was in vineyards; during Pedro's childhood, Andalucía marketed grapes that were exported as wine to the Indies.[16] After Cortegana's share in the American wine

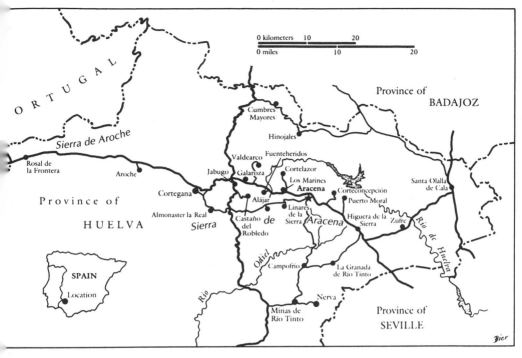

Map 1. Western Andalucía, Spain. Courtesy of Richard Maddox and the University of Illinois Press. Reprinted from *The Politics of Tradition in an Andalusian Town* (Urbana: University of Illinois Press, 1993), 3.

market in the late eighteenth century had disappeared, residents of Cortegana took up pottery and woodworking, increased the production of chestnuts to feed pigs, and became famous for the quality of their sausages. These were all signs of a population that reacted to its impoverished soil and limited opportunity by hard work and enterprise.[17]

Hill towns like Cortegana also specialized in the breeding of mules, which this region, as well as other parts of Spain, depended on for transport and commerce. The mules raised here transported commodities to the southern coasts from as far away as Almadén where the mercury used in refining silver ore in New Spain was produced. They were also essential to the provisioning of ships that served the colonial Indies.[18] The most lucrative enterprises in western Andalucía involved the Indies trade. Activities such as shipbuilding, supplying the Canary Islands with products for the outbound fleets, fishing, and trading contraband provided employment for local people. Emigration to the coastal cities and to the Indies, a tradition since the sixteenth century, constituted a significant export to a few families and attracted some capable young men.[19] Most of the hill towns were small, but they were not far from larger and more prosperous towns and cities.

On Spain's Atlantic coast, Huelva was an old town originally founded by the Romans as Onuba. It had long been an active port for the fishing fleet and for the export of copper, tin, and lead from the nearby Río Tinto mines. Not far from Huelva was the port from which Columbus sailed in 1492 and which served as a center for navigation and exploration. Other towns that played a significant role in the commerce of the hill towns were Seville, Cádiz, and Puerto de Santa María. Cádiz is about 200 kilometers to the southeast of Aracena, the principal town in the Sierra of Huelva. After 1717, Cádiz became the official port for the commodities that Spain sent to its colonies and was the recipient of the American silver that financed Spanish imperial ambitions in the eighteenth century.

The town of Cortegana presented special opportunities. It was located at the periphery of a prosperous region, acquainted with New World wealth through her access to the seaport that served the Indies market but also driven by adversity. It was a place of neither grinding poverty nor of great entailed estates. Cortegana bore an uncanny physical resemblance to a typical mining town in colonial Mexico. However, Cortegana's only mineral resource was marble, so difficult to access that quarrying it was as hard as mining precious metals, although far less remunerative. Marble had been produced in the town for at least a century and a half before the baptism of Pedro Terreros, and had been used to construct parts of the parish church, completed in 1552.[20]

Cortegana possessed little more than the promise of mineral wealth, but western Andalucía offered potential sites of exploitation for the earth's inert resources. An ancient Roman road called the "silver road" (*camino de plata*) linked the mountain ranges connecting the mines of Andalucía with those of Asturias. As well as proximity to the "silver road," Cortegana was located close to a thriving mining community, the Río Tinto mines, that had been mined centuries earlier by the Romans and still produced lead, tin, and some silver. In 1725, before Pedro Terreros's emigration to Mexico, a Swedish company rented the mines of Río Tinto and began to extract copper. Silver mining was also conducted in the nearby hill towns of Aracena and Cazalla de la Sierra as well as Guadalcanal by the first decades of the seventeenth century. The silver mines of Guadalcanal would continue to produce ore throughout the eighteenth century.

The many mining ventures not far from Cortegana were visible to Pedro Terreros during his early years, which might have inspired him to invest in mines when he was only thirty-one. He had certainly learned that the most lucrative enterprises in western Andalucía involved the Indies trade.[21] The hill towns had access to the mines of Almadén, the chief supplier of the element mercury, which was an essential ingredient in silver refining. In 1709, the mines of Almadén, which supplied Mexico with mercury, began a new phase of administration when oversight was transferred from the Royal Treasury to the Council of the Indies, indicating the crown's intention to dedicate Almaden's production to supplying the mines of Mexico. Muleteers, men who transported commodities on mules, from Cortegana and other hill towns contracted to deliver mercury from Almadén to the ports for shipping to the Indies.

During Pedro Romero de Terreros's more than fifty-year-long residence in Mexico, between 1730 and 1781, Spain remained central to his personal vision and aspirations. He craved and received the notice of the Bourbon King Charles III, sought elevation to nobility, provided for his family that still lived in Spain, recruited Spanish friars to proselytize in Mexico, and sent his sons to be educated in Madrid. He chose as his title the count of Regla, the name of a Spanish evocation of the Virgin, and his principal philanthropy, the Monte de Piedad, was modeled on a Spanish institution. An inveterate letter writer, Pedro Terreros kept in contact with Spanish colleagues throughout his life in Mexico as well as his family in the Peninsula. After leaving in 1728, however, Terreros never returned to Spain.

THE TIMES

For many centuries relations between Spain and Portugal had been difficult, even bellicose. One lasting testimony to this constant warfare are the many fortress-like buildings, whether castles or churches, that still dot the hillsides of the region. This is true of the hill towns, most of which constructed a secure stronghold that offered protection during periods of warfare. If political control over the hill towns was disputed for many years, so too was ecclesiastical jurisdiction. As late as the sixteenth century, the baptismal books in the Cortegana parochial archive identify the town as part of the bishopric of Lisbon, Portugal. By the early eighteenth century it was clear that Cortegana belonged to the archbishopric of Seville and that their city's political allegiance was to Spain, not Portugal.

Spain had annexed Portugal in 1580, and sixty years later, in 1640, Portugal successfully declared its independence from Spain, rekindling warfare between the two countries that continued sporadically until 1713 when the War of the Spanish Succession ended. In 1681 or 1682, the town of Cortegana was sacked by the Portuguese. Local residents provided billets and food for Spanish soldiers sent to defend the frontier and to protect Seville from Portuguese incursions. Later, during the War of the Spanish Succession (1700–13), combat between Spain and Portugal occurred to the north of the hill towns but Cortegana escaped damage.

The constant warfare from the seventeenth century on in this frontier region meant that the town of Cortegana and the surrounding area could not prosper. Nonetheless, during the later years of the War of Succession there were signs that the Spanish economy was beginning to improve. These signs included new mining ventures, plans for the revival of the Spanish navy, and, in 1717, the naming of Cádiz as Spain's legal port of transit to America. These positive developments in the Spanish economy, coinciding as they did with Pedro Terreros's birth in 1710 and his formative years in Spain, may have encouraged the young man to view the future with more optimism than had earlier generations of young men from his town. In addition to the Portuguese invasion of the 1680s, Pedro's forbears had experienced the misfortunes of plague, drought, and population loss.[22] Pedro was fortunate that his birth and adolescence coincided with this period of increasing prosperity for Spain.[23] These conditions allowed him to be confident about the possibility of becoming a rich and successful man.

MIGRATION

Migration from Spain's western hill towns to larger places in the Peninsula and then to the colonies provided one exit from the region's poverty. One conscious realization of this phenomenon is contained in a response to a government survey in the neighboring community of Almonaster. The survey asked whether there had been any distinguished men from this community, and the priest who wrote the response answered that there were "no illustrious men because the inhabitants were very poor and they did not have the means to place their sons in profitable employment."[24] This was a fact that several members of the Terreros family of Cortegana learned very early. As a result, they looked elsewhere to find opportunity. Migration facilitated by family connections was one response to the poverty in the interior of the Sierra de Huelva.

Pedro Terreros stands in the middle of a tradition of family migration that began well before 1685. Bartolomé Terreros, a great-uncle, was already settled in Mexico City by this date and had two sons who were well established in business by the first years of the eighteenth century. Bartolomé also had brought his nephew, Juan Vázquez Terreros (hereafter referred to as Juan Vázquez). Juan Vázquez, in turn, installed himself in the thriving city of Querétaro well before 1700. Both Pedro and his brother Francisco would be employed in the enterprises of their uncle. Pedro later brought two or three cousins to work in his own mercantile enterprises.

Like other young men from small towns, Pedro possibly began his training as a clerk in a counting house or merchant's establishment in either Cádiz or Puerto de Santa María in Spain. Evidence suggests that Pedro began his training in Puerto de Santa María working for the merchant Domingo López de Carvajal, whom years later he credited with starting him on his career.[25] Work in these counting houses in the larger towns did not provide vastly improved material conditions over the poverty in rural areas. Some twenty-five years after Pedro's departure from Spain, another young man complained to his relatives that while beginning his career he had never been able to earn enough money to buy shoes.[26] Not only did poor pay and low status motivate many clerks to migrate to American colonies, but stories of success in America that circulated in Spain attracted them as well.

The implications were clear: for an ambitious young man, neither his home-town nor Spain's port cities could provide adequate promise of prosperity.

Donations of substantial sums of money and silver sent by immigrants (called *indianos* when they returned to Spain) to towns in the Sierra of Huelva demon-strated to Pedro the wealth that might be obtained from the Indies. For ex-ample, a local immigrant in Oaxaca had donated a silver image of Our Lady of Solitude (Nuestra Señora de la Soledad) to the church in neighboring Tres Cumbres.[27] Elaborately decorated silver vessels to be used in the celebration of the mass abounded in the towns of the Sierra.[28] In Puerto de Santa María, where Pedro likely worked and where his friend López de Carvajal lived, there was a large silver retable donated by a relative of the Viceroy of New Spain. A less showy donation based on colonial profits, that of Bartolomé de Conjo from Cortegana, had established a fund to provide bread for the town's poor and may have arrived before Pedro Terreros's departure.[29]

In 1693, a wealthy immigrant from Aracena to Peru, sent to his birth place eight strong boxes of gold and silver. This immense treasure supported his sur-viving relatives, founded chaplaincies, instituted funds to feed the poor, and provided clothing for twenty-four people. By the middle of the eighteenth century, Gavino Villafranco's descendants had been able to use these funds to become the wealthiest family in the town, a position of local power they continued to hold through the twentieth century.[30]

Andalucian Spain influenced Pedro in still another way. Part of the title of nobility that he selected in 1759, that of the count of Regla, derived from his Spanish heritage. Many other men of his status selected titles based on Mexican landmarks or their own achievements, but Pedro Terreros chose a title derived from an evocation of the Virgin popular in Spain and among sailors, but of little importance in Mexico.

Many factors influenced this decision. The sanctuary for the Virgin of Regla was located on the last spit of land visible to ships departing from Cádiz toward America, thus making it a memorable symbol for emigrants like Terreros. The Virgin of Regla was also the name of a ship that often carried migrants and commodities between Cádiz and Mexico, and Pedro Terreros might even have sailed on this ship.[31] He clearly had a special affection for the Virgin. In New Spain, Pedro Terreros named three of his haciendas after the Virgin of Regla, and the region in which they are located is now known as the region of the Reglas. In this case, however, it appears that the memorial was not associated with the Virgin, but with the man who bore her title, the successful immigrant Pedro Terreros.

In one significant aspect, Terreros differed from his peers: he was one of the last immigrants from Andalucía to achieve high status in colonial Mexico. The other Spanish immigrants of his era who attained similar prominence after 1750 were likely to come from the northern Spanish Provinces of Vizcaya and Asturias.

In a society where ties based on place of birth continued to govern membership in important confraternities, access to investment capital, decisions in legal cases, as well as marriage arrangements, Pedro Terreros's success is all the more notable given the small number of successful Andalucians in New Spain.

CONCLUSION

Born in a small, somewhat impoverished town with distant and difficult access to the sea and Spain's American Empire, into a family with many older siblings, aware from his earliest days that he would have to make his name through hard work, he chose to leave his birthplace and his country. When he left Cortegana to learn commercial practices he followed a traditional course for those who hoped to succeed. But his fortunate career advancement, on emigrating to the Indies, he owed to his extended family, particularly his uncle, Juan Vázquez, in the provincial town of Querétaro. Like many Spanish immigrants to Mexico, he depended on relatives to start his career.[32] Despite the squabbles of his brothers over the amount of money they should receive from his gifts to them, his family exercised a powerful hold on him, as it did for most Spaniards. This was a world in which familial connections counted a great deal, and family considerations dictated the individual's most vital decisions, such as vocation and marriage.

Pedro Terreros clearly took his old world values and religious beliefs with him. He was imbued with the beliefs of baroque Catholicism, distinguished, among other elements, by its emphasis on worship of the Virgin Mary. While his region of hill towns might not have been dominated by the large estates and vast social disparities between rich and poor that characterized other parts of the southern regions, his desire to become a powerful patriarch was born here nonetheless. Pedro Terreros's later search for aristocratic titles and his embrace of the colony's hierarchical social systems suggests that he retained and esteemed the values and customs of his native land. His experiences in New Spain strengthened these commitments.

Pedro Terreros's position as the fourth son in his family taught him that assertive behavior was the only path to success. Endowed with exceptional intelligence and extraordinary determination, his position as a younger son was frustrating while in Cortegana since the best positions went to the older sons. Although there was no official rule of primogeniture in Andalucía, in practice the older sons in this family—Francisco, Joseph, and Diego—were given the best opportunities. Pedro would have to work his way into a position of prominence on his own with little support from his nuclear family.

While he did not forget his family in Cortegana, he was not as generous as they hoped. The sons of Pedro's brothers claimed the right to inherit a chaplaincy set up by Pedro Terreros and his wife to benefit Juan Vázquez's grandson, Juan Manuel.[33] In this, they displayed an arrogance and an entitlement toward their colonial relatives that masked their own disappointment at Pedro Terreros's failure to bestow a significant donation on them. Their reaction mirrored a more general disappointment felt in the town of Cortegana as a result of Pedro Terreros. Failing to provide gifts, endowments, or foundations for his native town, this disappointment continues until the present day.[34] After the silver treasures and the chaplaincy that he sent from the bequest of his Querétaro uncle, Pedro Terreros contributed virtually nothing to Cortegana itself. Even the chaplaincy from his uncle's bequest was set up with resources from another place and was enjoyed by a brother who did not reside in the town. By the time Pedro Terreros had disposable funds for charities from his mines, his aspirations had shifted from seeking recognition in his own hometown to having his name and fame recognized and honored in the highest echelons of Spanish and colonial Mexican society.

CHAPTER 2

Merchant in Querétaro: 1730–1750

> All gachupines [peninsular Spaniards] are addressed as "don"
> and are treated with great respect, all being taken for nobles, no
> matter what class they are, since to be European suffices.
>
> —Ajofrín, Diario del viaje

> The most miserable European, without education or cultiva-
> tion, believes himself superior to a white person [creole] born in the
> new continent.
>
> Alexander von Humboldt,
> quoted in Brading, Miners and Merchants

These observations, the first by a peninsular-born Capuchin friar and the second by the German scientist Alexander von Humboldt, who visited New Spain, describe the entitlement that immigrants from Spain typically claimed when they arrived in Mexico. Attitudes of presumed superiority on the part of these Europeans created tension between Spanish immigrants (*peninsulares*) and the men and women born to white parents (*creoles*) in colonial Mexico. These antipathies seemed to have hardened during Pedro Terreros's years in Mexico with the peninsulares becoming ever more disdainful of local inhabitants. Not only did Spanish immigrants denigrate the habits and customs of creoles, but also they looked with even greater contempt on the colony's Indians, mestizos, mulattoes, and Afro-Mexicans.

When Pedro Terreros first set foot in colonial Mexico around 1730, he auto- matically assumed the local style, becoming Don Pedro. The title of "don" was reserved in Spain only for those who held the rank of minor nobility. Pedro Terreros became the quintessential *gachupín*, the pejorative term adopted by the local community to refer especially to newly arrived peninsulares.

VERACRUZ AND QUERÉTARO

Pedro Terreros's first vision of Mexico was probably either of Tampico or Veracruz (see Map 2). The latter city was the chief transshipping point for the trade between colonial Mexico and Europe. From this port, European goods sent by Spanish merchants arrived in annual fleets and then traded to markets throughout Mexico and northern Central America. In return, Veracruz exported silver,

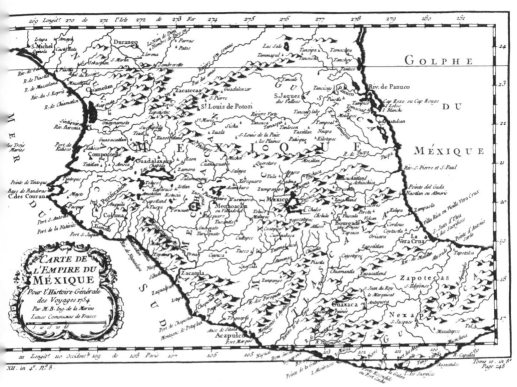

Map 2. Mexico in 1754.
Courtesy of the Geography and Map Division, Library of Congress.

hides, indigo, and other colonial products to Europe. It was a busy port only when the commercial fleets arrived from Spain. From the seventeenth through the nineteenth centuries observers have remarked on the depressing nature of this steamy port, where the bulk of immigrants came to New Spain. According to the Italian traveler, Gemelli Carreri, "Despite the fact that all the fleets and ships that come from Europe to New Spain, [land here], the city, far from being very large and rich, like Mexico [City] . . . is very small and poor."[1] Antonio Ulloa, appointed as a crown investigator at the apparent height of colonial prosperity, noted that Veracruz was "the most famous city in the world, through which the merchandise of Europe passes, and which is the depository for all the treasure of the kingdom . . . has only two principal streets, and a few churches and buildings, all ordinary except those which are used to store merchandise."[2] According to a later description of the city's condition at a time of relative poverty for all of Mexico, the "city was melancholy, forlorn, and dreary . . . nothing earthly can exceed the sadness of this city."[3] This was true in the eighteenth century as well.

The dismal aspect of Veracruz and the surrounding rural villages must have contributed to the sense of disdain that Pedro Terreros and other travelers felt toward the inhabitants of Mexico. Here, in a colony of legendary wealth, the residents lived in squalor and misery. During Terreros's four- or five-day trip between the port city and Querétaro, he passed through many humble villages. But with the one exception of the town of Jalapa, where the annual trade fairs occurred, these settlements were small, poor, and poverty-stricken, far more primitive than Pedro Terreros's hometown of Cortegana. They certainly presented a stark contrast with the urban amenities to be found in Spain's port cities like Seville or Cádiz.

Terreros's uncle's business was located in Querétaro, a city that with its hinterland had a population of between 20,000 and 30,000 in 1746. Certainly Querétaro must have been more impressive than the coastal areas with its smaller villages. In the 1730s Querétaro possessed large plazas, three Franciscan friaries, and one of the wealthiest convents in the Indies. In addition, it boasted Jesuit, Dominican, and Augustinian churches and foundations as well—all signs of a prosperous city. In fact, there could hardly have been a more favorable place for a merchant to begin his career. Querétaro, the third largest city in colonial Mexico, was flourishing artistically and economically.

Lying about 220 kilometers north of Mexico City, at the southeastern edge of a fertile plain that divides two mountain ranges, Querétaro was called by contemporary boosters the "garden of America," not only for the amenities that beautified it but also because of the opportunities that it offered for its wealthier residents. The surrounding area was well watered, with small rivers and streams for irrigation, and with adequate rainfall in most years. Wheat, corn, and rye fields alternated with extensive grazing areas for sheep. Added to this, Querétaro enjoyed a pleasant and equable climate.

The city's natural gifts were enhanced by its strategic location at the eastern end of a large region called the Bajío, which extended north and west toward Guadalajara. The region was known for its rich silver mines located mainly in the neighboring city of Guanajuato. But it was the combination of mining, agriculture, and manufacturing that gave the region an economic diversity that brought fortunes and power to those able to exploit these assets.[4] So attractive was the city to the inhabitants of other regions that as early as the mid-seventeenth century people in the frontier community of Monterrey complained that landowners in Monterey preferred to live in Querétaro, more than 370 miles away (600 kilometers). By the end of the eighteenth century, residents of Mexico City were coming to vacation in Querétaro.[5] A contemporary of Pedro Terreros described the city as "the most beautiful, grand, and opulent city of the archbishopric of Mexico, as much for the beautiful temples of sumptuous manufacture, the growing number of Spanish families, order of its streets and plazas, the perfect construction of their houses and the growing number of Spanish [23]families. . . .Two thousand houses and countless gardens."[6]

Querétaro lay at the convergence of the trade routes of eighteenth-century Mexico, located along the route that linked Mexico City to northern mining communities. The city was also an entrepot for European commodities from the annual fleets and from the trade fairs of Jalapa, San Juan, and Saltillo.[7] Not only were goods from the Atlantic fleets available, but consumers could chose from abundant stocks of silks, pottery, and other goods brought from East Asia and shipped through the Spanish-held port of Manila to Acapulco. The number of travelers to Querétaro in 1695 is suggested by a prospective inn-owner, who when seeking a license for an inn noted that the city needed places to "lodge travelers because of the heavy concentration of people and traffic bound for cities in the interior [of Mexico]."[8] All the productive enterprises of eighteenth-century New Spain existed here, but equipping silver mines provided one foundation of the city's economy.[9] Textile mills (both *obrajes* and *trapiches*, which designated larger and smaller mills), where woolen cloth from the coarsest blankets to the finest domestic *paños*, used as a fabric for blouses and certain kinds of skirts, were woven in the city.[10] Humboldt described Querétaro "as celebrated for the beauty of its aqueduct and for its factories of woven goods."[11]

One eighteenth-century observer noted that the city was the home for "persons who have flourished in every area which has ever emerged into light," using the Spanish expression for the birth of a child. A nineteenth-century enthusiast recalled that Querétaro garnered:

> the riches of half the republic, cultivating its fertile soil and controlling the rich silver dust from interior and exterior trade. With one powerful hand, the city collected specialties from Veracruz and from Querétaro, and with the other it changed them for the silver, the seeds, and the thousands of products of the Bajío and the Pacific coast. Querétaro was the confluence of incredible currents of traffic; the bazaar in which the commodities of the world were changed for the goods of the whole republic.[12]

Along with Querétaro's position at the vanguard of colonial Mexico's economic development, the city also trained missionaries for the church, especially Franciscans. As early as 1683, a missionary college had been established in Querétaro to train friars to proselytize among the Indians, both those in the immediate vicinity of the city and those to the north. These were the Indians of the Sierra Gorda, the branch of the Sierra Madre Oriental that begins around Zimapán in the present-day state of Hidalgo and continues through the north of the state of Querétaro. Periods of missionary activity began even in the sixteenth century, as Spaniards tried to settle this section of the colony, and the ecclesiastical and civil authorities undertook a major pacification and conversion campaign at the end of the 1730s.[13] The church often played a quasi-military role in its efforts to convert the Indians. No separation between church and state existed here. Franciscan friars also carried out campaigns for the promotion of orderly behavior of the often unruly urban population of this burgeoning frontier city, calming disorders when military forces were insufficient. Pedro Terreros would depend on the powers of both church and state to maintain order in Real del Monte, the community that he later controlled.

Franciscan institutions dominated Querétaro, which no doubt explains why Pedro Terreros was almost exclusively devoted to Franciscan causes. Two Terreros cousins also trained as missionaries in Spain and colonial Mexico and reached high positions in the Franciscan order, giving Terreros yet another link to this branch of the Catholic Church. The church of San Francisco served as Querétaro's principal church until the mid-eighteenth century. A Franciscan friary of the Holy Cross, on a small hill overlooking the city, was the site and source for the founding myth of the city. According to the legend, a cross and the image of the warrior Saint James, or Santiago, Spain's patron saint, appeared in a vision to the conquerors in 1531 while they stood on the hill, which at that time overlooked Indian settlements.[14]

The appearance of these images became a permanent fixture of the city's historical memory many years after the founding of Querétaro, when an image of Santiago on horseback with a sword raised above his head, trampling the bodies of warriors, rather than Moors as he would have been portrayed in Spain, was carved into the facade of the church (see Figure 3). This image appropriated Spanish iconography to represent a religious sanction for the city's militant conquest. The friary later became the site of the first Franciscan college for training missionaries, established in 1683. Adjacent to the house of Pedro Terreros's uncle, where Pedro probably lived as a young clerk, was a third Franciscan institution, the church of San Antonio, where the *descalzos* (the barefoot observant branch) had its first establishment in the city.

In the 1730s, Franciscan institutions for women were not as numerous as those for men in Querétaro, but the one that did exist was enormous. The convent of Santa Clara, the first women's convent in the city, "occupied four city blocks and had streets, gardens, fountains, and more than sixty houses, in which the nuns and their servants lived. It formed a true village closed to the outside world." Beside the convent church, there were ten chapels located in other parts of the complex. Four of Pedro Terreros's women cousins, as well as other female relatives, lived in Santa Clara, and this tied him even more closely to the Franciscan order.[15]

The religious foundations of Querétaro flourished during the period of Pedro Terreros's residence in the city during the 1730s and 1740s and probably directed his attention to the advantages and disadvantages of giving magnanimous gifts both to the church and to the city's poor. The man who may have served as a

Fig. 3. Stone carving of Santiago on horseback trampling a Moor or Indian
at the entrance of the church of San Francisco in Querétaro.
Photograph by Juan Romero de Terreros.

model for Terreros of philanthropic behavior was the marqués de Villa del Villar
de Aguila, who had organized the construction of the aqueduct in Querétaro.
Also, at the urging of his wife, the marqués funded a branch of already
established Franciscan nuns, called Capuchins. He would later complain that
his wife's lavish generosity and devotion to charities—she moved entire groups
of nuns from one city to another, and fed and clothed numerous people, not all
of them poor—threatened his financial well-being.[16]

The emphasis on the religious character of Querétaro was visible both in the
creation of magnificent ecclesiastical buildings, as well as in more ephemeral
events. In 1802 a chronicler wrote of the "magnificence and splendor that the [people
of Querétaro] employ in the divine cult, [including] . . . annual festivals, penitential
processions, devout sodalities, perpetual chaplaincies, and pious gifts."[17] Religious
and secular events reflected the prosperity of the town and the financial ability of
wealthy families to support splendid celebrations. Special occasions required
sponsors, and the patronage of a major fiesta was a sign of social recognition as
well as wealth. For example, when Jacinto Suasnabar y Sosa, a relative of Pedro
Terreros's uncle, organized and paid for the bull fights that were part of the city's
celebration of a royal marriage in 1729, the sponsorship marked his increased
importance in the city.[18] The ten-day-long celebration in 1738 to mark the
completion of the aqueduct, however, dwarfed all previous celebrations.

The city boasted a military as well as a religious tradition. Symbolized by the combination of the cross and the warrior Santiago on the facade of the church of San Francisco, the military aspect stemmed from the city's role as a frontier supplier and colonizer. It was also underlined by the number of local men who bore the title of militia captain, a role they combined with their economic leadership as owners of obrajes, livestock, and land. The rough and aggressive behavior of the militia captains led to violence in the 1730s, proving that certain men settled issues by means other than the law. So serious were these disturbances that the local authorities felt obliged to inform the authorities in Spain.[19]

While Querétaro in the 1730s and 1740s experienced growing prosperity, the number of poor also grew. Men and women from the region's smaller villages, towns, and farms came to live in the city, displaced by famines, epidemics, and the growing concentration of land owned by fewer men. According to an investigator in 1741, "The majority of the families who live here are poor and miserable and can hardly sustain themselves through their personal work in the [textile] obrajes."[20] The evidence of increasing poverty in the city failed to move Terreros. His future charitable acts neglected the very poor in favor of religious institutions and men and women who had fallen on temporary hard times. Like many Spanish merchants, he considered workers expendable factors of production.

In the seventeenth century, Querétaro depended on the wealth of Mexico City merchants. Even the most prosperous merchants in Querétaro served as factors or agents to more substantial business men in the capital city.[21] Given the absence of formal banks to extend credit, merchants acted as financiers. By the mid-eighteenth century, with the growth of silver mining in the neighboring town of Guanajuato, with more direct ties to expanding frontiers to the north, and above all with the expansion of the textile industry in Querétaro itself, more prosperous local merchants improved their economic position. They began to finance smaller local businessmen, while continuing to be dependent on Mexico City wholesalers for cash, credit, and merchandise.

Pedro Terreros's uncle, Juan Vázquez, may initially have been dependent on his cousin Bartolomé Terreros y Ochoa in Mexico City for credit, but in later years he and his partners financed others in Querétaro. These contracts conform to the arrangements that Pedro Terreros would make later, when he invested money in a local store or other enterprise; the storekeeper contributed his labor and a smaller amount of money and the profits would be divided between the two men.[22]

The citizens of eighteenth-century Querétaro boasted of being "hard-working and far removed from luxuries," but some spent lavishly on material goods, and the wealthiest built large houses, generously decorated with silks and satins, fine woodwork, rugs, china, silver, and gold.[23] Notarial records reveal a population of men (and some women) engaged in buying, selling, improving, and renting productive property such as herds of sheep, land, textile mills, mines, and material goods. These men spent profusely on luxuries, religious foundations, and fiestas seen as necessary for the impression that they produced on others and for their own personal satisfaction. They also paid for diversions such as bull fights and elaborate celebrations of saint's days both to entertain themselves and the plebeians.

The most successful entrepreneurs in Querétaro, as elsewhere in colonial Mexico, varied their investments both geographically and by sector. Pedro Terreros learned the wisdom of diversification early in his entrepreneurial career. Later in his life he furnished elegant houses, continually acquired and sold merchandise, purchased haciendas, and spent significant sums on religious institutions and public rituals and observances. He left an impression of being both parsimonious (as befit a successful merchant) and extravagant. The atmosphere of the city of Querétaro shaped Terreros during his twenties and early thirties, determining his aspirations. Here he found models of men to be emulated and to compare to his uncle who provided an example of behavior to avoid.

THE TERREROS FAMILY IN NEW SPAIN

Of the six offspring of Ana Gómez Vázquez Terreros and her husband, two migrated to Querétaro early in this eighteenth-century period of prosperity. Francisco Vázquez Romero de Terreros and his brother Pedro came separately to colonial Mexico to work for their maternal uncle, Juan Vázquez. As early as 1723, Francisco, the older brother, conducted business in the city of Zacatecas, about a six-day (629 kilometers or 370 miles) journey from Querétaro.[24] As an employee of his uncle, he brought merchandise from Europe, Asia, Mexico City, and other places in New Spain to Zacatecas and returned to Querétaro with silver. Francisco was close to his uncle and added his uncle's name of Vázquez. He later indicated his affection for this uncle by drafting a will in which he left him whatever property he had accumulated.

The penultimate report we have of Francisco's career is in August 1728 when he and his uncle executed two agreements in preparation for Francisco's imminent departure for Spain. These included descriptions of silver objects that Francisco was to take with him. Together with his nephew, Francisco, Juan Vázquez had paid for the fabrication of a monstrance, that is, a transparent receptacle in which the consecrated host would be displayed. Juan Vázquez also donated another lamp and candle holders that were to be placed in the church of San Salvador.[25] In addition to these silver objects with a value of approximately 1,520 pesos, Juan Vázquez handed over to Francisco 20,000 pesos in silver coins, 14,000 belonging to him and 6,000 to his nephew Francisco. Francisco had garnered his share of the money by trading on his own, leaving his uncle to keep the profits in a kind of informal trust for him. He received all the money from his uncle to "manage in the Kingdoms of Castile, in the ways which he considers appropriate."[26] Unfortunately, he never had the opportunity to deliver or spend the money in Spain.

While waiting for a ship to take him back to Spain in 1728, Francisco died of yellow fever in Veracruz, the unhealthiest of Mexican colonial cities.[27]

Why was Francisco preparing to undertake this journey? Had he failed to please his uncle? Did familial ties in Spain play a part in pulling him back? Alan Probert, a twentieth-century commentator, guesses that Francisco's parents wanted him to return in order to take over the family farms, and in exchange the parents sent their younger son, Pedro, to assist their relative. Another account, that of a contemporary, a Franciscan friar who knew Pedro Terreros, suggests that Pedro came to New Spain only to settle his brother's estate after his death. He then visited his uncle and resolved to remain because his skills were needed. What is known for certain is that the death of his older brother was the first fortuitous event in the career of Pedro Terreros, because it allowed him to take over his brother's position.[28]

Few records remain of Pedro Terreros's early work in his uncle's business. The first document is from 1730, when he was in Veracruz arranging for the shipment of the silver objects entrusted to his brother for religious institutions in Cortegana. About that time, he wrote a will quite similar to the one his brother had penned earlier, although Pedro planned to leave his property to his family in Spain and not, as Francisco had done, to his uncle in New Spain.[29] It was customary to draw up a notarized will before embarking on journeys, and Pedro signed his just before traveling to Jalapa, the town where Spanish merchants brought their imported European goods, thus avoiding the harmful and disease-ridden environment of Veracruz. Jalapa is about 70 miles west of Veracruz and 4,000 feet higher. Throughout the duration of their partnership, Pedro and his uncle purchased most of the goods to be stocked in their Querétaro store at the Jalapa fair.

Pedro Terreros, his brother Francisco, and their uncle, Juan Vázquez, formed a small group of family members who migrated from Cortegana to New Spain that had begun at least as early as the mid-seventeenth century, when one Cortegana cousin, Bartolomé Terreros y Ochoa, had established himself in Mexico City.[30] He may in fact have financed Juan Vázquez in the establishment of his business in Querétaro.

By 1708 Juan Vázquez had married María Antonia Suasnabar y Sosa, a widow who belonged to a local family related to the prestigious Mexico City family of the counts of the Valley of Orizaba.[31] As a sign of his ambitions and connections, he chose a woman with ties to the Mexico City nobility rather than marrying within one of the secondary Querétaro elite families.[32] Twenty-five years after his marriage, Juan Vázquez stated in his last will and testament that his wife had brought 3,000 pesos to the marriage. She also had some debts inherited from her first husband. At that time he possessed an estate of 14,000 pesos.[33] Unless he had married for love, his wife's paltry dowry indicates that Vázquez had married to improve his social position and family influence rather than to increase his wealth, a model that his nephew Pedro would follow nearly half a century later.

In the early years of Juan Vázquez's residence in Querétaro, he made several efforts to expand his investments beyond his mercantile business. At one time he owned some rural land, but apparently he did not pursue this type of investment. At his death he owned no rural land, no sheep, not even a small textile mill. He tried unsuccessfully to collect money from the estate of his wife's first husband, which apparently included a hacienda called Guadalupe and a house in a mining community.[34]

Juan Vázquez made loans to establish two small retail stores in Querétaro. He also invested 3,000 pesos in the business of a candle maker in the neighboring town of Celaya.[35] These expenditures offer examples of how the large wholesale merchants were able to influence smaller retail businesses. The system provided modest entrepreneurs the opportunity to be independent and furnished outlets for investment for wealthier men and women. A merchant from Mexico City supplied merchandise for Juan Vázquez's Querétaro retail store and financed the sale of his goods to mining areas.[36] His nephew Pedro in later years engaged in the same kind of investments.

In 1733, two years before Juan Vázquez's death, his mercantile business was worth 63,450 pesos in merchandise from Europe, China, and New Spain, a sum that made it one of the largest businesses in Querétaro. At his death, its worth had increased by about 6,000 pesos and constituted nearly half the value of an estate appraised at 138,000 pesos. It was in the administration of this business that Juan Vázquez employed his nephews.

In his will of 1733, Juan Vázquez named Pedro as the last of five executors, but by 1735, Pedro had become one of only two executors. Pedro had somehow managed to get control of his uncle's estate and eventually organized the funeral, settled the estate, and took over the administration of his uncle's business. Juan Vázquez's own son, no more than eighteen at the time of his father's death, had the wrong kind of experience to run this business. Even if he had been older, custom dictated that the creole son would not be permitted to inherit and manage the business, and the peninsular nephew would continue in control. The Spanish wholesale merchants formed a distinct group and did not welcome local-born participants, even if they were their own sons. As a result, few members in the merchant guild (*consulado*) were creole. Only through marriage of his daughter to a Spanish nephew could a wholesale merchant have his own flesh and blood continue in his business.

Since at least as early as the 1760s, commentators have observed this odd exclusion of creole sons from the businesses of wealthy immigrant merchants. José de Gálvez, who virtually ruled colonial Mexico as an inspector (*visitador*) wrote that "generally speaking the creoles do not enter trade even though their fathers have lived off it."[37] In the nineteenth century, Lucas Alamán wrote, "Rarely do the creoles conserve the economic order of their fathers and they do not follow the profession that has enriched them, . . .Nor do the creoles subject their sons to the severe discipline in which they themselves were formed."[38] The twentieth-century historian David Brading observed that merchants were a clan that included only those born in Spain. He added that these young men went through a seasoning process, or initiation rites, from which those born in America were barred.[39]

The exclusion of Mexican-born sons might have been a way of protecting them, for while commerce was the source of the largest fortunes, getting and keeping this wealth through trade included risks. The usual problems of premodern navigation—including shipwrecks, pirates, and lost cargos—were compounded by threats provoked by Spain's many wars. In the early years of the century, when Juan Vázquez was engaged in business, there was the War of the Spanish Succession (1701–13). Five years after Pedro had assumed control of the business, in 1740, the War of the Austrian Succession (or the War of Jenkins's Ear), disrupted normal commerce, although it also facilitated profits for the owners of smaller vessels that traded along the coast. It is perhaps understandable that a father might wish to protect his son from the hazards and jeopardies threatening an international trader and instead provide him with security. Hence, in the case of the Terreros clan, it was the maternal nephew from Spain who speculated and took risks, but who also enjoyed large profits.

Juan Vázquez's only son, Juan Manuel Terreros (who adopted his father's maternal name) was sent by his father at the age of sixteen to a Mexico City seminary where he studied philosophy and rhetoric, but learned little about commerce. Vázquez instructed the man who was to oversee his son's education, "that he should correct, subdue, and guide him by either gentle or rigorous means as [is] necessary." Vázquez also asked that he supervise his son's companions and, should the need arise, communicate with the governor and viceroy about any problems.[40] The suggestion that the highest officers of the colonial government could be called on for help and guidance indicates the social recognition and economic power possessed by Vázquez.

Unfortunately, we know nothing of Juan Manuel Terreros's years in Mexico City. His success or failure as a scholar, his relationships with "respectable" and obedient young men (or more dubious associations), and whatever recourse to the highest levels of government by the tutor to discipline him are not found in the documents. Sometime after 1735, when he returned to Querétaro after his father's death, he assumed a municipal position to which he was entitled by his high status in the town. Juan Manuel Terreros cemented ties with his older cousin, Pedro Terreros, by naming his first-born son after him and by asking him to be the godparent to the boy. In Juan Manuel's letters to his cousin Pedro, his son is referred to as "Pedrito," and as Pedro's godson (*ahijado*). In later years, Pedro Terreros and his wife set up a fund for a chaplaincy that would support "Pedrito" in his profession as a cleric.[41]

About his social life, we know that Juan Vázquez belonged to an unusually large number of confraternities (*cofradías*), eleven to be exact. Cofradías were brotherhoods of men and women who venerated a common saint or image, supported a particular church or chapel, provided burials for members, marched in funeral processions for their deceased brethren, and sponsored celebrations and Masses.[42] Memberships in a number of confraternities affirmed one's high social status.

We know a great deal about Juan Vázquez and his affairs through his last will and testament, a document written and revised during a period of two years between 1733 and 1735. It reveals a man who had multiple affiliations within the Catholic Church and contacts with members of lower social orders. He had lent money to Indians, and two of the eleven confraternities to which he belonged were composed of members of the popular classes—one in an Indian parish and the other in a mixed-race (*pardo*) parish. Juan Vázquez belonged to nine additional confraternities that were associated with almost all the leading religious orders in Querétero; he even belonged to one Mexico City confraternity. He had served as a patron of the Augustinian order since 1728.[43]

Like other men and women in Querétero, Juan Vázquez owned slaves: five females and four males. Although slavery was declining in importance in Mexico by the 1730s because of the increase in the free population, there still was no opprobrium attached to the ownership of other human beings. Although some people as an act of piety manumitted their slaves in their wills, Juan Vázquez did not do so. When he drew up his will, Juan Vázquez granted freedom to only one of his nine slaves, and this was an elderly female slave. As recommended by Juan Vázquez in the will, she chose to join her master's daughters in the convent of Santa Clara where she probably continued to serve the family as a free servant. Since this slave was old and perhaps unable to work long hours, her alternative to the convent might have been abandonment.

As was customary, the dwelling of Juan Vázquez served the dual purpose of housing his business and his family. Located behind the church of San Antonio in the city center, it bordered on small landowners' property as well as the lands of one of the principal families of Querétaro. The two-story house, with its two patios, was appraised at 8,000 pesos at his time of death, making it one of the most expensive residences in the city.[44] Business was conducted on the ground floor, which was divided into an entry, an office, a retail store, a warehouse, a coach house, and a portal (a covered walkway enclosing the patio). A staircase led to the family's living quarters on the second floor. The rest of the property on the ground floor consisted of a kitchen, a second patio, and stables.[45]

Surprisingly, the family's household furnishings were modest. The most valuable objects were religious paintings that were valued as much as all the other furniture and household goods combined. Many of the paintings show the Virgin in her various evocations—Afflictions, Solitude, and Sorrows (Angústias, Soledad, and Dolores). Female saints, Catarina, Ignacia, and Verónica, were also included in this collection. Among the paintings of male saints, Francis of Assisi had pride of place, as was appropriate for a family that had at least two male members in the order and already had sent three of its daughters to the Franciscan convent of Santa Clara in Querétaro.

At Juan Vázquez's death in 1735, his household furnishings included in the probate of his estate were exceptionally sparse for a wealthy merchant of his status, so sparse that all the family and household goods including paintings and books could be counted by court-appointed assessors in just one day. The most numerous household objects were chairs, almost all of little value.

More striking than the objects listed on the inventory are those that are missing or account for only a small portion of the estate. There are no beds, for example, but only old bed curtains made of threadbare fabrics and a well-worn silk counterpane. There are a few pieces of imported china, and no pillows and *rodastradas* (platforms on which women piled pillows and rugs to sit on rather than on chairs). The silver and jewelry comprised less than 3 percent of the total value of the estate, a figure that is significantly lower than in comparable wealthy Mexican families.

However, when it came to public appearances—a matter of importance to any family of status, including a major wholesale merchant—a more opulent impression was required. Juan Vázquez owned a carriage, an indispensable piece of equipment for a merchant of his status. And his personal wardrobe, worth 358 pesos, was valuable enough to be acceptable for appearances at public functions but was not excessive or showy. Juan Vázquez may have preferred an austere private life, spending little on furniture and silverware, but in order to maintain his position he dressed well and appeared in public in an appropriate vehicle.

In only one category, that of books and art, did Juan Vázquez seem willing to freely spend his wealth. He had accumulated nearly 290 pesos worth of books. Only one of these books was secular, and it dealt with commercial contracts. All other books in his private library were religious, with titles such as the *Mystical City of God*. He also owned books about a seventeenth-century Spanish nun, a book of Catholic virtues, and six copies of a book called *David Perseguido* by Cristóbal Lozano, which narrated and then commented on the biblical story of Saul and David. Lozano used the story of King Saul, who persecuted David because he killed ten thousand men while Saul himself could kill only one thousand, to discuss envy. Aimed at a society in which envy of the achievements and possessions of other people often reached particularly virulent heights, the author tried to teach readers to accept with equanimity the praise and rewards given to their rivals.

We have no idea, of course, whether Pedro Terreros ever read *David Perseguido* or any of the books in his uncle's possession. Years later, at Pedro Terreros's funeral service, a friar commented that the most valuable objects in Pedro's household were books of devotion. But this investment in religious works had been far more true of his uncle's house in 1735 than of Pedro's house in 1781. There is the possibility that the image of the persecuted David might have resonated with Pedro Terreros, who sometimes believed that royal officials, his business associates, and even his employees either failed to value his contributions or envied his achievements.

The religious titles that dominated the library of Juan Vázquez, his affiliation with so many confraternities and religious institutions, and the large number of his testamentary bequests to religious foundations underline his pious nature. The provisions Vázquez made for his daughters, all of whom took religious vows, further confirm this religious vocation. In colonial mercantile families it was customary to arrange the marriage of daughters to nephews, or other able clerks (*cajeros*) who worked in the business. Juan Vázquez did not follow this custom. It may have been because his daughters desired to enter a religious life. Or, perhaps, this resulted from his own determination to dedicate his daughters to the church. There is also the possibility that his nephews, Francisco and then Pedro, resisted marriage with their cousins. We do know that by the time that Vázquez wrote the final codicil to his will in 1735, three of his daughters had already entered the Franciscan convent of Santa Clara in Querétaro, joining maternal aunts and cousins; the youngest sister, not yet old enough to be a novice, already lived there.

The four sisters who lived in the convent of Santa Clara may have taken many luxury items from the paternal house to the convent, thus explaining why this apparently wealthy man had such modest possessions at his death in 1735. It is also possible that they never purchased many material goods because they sought to maintain a lifestyle that imitated the Franciscan ideal of poverty.[46] Yet another explanation, and perhaps the best, is that this modest household reflected a financial necessity imposed by the conditions of a business that had endured severe losses despite its apparent value reflected in the will.

The variety and complexities of investments characteristic of other successful mercantile families in the colony is missing from the Vázquez estate's portfolio. Evidence suggests that in his later years Juan Vázquez had begun to lose his skill and possibly even his interest in business. Despite the contemporary belief that Vázquez had one of the most prosperous businesses in Querétaro, there are indications in surviving documents that things were not going well. We do not know what may have caused these reverses. It might be speculated from the experiences of other merchants that he lost valuable cargo when a ship went down at sea, that he had uncollectible debts, or that he had made unwise investments. Whatever the cause of his "fatal losses," they may explain why the family lived in such modest circumstances within their home and possessed few silver objects and little jewelry.

These were, after all, the easiest items to sell or pawn when one needed cash.

One drain on the family's wealth was the expenditure, which soon reached astronomical heights, that Juan Vázquez had made for his daughters in the convent of Santa Clara. The three older daughters had received dowries of between 7,000 to 10,000 pesos when they entered the convent. This was at a time when the average dowries for entering a convent generally ranged from 3,000 to 4,000 pesos. Women entering convents had to have dowries for both material and spiritual reasons. Money from the dowries was invested in real estate and loans to provide income for both the convent and the individual nun. Entering nuns also had to have dowries because this was a marriage to Christ, and the same offerings or generosity needed to be made for this kind of marriage as for a secular marriage. Finally, quarters in this convent were of varied quality and cost. Some nuns lived in dormitories while others enjoyed their own houses.

Other Querétaro families of similar social status provided their daughters entering the Santa Clara convent with similar dowries and living quarters. Juan Vázquez nearly always emulated the customs of other well-to-do families in his own community. He had been forced to borrow to pay for his daughters' dowries and living expenses by placing a lien of 34,000 pesos on properties that he had then owned. In the will, they also received additional funds of 3,000 pesos to build their own "cell," or house, in the convent complex, which might have been two stories high and contained many rooms. Considering that Juan Vázquez's house, which included a large percentage of space dedicated to business, was valued at 8,000 pesos, the sum of 3,000 should have been adequate to construct a house of considerable size to be shared by the daughters. The will also directed that an additional 3,000 pesos be taken from his estate to provide his daughters necessities in the convent. Three nieces who were in other convents also received generous gifts from the Vázquez estate. Responsibility to help maintain these nuns continued under Pedro, who in future years, received requests for money and attention from the daughters of Juan Vázquez as well as other family members who were nuns.[47]

In addition to the half of his estate that his youngest daughter, María Teresa, would inherit (the other half would be inherited, as the law provided, by his son) Juan Vázquez bequeathed an additional 3,000 pesos to be invested to meet the needs of his youngest daughter. According to Spanish law, what remained after these bequests had to be divided between his son and youngest daughter, who was not yet a nun. The right of children to inherit their parents' estate was a fundamental principle of the Laws of Toro, which governed inheritance throughout the history of the colony.

Before his death in 1735 at the age of fifty-five, Juan Vázquez left instructions for his own elaborate funeral. This commitment of extravagant funds was made even though the custom of expensive, ritual-laden funerals was waning in colonial Mexico and his business was no longer robust. Pedro Terreros, who was charged with arranging the funeral, had little choice but to heed his uncle's wishes regardless of the cost. Juan Vázquez directed that Masses be said for him and his wife in all the churches of Querétaro. Money was also allocated to dress poor women for mourning at his funeral. Other expenses included the mourning clothing for his family as well as six bushels of wheat, twelve lambs, money for wine, and 538 pesos for candles for the funeral feast. The costs reached 25,048 pesos. Nearly fifty years later (in 1782), the eulogist at Pedro Terreros's own funeral mentioned the extravagant cost of this funeral, characterizing Pedro as an Isaac in blind obedience to his uncle's will, even if the funeral expenditures put at risk the business and the estate.[48] Here he used the biblical narrative of Isaac's submission to his father, Abraham, when permitting himself to be bound in preparation for sacrifice as a metaphor for Pedro's obedience to his uncle's funeral instructions.

Historians might observe that by arranging this funeral Pedro Terreros celebrated his own person at the same time he memorialized the life of his uncle. Organizing a procession of clergy in splendid dress, with confraternity members robed in their official garb and female mourners wearing black garments donated by the estate gave Pedro Terreros his first opportunity to sponsor a major ceremony. The death of his uncle also allowed Terreros to become an independent merchant-entrepreneur. From this date he was able to risk both his own and his uncle's capital in mines, merchandise, and loans. His uncle's demise was the second of three fortuitous deaths that afforded Pedro Terreros the opportunity to test, develop, and hone his business talents.

INDEPENDENT ENTREPRENEUR AND FAMILY MATRIARCH: 1735–1743

When Juan Vázquez died, his two youngest children inherited whatever remained of his estate after the payment of funeral expenses, debts, and bequests. As nuns, his older children could no longer claim a share of their father's money or property. His nephew, Pedro Terreros, could not, by law, inherit more than a small part of his uncle's estate; indeed, his uncle's will mentions him not as an heir but as an executor. It was in this capacity that Pedro Terreros began his independent career as an entrepreneur.

In a codicil to Juan Vázquez's will signed shortly before his death, he decided to reduce the number of executors from five to two: Pedro and another nephew, Jacinto Suasnabar y Sosa. In a statement added to the will two days later, Pedro Terreros's share of any future profits from the business were increased from one-fourth to one-third. Juan Vázquez included a phrase praising his nephew for his "activity, accuracy, and good work," adding that he wished Pedro to "maintain the company on its current course in the same manner as agreed upon."[49]

What was the character of the business on which Pedro Terreros's future career depended? He told the Franciscan friars that when he arrived in Querétaro in the late 1720s, his uncle's business "suffered fatal losses" for several possible reasons. Whether this relatively young man was able to reverse these losses during the years when he worked for his uncle is impossible to determine, but once he controlled the business there is no doubt he made it profitable. As a vigorous man of twenty-five, Pedro brought energy and dynamism to a business; these traits would characterize his career. Through his management of the mercantile enterprise, Terreros could and did invest in a wide range of commercial activities for which there are few surviving records. What is clear is that it supplied him with handsome returns. In 1743, he rented another store in a different neighborhood in Querétaro.[50] Four years later, he invested 16,000 pesos in a partnership with Pedro Ochoa, who bore a Terreros family name but who came from Vizcaya rather than Cortegana. Out of this partnership Pedro Terreros was to receive between one-half and two-thirds of this company's profits.[51] Several days after the establishment of the company, Ochoa signaled the depth of the relationship by issuing a document making Terreros his executor and heir. Imagine the amount of control that Terreros exercised over this partnership! But such asymmetrical authority was not dissimilar to the arrangement that Pedro's brother, Francisco, had made with his uncle Juan Vázquez in earlier years or partnerships between other Spanish merchants. Pedro Ochoa became a trusted, dependable, but dependent servant, someone who often assumed Pedro Terreros's responsibilities in Querétaro when the growing complexity of Pedro's affairs drew him away.

By 1741, six years after the death of his uncle and his assumption of responsibility for the administration of both the Vázquez estate and business, Pedro Terreros began to invest heavily in silver mines. Where did he get the money for this investment? His uncle's business was worth around 70,000 pesos in 1735 or 1736. This probably represented a wholesale value, in which case we might add 70 percent to the value of the merchandise.[52] Pedro Terreros enjoyed one-third of the profits from the business; Juan Vázquez's two children divided the other two-thirds of the profits between them. Pedro Terreros had his own investment in the mercantile business of approximately 4,000 pesos.

Another source of capital for Pedro's early investments might have been money garnered from executors, the customary executor's fee of 10 percent total of the estate's value. Another source of funds might have been the profits gained by executors from conducting the estate's business. These substantial fees and the possibility of borrowing money from the estate might well have been the major source of Pedro's working capital. It should be noted, however, that the amount of time involved in working on the settlement of an estate could be heavy, as well as psychologically draining, particularly if the family suffered internal disputes over the division or if the family distrusted the executor.

In later years, Pedro Terreros did not acknowledge that his uncle's estate had provided him with crucial investment capital. In fact, according to his memory, the large bequests and extravagant funeral plans mandated by Juan Vázquez's will threatened the stability of the business. Nevertheless, Pedro's position as both the person in charge of the business and the principal executor of the estate accelerated his economic and social ascension. He hardly seemed like the helpless and compliant Isaac agreeing to be sacrificed as characterized in the eulogy delivered at his own funeral.

Pedro Terreros's difficulties as executor grew in 1737, as his youngest cousin, Ana María, decided to become a nun and made the customary will when she took vows as a novice. Her half share of her father's estate was 37,000 pesos, which she now transferred to charitable and religious foundations. Pedro Terreros postponed the payment of these legacies, observing that the estate would suffer enormous losses because the money was invested in "properties, household goods, merchandise, and businesses." Terreros argued that this gift would force the immediate sale of properties and liquidation of investments at low prices. Six years later, in 1747, the money still had not been paid, and Ana María appealed to the other executor of her father's will in the hope of forcing action. Soon after this appeal, Terreros arranged the settlement of the wills of both father and daughter, agreeing to pay 50 pesos a month to each of the four daughters of Juan Vázquez for the duration of their lives. He then promised to provide an additional 23,310 pesos within the next four years to pay all other bequests and debts attached to the estates. With this arrangement, Terreros ended his responsibilities to the estates of father and daughter and provided money to the nuns for luxuries such as chocolate.[53] Apparently, the generous dowries already provided would not cover the expense of small luxuries like chocolate. In 1760, one of the Terreros sisters requested a contribution (*limosna*), from Pedro Terreros telling him that "what is administered to us is not enough as we have debts and we have no other place to turn for assistance." It is clear that the nuns valued their connection to their powerful cousin and the benefits and luxuries he could provide, often expressing a desire for news of his children and requesting that he write to them.[54]

To his cousin Juan Manuel Vázquez Terreros, Pedro turned over some of his father's properties in Querétaro. Juan Manuel also acted as the collector of debts for Pedro and performed other services for him. At least once, Juan Manuel got himself into considerable difficulty by borrowing money from the Jesuits, the wealthiest religious order in colonial Mexico. Juan Vázquez's son, who was educated under the supervision of the viceroy, lacked a sense of fiscal accountability. Perhaps the presence of a powerful and successful cousin and guardian who acted as his patron inhibited the growth of an independent and self-reliant character; or perhaps Pedro Terreros saved his younger cousin from ruin and bankruptcy.[55]

Assessing Pedro Terreros's administration of his uncle's estate and business is perplexing. We can be fairly certain that he stole no money from the estate because it was not consistent with the moral nature of his character. But he paid the legacies due his cousins slowly and benefited from the use of the monies and goods, a not uncommon strategy. The priest who served as eulogist at Pedro Terreros's funeral service remembered that the deceased had managed the estate, "not as executor, but as a loving father, fulfilling the commands and legacies so that the heirs were fully satisfied, and that Don Pedro knew how to protect them until they were settled in the position that they themselves had selected."[56]

It is obvious that his uncle's mercantile business was crucial to Pedro's success and his later success would be crucial to the prosperity of his five cousins. Without a peninsular family member with contacts in the international mercantile trading networks, who could continue the family's business and postpone the final settlement of the estate and its liquidation in a forced sale, no beneficiary of the estate was likely to have been left much money or property.

CONCLUSION

Family and city established Pedro Terreros's career in the 1730s and 1740s. The prosperity of Querétaro, with its ties to the expanding frontiers to the north, favored merchants and obraje owners, and Pedro Terreros was in a good position to take advantage of these circumstances. The city provided him with one of the many sources of slaves, whom he believed to be essential to his future.[57] In later years, he purchased haciendas close to the city and lent money to Querétaro residents. He continued his mercantile career, with the help of family members, some from Spain who resided in Querétaro, and with members of his uncle's extended kin. His successful business operations would not have been possible without both family assistance and a thriving city, which provided him with a workforce and a market. This in turn enabled him to diversify his investments, which was essential for success in colonial Mexico. A member of a peninsular group of merchants who later dominated the geographic center and wealthy enterprise of Querétaro, Pedro Terreros and other Spanish migrants directed the economic life of the city in the latter half of the eighteenth century.[58]

In the broader picture, it is indeed within the family circle that we must look for the origins of the complex process of entrepreneurship and fortune making that would transform Pedro Terreros into the count of Regla. Kin and friendship ties were nurtured by the willingness of well-established peninsulares who dominated Mexico's European trade to sponsor and promote their young male relatives. As Juan Vázquez had brought over his two nephews, Francisco and

Pedro, so Pedro would bring two relatives, José García Terreros and Pedro Ochoa. This castelike character of the Spanish international merchant elite relied on the willingness of young peninsular male relatives to brave the Atlantic crossing and live in almost monastic conditions. Their initiation to Mexican society was in stark contrast to the upbringing of creole sons who enjoyed an education as gentlemen, and generally proved to be less hard-working and less ambitious than the immigrants. In fact, we have in this phenomenon another explanation, in addition to monopoly privilege, for the vitality of the Spanish business class in the colonies. The interlocking dynamism of relatives and friends on both sides of the Atlantic resulted in a migratory stream from one shore to the other. The maintenance of family connections continued by sending gifts to the Spanish village or town and by economic support for poor relatives there.

As Pedro Terreros's business expanded, his colleague, partner, and financier, Domingo López de Carvajal, supplied him with clerks and accountants from Spain, recommending desirable candidates.[59] This demonstrates a defining characteristic of colonial business in which the metropolitan country and its population assumed that the lion's share of opportunities and profits belonged to Spain and its Spanish subjects.

In time, the ties that Pedro Terreros established in Querétaro and later in Mexico City overshadowed his connections with his native community in Spain. Later, many years after Terreros had relocated from Querétaro to Mexico City and Pachuca, he continued to identify himself as a citizen (*vecino*) of that city. Other men of influence and power in New Spain had multiple residences, but they were nearly all based in Mexico City; so in this respect, as in many others, Pedro Terreros differed from his peers. It was not until the last years of his life that he unambiguously identified himself as a vecino of Mexico City. Throughout his career Querétaro would offer him a secure base as a citizen, a merchant, and the holder of positions in the city, in which his relatives and friends acted for him.

Although famed as a miner, landowner, and philanthropist, Pedro Terreros began his career as a merchant and continued to dedicate himself to commerce, at least through the 1760s.[60] His dedication to commerce and to material success was fired by the atmosphere of Querétaro, the city where he spent his first decade and a half in colonial Mexico. Nonetheless, he could not become a merchant with the importance of the Basque and Asturian merchants who came from the north of Spain and who dominated the merchant guild (*consulado*), which controlled international trade between Spain and Mexico. Merchants from these two ethnic groups controlled the largest concentration of capital in Mexico. Since Pedro Terreros was neither a Basque nor an Asturian and came from a provincial mercantile house rather than one in Mexico City, he could achieve the highest positions in society only through the acquisition of the kind of money available through investment in colonial Mexico's most valued export: silver.

44

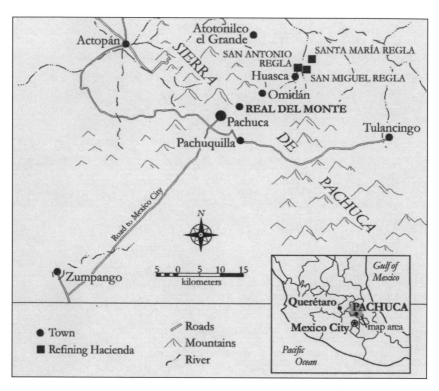

Map 3. Pachuca, Real del Monte, and the Regla Region.

CHAPTER 3

Silver Miner in Pachuca and Real del Monte: 1741–1766

God has determined that New Spain will have silver mines,
just as the author of nature has decided that other provinces and
kingdoms will produce linen, wool, or have a textile industry. For
gold and silver are the means by which this kingdom trades with
the rest of the Spanish provinces. From this it follows that precious
metals are necessary for the maintenance of the universal commerce
of the whole world, and for this reason the Spanish kings have
persistently recommended special care for the mines of New Spain.
—AHPM, José Alejandro Bustamante, Representación
hecha al Virrey, 1748; also published in Velázquez,
"José Alejandro Bustamante"

These were the opinions voiced by José Alejandro Bustamante, the partner and friend of Pedro Romero de Terreros, in 1747. It was Bustamante who began the mining enterprise that would eventually give Terreros an impressive fortune. Bustamante's statement correctly declared that colonial silver mining provided the lifeblood of Spain and the Spanish Empire. From the time of Spain's settlement of Española, the supplies of silver and gold from American colonies allowed Spain to become an arbiter of power in Europe, facilitated Spanish imperial expansion throughout the world, fueled its armies and navy, and encouraged Spaniards to emigrate to the colonies with the promise of enriching themselves and their families.

One of the earliest mining centers in New Spain was Pachuca and its satellite Real del Monte, 84 kilometers (60 miles) northeast of Mexico City, located in the present-day state of Hidalgo (see Map 3). It was here that Pedro Terreros began to invest in 1741. The road to Pachuca ran through a region filled with maguey plants and bounded on both sides by distant mountains. It is here, on the east, that the Sierra de Pachuca, a branch in the Sierra Madre Oriental, rises up. Pachuca derives its name from a Nahuatl word that indicates one of the town's principal geographic features, a narrow opening or pass in the mountains. A traveler in the late nineteenth century described the town as "enclosed within a semicircle of bare brown hills, by which it is hidden until nearly approached, Pachuca fills a little valley with low-walled houses of stone"[1] Real del Monte,

Fig. 4. Real del Monte in 1840. Lithograph by John Phillips.

about 10 kilometers to the northeast, appeared to be perched on the side of the mountain. A seventeenth-century traveler described Real del Monte as "a city of mud houses covered with wood . . .[where] twelve thousand people seek their bread in an abyss (see Figure 4). In the space of six leagues there are around a thousand mines."[2] In 1762, when the Real del Monte mines were again at the height of their productive cycle, Friar Ilarione da Bergamo described Pachuca as "nothing more than a small, somewhat decaying village, while in Real del Monte 12,000 people resided and more than 900 people were employed in mining."[3]

Like most other mining towns, both Pachuca and Real del Monte were built haphazardly. Mining communities, exempt from the strict rules that governed the placement of buildings and houses in other Mexican municipalities, located their buildings in a random fashion, following the mountains and rivers and displaying the disorder typical of boomtowns, which grew up overnight. These towns grew so rapidly that there was no time to impose formal plans; instead, they fanned out irregularly along the banks of the river in the case of Pachuca, or centered around a small plaza anchored by the church, with the houses of the workers scattered throughout the surrounding hills in the case of Real del Monte. A nineteenth-century traveler, Mme. Calderón de la Barca, approaching from the other direction, glimpsed Real del Monte from far above, "[with] its sloping roofs and large church, standing in the very midst of forests and mountains." Another nineteenth-century traveler, William Robertson, observed that "the houses [were] clustered on different hill sides, which formed, however, a continuous ravine, and showing . . . a variety of eminences and buildings jumbled about, here isolated, and there forming two irregular and curious-looking lines."[4]

Beginning in the mid-sixteenth century Pachuca and Real del Monte established long histories as mining centers. It was in Pachuca in 1554 that Bartolomé Medina, a Spanish merchant, introduced the industrial process of refining silver. By using mercury and copper pyrites "to amalgamate with the silver atoms in the ore . . . and applying enough heat to volatilize the mercury." Medina initiated a new method (based on European experience) to separate the silver from the ore. In Mexico, the chemicals were spread out on a paved surface and blended, hence the name "patio process."[5]

By the eighteenth century, Pachuca had become a well-organized community despite its inauspicious beginnings. In 1746, about five years after Pedro Terreros began to invest in Mexican silver mines, an official report described Pachuca as possessing a "well-proportioned material structure and a beautiful appearance thanks to the harmony of its streets, plazas, and buildings, a parochial church of exquisite architecture, a missionary college of Franciscans, a hospital of San Juan de Dios, and a poorhouse [*hospicio*] as well as small hermitages for the Indians." In this same report, the government surveyor mentioned that there were more than nine hundred Spanish, mestizo, and mulatto households, and a hundred and twenty Indian families in the community. Assuming an average family size of five, there were an estimated five thousand people in the town of Pachuca and its satellite of Pachuquilla, which housed the bulk of the local Indian population associated with the mines. Real del Monte at this time had a population of eighty white and *casta* (mixed-race) families, or about four hundred non-Indians. There were also uncounted numbers of Indian families who either worked in the mines or grew the corn and beans that fed the community. Regarding Pachuca, the report concluded with the statement that the "mines of these mountains had fallen into decay because of floods although [the miners] still hoped for success from new drainage works."[6]

It was in this mining community that the thirty-one-year-old Spanish merchant of Querétaro, Pedro Terreros, began to invest in 1741. He began by joining Bustamante in investing in a gigantic drainage project or adit (*socavón*) to rid the mines of water. Terreros appears to have been moved to invest in mining— the most difficult, dangerous, and profitable of activities in eighteenth-century New Spain—by a mixture of self-seeking and charitable impulses. No doubt he was motivated by the wealth he had seen displayed by successful immigrants to the Indies, including the rich gifts they had given to their communities, and he, like other merchants, had no profitable place to put money other than the silver mines. His early exposure to mining in western Andalucía may also have been a factor, coupled with the need to make money to pay the charitable bequests in his uncle's and cousin's wills. A pledge he had made to the Virgin of Regla that he would become a wealthy man may also have stimulated him

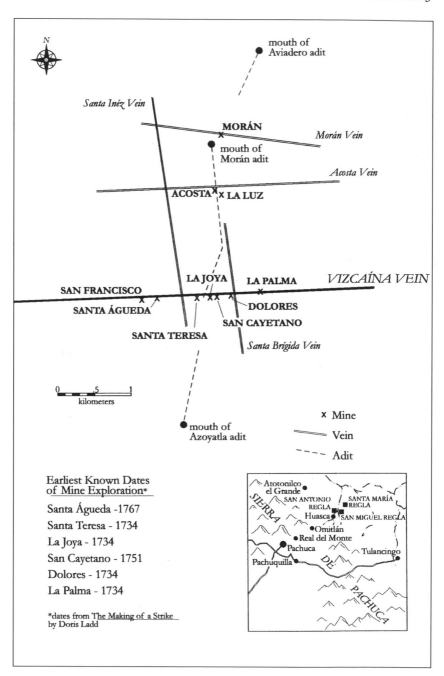

Map 4. Vizcaína and Other Mines.

to invest in silver mines. In addition, he appears to have been expressing an enthusiasm for gambling, not on cockfights, cards, or dice, but on a productive enterprise in which he believed that the chances of winning were very high. Terreros's own explanation of his motives, an explanation repeated many times in the course of his life and even reiterated at his funeral by a Franciscan friar, was:

> Understanding the unhappy state to which the citizens and residents of these mining towns [*reales*] had been reduced because nobody dared to rehabilitate and drain the mines . . .[and knowing that] for many years, the mines had been deserted and not worked . . .[he was] desirous of sacrificing their [his partners' and his own] fortunes for the benefit of the public and the Royal Treasury and helping the friaries and churches.[7]

Pedro Terreros rarely failed to assert that philanthropy had motivated him to invest in silver mines in Real del Monte. He claimed that his purposes were altruistic: to help the poor, to provide employment, to aid religious institutions, and above all to provide the Spanish treasury with money. Only silver mining promised profits large enough to achieve these ambitious aims. José Alejandro Bustamante, later joined by Terreros, decided to restore the mines at Real del Monte by investing in a gigantic drainage project.

Terreros was a man of enormous energy, driving ambition, and insatiable craving for recognition at the highest levels of Spanish society. To attain this goal, he sought wealth through the mines. In this he followed the trajectory of generations of both creole and Spanish immigrant entrepreneurs in Mexico. As explained by one historian, "to the immigrant from Spain or the poor colonist, mining offered a quick, if perilous short-cut to social distinction."[8] Even the merchants and members of the nobility at the top of the colonial social pyramid invested in mines, lured by the promise of enormous profit.

Pachuca and Real del Monte had been among the five or six most productive silver centers in colonial Mexico, so they were a good place to invest. By the end of the seventeenth century, however, the chief deposits of silver ore lay deep within the earth. The Veta Vizcaína, the wealthiest vein of silver-bearing rock in the region, extended about 5 kilometers to the east of Real del Monte with an extraordinarily wide diameter. It ran a long distance without either changing direction "nor coming in contact with other veins which could traverse or subvert it." (See Map 4.) Production from this vein eventually came to surpass all other sources of silver in the region.[9] After 1750, Pedro Terreros gained control of the Veta, which provided the principal basis of his fortune.

Under Spanish law mineral wealth found in the subsoil belonged to the crown and could not be alienated permanently. Thus, anyone who hoped to work a mine had to seek government permission and obtain a license (*denuncio*), which conferred the right to use the resources. Licenses could be revoked after only four months if a miner failed to work the mine. At this point, another person could then "denounce" or receive a license to the same mine. Nonetheless, the men who controlled the Veta Vizcaína, especially Pedro Terreros, referred to themselves as the owners of the Veta, that is, of the eight or nine productive mines that were included in the vein. He also owned, or leased from the crown, another lucrative series of mines, La Palma, Dolores, San Cayetano, and La Joya, which were sometimes identified as part of a separate vein called Santa Brígida, also located in Real del Monte.

ISIDRO RODRÍGUEZ DE MADRID

The fate of the miner Isidro Rodríguez de Madrid, Pedro Terreros's predecessor in working the Veta Vizcaína, is worth recalling.[10] Rodríguez de Madrid was buried as a pauper just as Pedro Terreros began his own ascent into the colonial elite. Later Terreros commented on the misfortunes that had ruined his successor. In reports to royal officials, Pedro Terreros described the principal problem—flooding—confronted by Rodríguez de Madrid and the reasons for his failure to resolve it. Many mines had been worked continuously since the mid-sixteenth century, and the surface veins had been quickly exhausted, forcing miners to dig deeper into the earth for ore-bearing rock. This rich vein had been mined since the early seventeenth century, and even before 1700 the shafts had reached phenomenal depths. This led inevitably to flooding from underground water. As early as 1696, after inspecting shafts that reached 160, 184, and 200 yards, the Italian traveler Gemelli Carreri reported that the mines extended virtually into the bowels of the earth.[11]

Born in Mexico City around 1684, Isidro Rodríguez de Madrid was identified as a *comprador de plata y oro*, that is, a person who purchased silver and gold from refiners or miners and converted it into usable coin.[12] Sometime before 1708 he had founded a silver bank that lent money to miners, arranged for the final smelting of the silver into bars, and then exchanged the silver bars for coins to facilitate this business. By 1716, Rodríguez de Madrid, one of only two silver bankers in Mexico, entered mining himself, receiving a license to mine in Real del Monte.[13] As a miner he enjoyed great success. He dramatically increased production at the Pachuca mines. It was noted by nineteenth-century British commentator Henry Ward that before his time silver was shipped from the Pachuca provincial treasury (*caja real*), where the miners and refiners sent their silver to be taxed, to Mexico City to be minted as coins about every six months; by 1725, shipments left Pachuca every two weeks.[14] Ward also reported that in the year 1726 alone Rodríguez de Madrid had produced 388,386 marks of silver, or 3,401,884 silver pesos, one of the largest sums ever recorded. But this figure is disputed by an eighteenth-century source.[15] According to the *Gazeta de México* the Pachuca treasury sent only 240,000 pesos of silver to Mexico City in 1728. This was a large sum, but was certainly less than the figure given later by Ward.[16]

In 1725, the Veta Vizcaína flooded, consuming the fortune of Rodríguez de Madrid, as "the uncontrollable force of the waters buried his wealth and submerged his mines."[17] The unfortunate Rodríguez abandoned mining soon after, causing the Pachuca-Real del Monte region to suffer depopulation and poverty. According to Pedro Terreros's narrative of these events, the community's relief arrived only in 1739, when Terreros's own partner, José Alejandro Bustamante, applied to the government for permission to exploit these same mines. Two years after Bustamante's decision, Pedro Terreros became his financial backer (*aviador*).[18]

Underground water challenged nearly all Mexican silver miners. Rodríguez de Madrid had used whims or winches (*malacates*), a type of hoist to which leather buckets were attached, to drain the mines. Because of the labyrinthine nature of the underground workings with shafts shooting off in many directions, drainage, either by men or malacates, was necessary at many points along the vein. These extra points of entry, although necessary for this technology, made it impossible to guard the mines. As a consequence, ore-bearing rock was stolen and profits were lost. Turning to improved technology in the hope of finding more efficient draining methods, Rodríguez de Madrid contracted with his cousin, López de Diéguiz, to design and import machinery from Europe.[19] The machinery arrived after the flood of 1725, but it was not made to drain such a tremendous amount of water. Although the flood was a disaster for the production of additional silver ore from the now flooded richest vein, apparently enough ore came from other sections of the Pachuca region to compensate some people in the community. The mines worked by other men in the Pachuca region continued to function for many years after the flood.

Rodríguez de Madrid remained in Pachuca at least until 1733, but silver mining was only one of a number of enterprises in which he invested. He held the local monopoly for the distribution of playing cards. In the interest of making this monopoly even more profitable, he tried to have the government suppress cock-fighting, a competitive venture, so that he would effectively control all games of chance. When the government refused, he invested heavily in locations where cock-fighting was permitted so that he might share in these profits as well.[20] But neither Rodríguez de Madrid's silver bank nor his other activities like card monopolies and cockfights could provide the capital necessary for draining the mines. By the end of the 1730s, his name had disappeared from the colonial economic records. It surfaced again in 1754 when charitable donors paid for his funeral.

There were many differences between the careers of Pedro Terreros and Isidro Rodríguez de Madrid. Terreros would avoid many of his predecessor's investments, including his experiments with costly machinery and untried technologies, his silver banking ventures, and his purchase of government monopolies. But the two did follow the same basic paths in their public careers and philanthropies.

Table 1 Remissions to Mexico City from the Pachuca Treasury
before Bustamante and Terreros, 1721–1739

YEAR	PESOS
1721	148,651
1722	233,701
1723	249,996
1724	261,662
1725	179,093
1726	291,180
1727	366,472
1728	142,536
1729	***
1730	**405,373
1731	141,322
1732	***
1733	**464,586
1734	78,533
1735	249,922
1736	98,565
1737	136,744
1738	85,424
1739	71,807

Source: TePaske and Klein, *Real Hacienda de Nueva España*, II:13–16.
** May include production figures for the reported year and the
previous year in which no figure was reported.
*** Figures missing.

Rodríguez de Madrid was a trustee (*síndico*) of the convent for Indian nuns
called Corpus Christi in Mexico City. Terreros was a síndico of Franciscan
institutions in Querétaro and Pachuca, sponsored and paid for the celebration
of the coronation of Charles III in Pachuca, and sought to establish a convent
similar to that of Corpus Christi but for Spanish nuns. Rodríguez de Madrid
was, like Terreros, famous for his elaborate fiestas and he too boasted of his many
achievements.[21] In their desire to impress their contemporaries and to dominate
the mining region, especially the Veta Vizcaína, these men shared common
aspirations. They did not, however, share the same tragic death as a pauper.

Pedro Terreros himself often emphasized the poverty of the Pachuca region
during the period 1725 until about 1750. It was after this later date that his drainage
of the Veta Vizcaína began to yield some success and significant amounts of
silver could again be extracted from the previously flooded shafts. The annual

figures of silver passing through the Pachuca provincial treasury from 1721 to 1739 reveal an ambiguous history with sharp rises and precipitous declines. The decades of the 1720s to the 1730s were a period when Rodríguez de Madrid dominated the region and then lost his mines, and when there was no dominating figure of the mines at Pachuca or Real del Monte.

A crisis may have occurred in 1731–32.[22] One contemporary statement made in this time period concerned an argument over the collection of the *alcabala* (a sales or transfer tax); one miner commented that "there was little activity in the mines."[23] Unusually large figures from the treasury contradict this qualitative statement, but the discrepancy might be explained by the fact that the silver mines produced little ore, while the refining mills were exceptionally active, working with ore that had already been removed from the earth.

The historian Herbert Klein's published summary of silver production coming from the Pachuca treasury was compiled in ten-year periods. He finds that the Pachuca treasury produced an annual average of 241,046 silver pesos during the 1720s, an amount not equaled in the lifetime of Pedro Terreros. Klein and TePaske's figures (see Table 1) demonstrate that in the decade of the 1730s production dropped about 90,000 pesos in an average year, a decline arrested in the last years of the decade of the 1740s.[24] Pedro Terreros reported a decline in the region's normally richest mines in the Veta Vizcaína. Smaller miners and refiners in the 1730s, however, continued producing silver bars at earlier levels. Pedro Terreros's insistence on the poverty of the region, before his infusion of cash, may have been exaggerated.

JOSÉ ALEJANDRO BUSTAMANTE: THE EARLY YEARS, 1700-1740

Given the revived political ambitions of the kings of Spain in the eighteenth century, royal officials probably sought an investor-miner to undertake the work of draining the Veta Vizcaína. The crown shared the local population's concern over the decline of income from the Pachuca-Real del Monte mines. Convinced of the region's wealth, royal officials conducted an inspection of the Veta Vizcaína beginning around 1732.[25] They found that in many mines there were no workers and that owners guarded their mines so poorly that independent "entrepreneurs" called *buscones* (pilferers) freely roamed the underground tunnels looking for places in the walls where silver ore might be profitably extracted from the rocks. These scavengers then dislodged the ore, expropriating the richest stones and selling them to an independent ore refiner. Buscones often found the most promising ore. Because these ores were sometimes embedded in the pillars that held up the walls of the underground mining works, there was a heightened possibility of collapse in the intricate tunnels at the interior of the vein.[26] Royal officials clearly saw this danger. Seeking a single investor to control the entire lode, the viceroy welcomed the application of José Alejandro Bustamante, someone who enjoyed ties to the mercantile wealth in Mexico City and also owned substantial agricultural properties in the Pachuca region. Bustamante was one of three Andalucian immigrants who came to dominate the mining region in the 1740s; the other two were Pedro Terreros and Agustín Moreno y Castro, the marqués del Valleameno.

José Alejandro Bustamante was the oldest surviving legitimate son of a former viceroy of the Philippines. After years of living in Spain, Mexico, and the Philippines, Bustamante settled in Mexico in 1721. In May 1739 Bustamante asked for a license to drain and operate the mines of the Veta Vizcaína. The government granted his request the next month; this was an alacrity not typical of the Spanish colonial bureaucracy. It might be that the viceroy or other government officials pressured him into undertaking this work, since it almost coincided with the release of a part of his paternal inheritance. This inheritance had been held for more than two decades by the government as a result of a dispute over the possible embezzlement of funds from the Philippines or the division of the estate with his sisters.[27] The general license that conceded the right to exploit all the mines in the Veta Vizcaína gave Bustamante the right to exploit forced labor from surrounding Indian villages. It also granted him exceptionally large boundaries in his mines and countermines and gave him favorable interpretations of the mining code.[28] This license was so unusually broad that the viceroy reported it to authorities in Spain.

José Alejandro Bustamante y Bustillo would be another formidable presence in the life of Pedro Terreros. Bustamante's influence is acknowledged in Terreros's own chronicles of his participation in Real del Monte, as well as in accounts of other contemporaries.[29] The men had two biographical points in common. Both came from Andalucía and both had fathers who had fought in the War of the Spanish Succession. Bustamante was born in Seville to a wealthy family. His father, Fernando Manuel de Bustamante y Bustillo, served as chief Spanish official (*alcalde mayor*) in the Indian town of Tlaxcala in central Mexico, where he rose to an unwanted prominence by provoking a riot in 1692. His father later returned to Spain, fought in the War of the Spanish Succession as an officer, and then became governor of the Philippines, a difficult but lucrative position. The family accompanied him to Manila but two years later the father and his oldest legitimate son were killed in a riot that the viceroy may well have provoked. Defenders of Bustamante's father claimed that he was trying to eliminate corruption, but evidence suggests that he amassed a hefty fortune of his own. His executors brought back 504,872 pesos from the Philippines to Mexico, which were then held in escrow by the crown. This money would remain in litigation for many years.[30]

The young Bustamante returned to Spain to be educated and then came back to Mexico. It is unclear whether he learned about mining in Mexico or Spain.[31] In 1732, he acquired, either through purchase or gift, a series of haciendas in Zumpango de la Laguna, not too far from Pachuca and Real del Monte.[32] (See Maps 2 and 3, above.) Bustamante married exceptionally well to one of the eight daughters of the wealthy Pablo Fernández family. The marriage provided him with a dowry of 8,000 pesos as well as a source of loans for his mining properties.[33] In 1740, a part of his father's estate was distributed to some of the heirs, and José Alejandro received a share of 37,738 pesos. Once paid by the treasury in Mexico in 1740, it was directly invested by Bustamante in the mines of the Veta Vizcaína.[34] He later invested another 20,000 pesos in the mines.

It was Bustamante's idea to drain the flooded mines by digging a countermine or adit below the level of the Veta Vizcaína into which the flood waters would drain.[35] This was a more expensive solution than using buckets and winches or machinery, because constructing either a deep vertical shaft or a horizontal adit for drainage "cost as much as to build a factory or a church."[36] In the end, Bustamante and his partners spent almost the whole decade of the 1740s digging adits at three different locations until lowered water levels permitted them to find significant amounts of new silver ore. Only in 1762, more than twenty years after they had begun the project, did the adit actually reach all the mining shafts.[37]

Bustamante's permission to mine granted him the right to all the mines in the Veta Vizcaína. Other mine owners in the Veta Vizcaína refused to give up their property, however, despite Bustamante's royal license. His efforts to enforce his control led to endless disputes over such issues as whether the mines had been operated during the last four months, or whether the mine's owners had in fact placed a minimum of four workers in a mine shaft. What royal officials had given as a grant to Bustamante in 1739 had, in fact, to be negotiated over and over with other miners until 1746.[38]

By March 1741, Bustamante had already established a partnership with Pedro Terreros, who had initially entered the mine fields as the aviador or financial backer of Bustamante. In the Pachuca mining region, an aviador enjoyed special privileges. One of these was permission to extract high interest payments, which doubled every two weeks.[39] This gave the lender both a legal and financial advantage. The Mexican saying, "A mine needs a mine" [*una mina quiere mina*], suggests the dependence that a miner could have on his aviador. This was certain the case with Bustamante and Pedro Terreros, who by March 1743 became an equal partner.[40] By this date, they were not only equal partners in the mine but also jointly rented the refining hacienda of Ixtula in the municipality of Guascasaloya (modern Huasca). The men held the license to provide meat to the city of Pachuca and ran a retail store that was administered by their (merchant-clerk) cajero.[41]

Aside from their deepening business partnerships, the two men became personal friends. Terreros was asked to become the godparent for one of the Bustamante children. As coparents, or *compadres*, the two were prohibited from disputing and enjoined by the church to the highest standards of moral behavior toward each other. In many of the documents that Bustamante later signed, he asserted that he also represented his compadre, Pedro Romero de Terreros. Contemporaries often attested to their friendship. Pedro Terreros's cousin, Friar Giraldo Terreros, even wrote a letter to Terreros praising his partnership with Bustamante.[42]

In the joint mining venture at Real del Monte, Pedro Terreros supplied additional money and also bought slaves to labor in the mines. It was Bustamante, however, who had made an initial investment in the mine and who had the license. Bustamante also possessed both mining knowledge and familial contacts in Mexico City. Terreros described their partnership as one in which he "put his total wealth and Bustamante [invested] only his hard work," a statement only partially true since Bustamante had, of course, made the original financial investment in the mine. This was, however, for the most part a division of responsibilities and investments among partners that both Terreros and his uncle had earlier had in other commercial and industrial schemes. In this case, however, Terreros's statement ignored the financial contribution of his partner.[43] The 1743 partnership with Bustamante marked the beginning of the path that would lead to Pedro Terreros's domination of the Pachuca-Real del Monte region.

Of his many relatives and business partners, none was more important in the career of Pedro Terreros than Bustamante. Bustamante's original license established Terreros's claim to the Veta Vizcaína. He himself never received any license directly from the crown, but acquired the mines on the death of Bustamante. Before he died, Bustamante fervently argued for the significance of silver mines to both community and crown, while he also advocated for the rights of the original mine owners. In his writings requested by the crown, Bustamante pointed out that owners had to raise the capital to exploit the mines and struggle to control some fifteen different types of workers and administrators whose labor made possible the extraction of the underground wealth. Bustamante mourned not only the industry's shortage of capital, but also the ways in which the aviadores and mine workers victimized mine owners. Squeezed by both the aviador (capitalist-financier), whose investments in the mines made him a dominant presence, and by the workers, who, Bustamante claimed, stole tools provided by miners and the richest ores from the mines, many mine owners were ruined.[44] Bustamante's general economic views and his argument for the rights of mine owners were later adopted by Pedro Terreros, who began as an aviador and learned mining skills from Bustamante.[45] In fact, Terreros found himself, in the course of his almost decade-long relationship with Bustamante, in an ambiguous position. In the early years he safeguarded his investment through partnership, but later as he assumed a greater role in managing the mines, any inability to raise money placed him in the perilous position of losing his mines.

The very qualities that made Bustamante a notable and respected person among his contemporaries and to posterity also weakened his financial position. Both he and his brother-in-law, the marqués of Valleameno, provided workers with hospital care. He also refused to use *recojedores*—men paid to force free laborers to work in the mines at the regular rate of pay but against their will. His frequent attention to the needs of his community and, above all, his dedication to improving the conditions under which all owners operated took time and energy from the administration of his mines.[46]

In the decade of the 1720s, when Isidro Rodríguez Madrid controlled the Veta Vizcaína, the crown enjoyed the largest annual tax receipts of any period during the eighteenth century, which averaged nearly 154,000 pesos. The 1730s had an annual average of 93,500 pesos and in the 1740s, when Bustamante and Terreros controlled the Veta Vizcaína, the amount decreased to 67,000 pesos.[47] In the decade of the 1740s, the amount of silver sent to Mexico City from Pachuca continued to decline from its high point in the 1720s, although not so rapidly as in the previous decade.[48]

Draining the mines was the key to success at the Veta Vizcaína. It was hoped that while Bustamante and Terreros were building the adit to drain the mines in the 1740s that they would also discover more silver as workers dug in new places. But Bustamante found no bonanza, no rich vein of silver ore, in Azoyatla, where he had begun to build the horizontal drainage tunnel that would connect to the flooded mines of the Veta Vizcaína.[49] (See Map 4, above.) Around 1745, the viceroy permitted Bustamante and Terreros to abandon the Azoyatla site while giving them an additional series of mines on the other side of the mountain near Omitlán. These mines were located nearly 12,000 feet away from the Vizcaína and about 1,000 feet below the surface at a mine optimistically called La Joya (or, the Jewel). This site also eventually proved unproductive, and the smaller mine owners who had been attracted to invest in this venture dropped out. Bustamante and his partners then tried a third site, which they called Nuestra Señora de Aranzazu. It was here toward the end of the decade that they finally gained a bonanza at a formerly flooded mine appropriately called La Rica, or the rich mine, which contained silver-bearing ore that could be carried out on the barges that Bustamante had built.[50] Pedro Terreros later claimed to have spent 267,553 pesos on drainage projects alone, although some of that money may have been invested after 1748.

Pedro Terreros invested in a variety of businesses in the 1740s. He also traveled a lot, especially to Querétaro and Mexico City, where he bought slaves and established new businesses. He also frequented Pachuca, visiting with his compadre Bustamante but also overseeing his investments. In 1743, the year he became an equal partner in the mines with Bustamante, he assembled a record of his mercantile business, which had a total value of 143,000 pesos in commodities and various kinds of outstanding loans and expenses. He recorded having paid some 26,000 pesos to import goods from China and the Philippines. The account also notes the purchase of fabrics ranging from luxurious velvet to the simplest woven cotton cloth in addition to such luxuries as cacao from Caracas.[51] These commodities were sold in his stores in Real del Monte and Querétaro.⁵² By 1743, Terreros had probably already accumulated resources far beyond those he had received as the administrator of his uncle's estate. In 1748, he asserted in a statement to the crown that since 1741 he had invested 200,000 pesos in the mines of the Veta Vizcaína.⁵³ He later claimed to have invested 76,000 pesos more in the projects for draining the mines. Some of this money may have come from his friend and fellow merchant, Domingo López de Carvajal, who resided in Puerto de Santa María, Spain, and also in Mexico.⁵⁴ This infusion of outside capital exceeded the funds that Bustamante brought to the task of draining the mines.

BUSTAMANTE, TERREROS, AND THE MINING COMPANY: 1743-1755
Problems of financing the mines continued to trouble the partners and the government. The Spanish crown, always hungry for money, vastly increased pressure on their richest colony when war broke out between Spain and England in 1739. England's naval supremacy threatened shipments of silver from the colonies to Spain. This reached a crisis that erupted into the War of Jenkins's Ear and later expanded to the European continent as the War of the Austrian Succession (1740-48). The war affected the Spanish Empire's traditional methods of carrying on international commerce and the crown pressured merchants for large donations to aid the war effort.⁵⁵ But since no fleets sailed from Spain to the colonies, merchants in Mexico City were unable to provide traditional luxury commodities to their customers. These merchants sought other sources, such as mining to produce profits.

During the course of the war the Council of the Indies suggested that the viceroy, the count of Fuenclara, establish a new bank in 1743 to be dedicated to increasing investment in the silver mines. The new bank was to be funded by a forced loan from Mexico's wealthy citizens in which 2 million pesos would be raised by selling shares worth 500 pesos each in an enterprise called Company of Investors in the Mines of New Spain (Compañía de Aviadores de Minas de Nueva España). The leading merchants convinced the viceroy that the idea as conceived was impractical, and the general company never got started. However, the shortage of investment capital continued, and the idea for the creation of a company to invest in mines persisted.⁵⁶

In the 1740s, the pressure on the local people in Pachuca increased with the arrival of a new and more active viceroy, Juan Güemes de Horcacistas, later the count of Revilla Gigedo. He ordered the publication of a proclamation (*Bando*) setting forth the rules and conditions for a new company of miners. Bustamante was asked to serve as the viceroy's adviser on mining, and he also contributed to the company.⁵⁷ Bustamante took advantage of his position to publicize the significance of the silver industry and to explain the difficulties that bedeviled the colony's miners.⁵⁸ At the same time, Bustamante, whether coerced or voluntarily, recruited a company of investors to create a bank to provide capital to miners. Shares were sold to the public to raise funds for the more limited, but still costly, objective of providing money for the mines in Pachuca. The alcalde mayor of Pachuca on June 30, 1747, informed the viceroy of this new bank and told him what each miner had pledged to contribute.[59]

Bustamante's fellow investors in this venture included Tomás Tello, the son of a miner and a miner himself; Bustamante's own brother-in-law, the marqués del Valleameno; and Juan de Barandarián, a miner who was associated with Manuel Aldaco, an aviador tied to many Mexican miners. The mining company more closely resembled a limited partnership rather than a modern corporation. Through Barandarián and Aldaco the company gained the support of the silver banking family of Fagoaga, which controlled both a silver bank and the mint where silver bars were made into coin in Mexico City.[60] Tello provided intimate knowledge of the mining region. The marqués del Valleameno administered the vast properties of Hernan Cortés and had a pending appointment as governor of New Mexico, lending prestige to the venture. Valleameno's brother was also dean of the Mexico City cathedral, giving him the personal and political resources that, combined with Terreros's provincial fortune and assisted by capital from a Puerto de Santa María merchant, López de Carvajal, buttressed the banking company.[61]

Despite this impressive support from wealthy and powerful men, the company proved to be more advantageous for aviadores than for miners. Two years later, in 1749, Bustamante and Tello in fact tried to suppress it, because the financial obligations for supplies had driven them further into debt.[62] Since these men were experienced miners in the region, it appears that the banking company exacerbated the unfavorable position of the miner in Pachuca.

There are indications that Bustamante was already short of cash in 1745 when he began to sell his agricultural haciendas to Pedro Villaverde, whom he employed as a hacienda administrator. Pedro Terreros lent money to Villaverde, a creole from Michoacán, to pay for Bustamante's haciendas.[63] Villaverde would become an essential employee of Pedro Terreros, and he and his descendants served the Regla family for several generations. Pedro Terreros and Bustamante's brother-in-law, the marqués del Valleameno, continued to work with the banking company, Valleameno as a director and Terreros as an investor. In later years, Terreros alleged that the company owed him 48,103 pesos for about seventy-eight payments that he had made.[64]

During the 1740s Bustamante's financial position worsened, in part because the mines did not produce much silver. He lacked other businesses or sources of capital. He also had many time-consuming commitments in his roles as general attorney (*procurador general*) of the city and as the treasurer of the Franciscan college of Pachuca.[65] It is probable that he personally served in all positions, because he lacked the numerous relatives (*parentela*) who could represent him.

A wealthier, more powerful man would not have taken the time to fulfill these obligations. Only one half-brother, Fernando Bustamante, assisted José Alejandro as a representative in Mexico City, while Pedro Terreros called on Spanish and Querétaro cousins and nephews to aid him.[66]

Bustamante and Tello did not succeed in suppressing the company. Almost a year after Bustamante's death in August 1750, the marqués del Valleameno took over as banking company director. The end of the company is not certain, but it must have lasted at least until 1754, because Pedro Terreros still had an active account of about 4,000 pesos at that time.

To further his mining interests, Terreros maintained individual dealings with two banking company members: Juan de Barandarián and Tomás Tello, both experienced miners. Juan de Barandarián, who had begun working in the area in 1734, had originally been financed by the Fagoagas, the silver banking family in Mexico City. By 1752, Pedro Terreros had become another of his backers, and Barandarián owed him more than 72,000 pesos of principal and interest. In addition he had a debt of 6,013 pesos for mercury used to refine his silver ore. He was also forced by debt to cede to Terreros the important silver veins of Santa Brígida adjacent to the Veta Vizcaína in 1753.[67]

The history of the Tello brothers dealings with Pedro Terreros illustrates one of the ways in which Terreros rose to dominance in the region. Tomás Tello and his brother had inherited from their father mines and refining haciendas (*haciendas de beneficio*) built to process silver ore. They then formed a partnership with Pedro Terreros to purchase salt and the roasted copper pyrites (*magistral*) used in refining, as well as to buy commodities in Jalapa and Veracruz. They also experimented with the use of gunpowder for opening mine shafts and dislodging ore. In 1761, less than ten years after the founding of this partnership, Tello ceded the refining haciendas of San Antonio and San José to Terreros in return for his forgiving a debt of 26,000 pesos. In 1766, Tello borrowed 16,000 pesos from Terreros in order to cover another debt.[68] Terreros and Tello continued to have business dealings throughout their lives. When Tello died in 1780, one year before Pedro Terreros's death, his estate was auctioned, and Terreros obtained his old partner's house in Real del Monte and the hacienda of San Juan Hueyapán.[69] These purchases enabled Terreros to expand his control over the agricultural lands to the east of Real del Monte, centering around the municipalities of Huasca, Acatlán, and Tulancingo.

Terreros's relationship with Tello and Barandarián demonstrates a pattern followed by the financier in many of his other business dealings. He lent large sums of money to many different individuals, most of whom had difficulty repaying their loans. This money may have come from his commercial businesses or he may have acted as a conduit for peninsular merchants. When an individual could not repay his loans to Terreros, he received the debtor's property in lieu of payment. His dealings with Barandarián and Tello show how Terreros, in his role as money lender, could come to control, dominate, and fatally weaken the original mine owner and to increase his own wealth.

Although Pedro Terreros received refining haciendas, cash, and some additional mines from two of his partners, his association with Bustamante yielded a much more spectacular inheritance, the wealthiest series of mines in the Pachuca-Real del Monte region—the Veta Vizcaína. Since 1743, Terreros and Bustamante had worked the mines as equal partners, but at Bustamante's death in 1750, Pedro Terreros became, along with the marqués del Valleameno, a dominant figure in the mining region. His physical presence followed his investments, and after 1750 he spent much of his time in Pachuca and Real del Monte.

Bustamante's death in 1750 was not unexpected. He had been ill for more than a year, which may help to explain some of his business reverses. His illness might have been aggravated by knowledge of his financial precariousness as well as by the death of his wife, who probably died in childbirth and who had left him with many daughters. By 1750 he had few resources to provide for them in the future. One observer at this time commented on "Bustamante's notorious bad health." Another contemporary reported that José Alejandro "was afflicted with a bad leg which has so affected him that he cannot ride horseback and is often bed-ridden."[70] We know that he had resigned from some of his many positions in charities and politics, but continued to oversee the work of the mines. Returning in August 1750 to his home in Huasca, Bustamante fell from his horse and reinjured his leg, aggravating the earlier injury.[71] He died within a week on August 17, 1750.

Following Bustamante's death, Terreros opened a new ledger (*libro de caja*, a book listing his loans or credits organized by the name of the individual), which began by implying that Bustamante had ceded his interest in the Veta Vizcaína to Pedro Terreros. Terreros alleged in a letter to the viceroy copied into his ledger in 1750 that Bustamante had written that the mines belonged to his partner "because he had advanced the money which facilitated the work, and the offspring of Bustamante could only aspire to a certain [limited] amount."[72] He also wrote to the viceroy that "God has taken my compadre, and I [Pedro Terreros] remain in control of the mines." Pedro Terreros recorded that he had paid the 300 pesos still owing to Bustamante from their business ventures. During the course of the next years, he paid approximately 16,000 pesos to help care for the daughters of his former partner.[73] This money, partly dedicated to providing dowries for Bustamante's daughters to enter convents, may have satisfied a moral debt rather than a business obligation.

In his will, Bustamante requested that Terreros act as guardian of his children. While it had been advantageous in 1735 in Querétaro for Pedro Terreros to act as executor of his uncle's estate, fifteen years later, when he undertook the complete ownership of the mines, seemingly with abundant resources, administering

Bustamante's estate would have been a burdensome demand on his time and money. Instead, José Alejandro's half-brother, Manuel Bustamante, was substituted as the guardian and executor, serving simultaneously as one of Terreros's representatives for both family and business matters in Mexico City.[74]

The death of Bustamante both helped and hindered Terreros's ascent. He could now operate independently without consulting a partner, an arrangement he apparently preferred. By contrast, he had gained only a restricted title to the Veta Vizcaína with Bustamante's passing. The grant had been given to Bustamante alone, and mining ordinances prevented a second owner (such as Terreros taking over from his partner) from claiming the same rights to the mining vein that Bustamante had originally received in 1739.[75]

Bustamante had operated in ways that Pedro Terreros found deleterious but could not change while Bustamante was still alive. For example, Bustamante ceded the ownership of a mine to his brother-in-law, Valleameno, in order to receive more assistance from him in draining the mines. This same brother-in-law blocked Terreros's path to total control over the Veta Vizcaína. The peninsular Valleameno may have begun to mine in Real del Monte after his arrival in New Spain in 1742, where he became a major contributor to another company that rivaled Terreros's claims for the position of the most powerful miner in the region. The two men were almost contemporaries (Valleameno was seven years older) and both came from Andalucía. As such they were part of a less influential network of Spanish immigrants than those from northern Spain that dominated the colony's economy. But the commonalities of age and point of origin were counterbalanced in this case by the differing social and political position of the two men. Aside from his obvious social distinction as an aristocrat, Valleameno's political connections and his marriage into the same affluent mercantile family as Bustamante ensured him power and visibility in the community.[76] Valleameno had been working an unproductive mine in Pachuca in 1747 when Bustamante, probably influenced by family ties but also needing the financial contribution of his brother-in-law, decided to cede him a mine of the Veta Vizcaína named San Vicente.

The death of Bustamante removed any barrier to overt hostility between Valleameno and Terreros. Sometime between 1750 and 1754 Terreros attempted to retrieve the mine of San Vicente, alleging that it formed part of his inheritance from Bustamante. This move provoked a struggle with Valleameno, resulting in an argument over who owned the mine of San Vicente. The law suit to determine the rights of each litigant involved by extension three or four of the principal families of Mexico City. This meant that leading jurists, mining officials, the alcalde mayor of Pachuca, the *audiencia*, the viceroy, and in Spain, the Council of the Indies, and the king would all be pulled into the struggle. It also led to acts of violence when Pedro Terreros attempted to seize the mine, provoking small numbers of partisans of the two sides to at least one battle in the streets of Pachuca. While royal officials deplored the misplaced energy and cost of this conflict, a substantial amount of silver wealth was at stake as well as domination of Real del Monte.[77]

The dispute was focused on whether Valleameno had temporary or permanent possession of the mine of San Vicente and whether he had contributed financially to the digging of the adit that had drained the shafts. Before Bustamante's death, Valleameno had offered to keep his section of the vein drained by malacates (winches). The next year, in 1748, he had also agreed to pay one-quarter of the costs of a second attempt to dig an adit in the southern part of the Veta. Bustamante and Terreros were expected to pay half while other minority partners paid the last 25 percent. A year later, the investors abandoned that effort and tried again in a third location. They changed the name of the site from the humble Doña Juana to the grand Nuestra Señora de Aranzazu. At this point the minority partners withdrew, the two major investors absorbed these extra costs, and Valleameno acquiesced in the plan to continue his 25 percent contribution until the adit reached another mine.[78] In the year 1749, the men digging the adit discovered a rich ore-bearing section of their underground workings, apparently quite close to where the water would eventually drain from the interior of the earth.[79]

But Terreros's joy at this find was embittered by the fact that Valleameno's mine of San Vicente also contained rich veins and was in bonanza by 1750. To make matters worse, in 1753 Valleameno struck a second rich vein at his mine of Todos Santos.[80] Not surprisingly, Terreros chose this moment to initiate efforts to get back the San Vicente mine from Valleameno by claiming that the marqués was not obeying the royal mining ordinances. Valleameno's lawyer, Francisco Javier Gamboa, disputed this charge by asserting that his client had continued the work of the adit when Bustamante had become fatigued and was ready to abandon it. The mining judge rejected Terreros's claim to San Vicente, either because he had a poor case or because he lacked appropriate connections in the appeals court of the audiencia in Mexico City.[81]

The quarrel between the two men was intensified by the issue of mine worker and muleteer wages. Some unknown numbers of mine workers had been lured by Terreros from Guanajuato, but after their arrival in Real del Monte Terreros had reneged on his promise to pay them 4 reales a day; instead, he paid some of them only 3 reales. Workers possibly elected to work in Valleameno's mines because both pay and conditions were more advantageous there. This left Terreros short of workers.[82] According to the Valleameno representatives, Terreros's men invaded their mines on at least one occasion, forcibly carrying off workers and mistreating them.

Testimony given in this case in the audiencia indicates that from 1750 to 1755 Valleameno was a more successful mine owner than Terreros. Bernardino Díaz, the administrator of the Valleameno mines, testified that his employer had always paid the same amount as Terreros to dig the "exalted" adit and, moreover, that Valleameno's mines were producing more silver than Terreros's mines.[83]

In 1755, in the midst of this quarrel, Valleameno died at age fifty-two. He left a pregnant wife and three small children to inherit his rich mines. His heirs also inherited the need to continue defending family interests against Terreros. The latter task his wife accepted with alacrity. The marquesa filed suit to set aside the 1739 license to mine that Terreros had inherited from Bustamante. She also sought to deny Terreros the right to use forced Indian labor, a critical advantage of his original license since Indian villages in the surrounding region were obliged to contribute men to labor in the mines who were paid less than free workers.[84]

Between June 1756 and April 1757 two events altered the larger struggle between the two factions. One was Terreros's marriage into the prominent Miravalle family, giving him direct access to audiencia judges and to the viceroy. The countess of Miravalle, his mother-in-law, arranged that the audiencia judge assigned to hear the case would be her second cousin, Joaquín Antonio Rivadaneira, an important intellectual and writer in eighteenth-century Mexico.[85] Unfortunately, at the same time, Terreros's mines also flooded. Terreros's desire for the San Vicente mine grew appreciably after this incident, as did his need for forced Indian labor to drain the mines.

In the early days of 1757, fighting occasionally broke out in the streets of Pachuca between the representatives of the Terreros and Valleameno factions. These fights continued sporadically until 1759, when the courts ruled against Terreros.[86] The Valleameno faction claimed possession of the mines, but Terreros asserted in a legal case that since the family had ceased to pay any of the expenses for the drainage works, they had no right to the mines that benefited from it. Francisco Javier Gamboa, one of the colony's leading jurists, represented Valleameno's interests in this conflict. He alleged that his clients had invested in timbering, in opening mines, and in the creation of new ventilation shafts. However, it is not certain that any of this contributed to the actual drainage project.[87] As flooding became more severe, the Terreros interests tried to hide this problem from their opponents because it exposed their financial vulnerability.[88]

The legal process continued as the case wound its way through courts. After the decision of the local alcalde mayor of Pachuca awarded the disputed mine to Terreros, the case reached the audiencia on appeal. This court awarded the mine to Valleameno when the countess of Miravalle's cousin could not exercise his influence due to a conflict of interest. This decision was called into question when the Viceroy Amarillas, a good friend of both Miravalle and Terreros, disagreed. The case was appealed to the Council of the Indies in Spain by Terreros, who also asked for special favors. In 1759, the king and council decided that Terreros had no right to own San Vicente.[89]

It was, therefore, in the summer of 1759 that Terreros decided to take matters into his own hands. On Holy Trinity Sunday—which falls on the Sunday after Pentecost, either in April or May—when the mine of San Vicente was left unguarded,

Pedro Terreros and a group of his men entered the mine of San Vicente. This force included three foreman, a number of pickmen (*barreteros*, the leading men in a crew working in the mines), plus a contingent from surrounding haciendas provided by Terreros's employee Pedro Villaverde. They claimed that Terreros owned this part of the mine, a crucial area that was needed in order to connect to two points in Terreros's mine of La Joya. The marquesa del Valleameno's administrator, Bernardino Díaz, a local merchant and also one of the most capable miners in Real del Monte, accused Terreros of criminal trespass in a judicial process. After evaluating the evidence the courts ruled in favor of the Valleameno interests and levied a fine of 5,000 pesos on Terreros. Terreros paid the fine after some delay, but he refused to give up the section of the mine that he had seized. Nor would he cooperate in any effort to measure the boundaries within the mine. When officials came to find him at home, the doorkeeper tried to stop them, but they entered forcibly and were then invited to join Terreros in his meal. It seems that this display of power and supreme confidence put off the officials. Whether Terreros still possessed the mine of San Vicente is not clear.[90]

While the marquesa won the legal case, she neither possessed the mine nor its revenues. The death of the dean of the Mexico City cathedral, the executor of her husband's will, only added to her woes, for with his death she lost an influential male advocate. The marquesa's remarriage in 1760 to a widower with eight children, the treasurer of the mining region of Zimapán, should have improved her position, "because she now had someone to look after her interests," as Pedro Terreros's mother-in-law wrote to him.[91] Perhaps she remarried because she perceived the weakness of a woman in a conflict with a dominant local patriarch who could ignore legal decisions.

Terreros finally received legal title to the San Vicente mine in January 1766 after eleven years of conflict when the guardian of the Valleameno children returned the 1747 Bustamante letter of donation to Terreros.[92] With this private settlement that became a part of the official record, Terreros, the youngest and socially the lowest of the Andalucian trio, single-handedly dominated the richest mines in Pachuca and Real del Monte. Nonetheless, other miners and investors continued to operate in the region and to challenge Terreros's attempts at complete control.

SUCCESSES AND TRIUMPHS: 1750-1766

We know that Pedro Terreros possessed abundant resources by 1752, because in this year the military order of Calatrava accepted him as a member, an honor only bestowed on men of financial substance. In the same year, the archbishop of Mexico gave him the honorific title of "Father of the destitute and faithful supporter of religion" [Padre de desválidos y fiel apoyo de Religión]. This was another recognition that was only granted to wealthy men.[93] By 1754 Terreros had agreed to contribute 1,000 pesos a week for the construction of the altar of the church of San Fernando in Mexico City and to provide expensive dowries for the daughters of his deceased partner, Bustamante. According to his own statement when he applied for a noble title later in 1759, he had "substantial wealth" (*crecido caudal*). As recognition, wealth, and power accumulated in his hands, he began to add the name Regla to the names of saints and geographic landmarks that he used to designate his refining haciendas: El Salto, meaning waterfall, became La Regla, and San Miguel Archangel became San Miguel Regla.

Terreros got the capital to invest in the mines from his mercantile business and the management of his uncle's estate. Domingo López de Carvajal, a Spanish merchant and occasional resident of Mexico City, also invested at least 600,000 pesos. Another 500,000 pesos came from the Fagoaga family.[94] From 1750 to 1766, Terreros continued to invest in mining enterprises, with a substantial proportion going to fund the huge drainage project initiated in 1739. This was an immense project indeed. According to his own estimate, he had spent "a long time of twenty-three years, two months, and three days of mounting costs and such indescribable troubles, and labor, and suffering in the course of the work of the adit," not ceasing until most of the mines composing the Veta Vizcaína were connected. Humboldt, the German scientist who visited Mexico in the early years of the nineteenth century, reported that the drainage tunnel traversed 7,715 feet (2,352 meters) from its beginning to the point where it crossed the Vizcaína. When completed in 1762, Terreros claimed that he had spent 268,153 pesos for two failed drainage adits that uncovered no rich veins of ore. He requested another inspection of his mines in order to ensure his ownership of the mines, asserting that by September 1762 he had spent a total of 1,428,706 pesos on the mines without including the cost of purchasing the slaves. He also invested an undetermined amount of money to develop or improve a series of mines within the Veta Vizcaína—Santa Teresa, Jesús Nazareno, La Palma, Cristo, and Las Animas. These improvements included digging new entrances to mines, timbering inside the mines, and other activities designed to permit access to rich ore-bearing rocks. (See Map 4, above.)

It is unclear when Pedro Terreros (and Bustamante) began to reap large amounts of silver from their investments and labors. Profits could have been earned anytime from 1749 to 1759. Francisco Canterla placed the earliest profits in 1759 when Terreros brought 60,000 silver marcos (multiplied by eight, this comes to 480,000 pesos) to register with officials in Pachuca.

Spanish law required miners in the region to first bring silver to Pachuca to be weighed and taxed before sending it to Mexico City to be minted. The assayer at the treasury in Pachuca weighed the silver and subtracted one-tenth of its total weight, which was given to the crown as tax. The results give a rough, but probably reliable, figure as to the amount of silver Terreros and other miners sent to Mexico City where the silver bars were minted as reales and pesos.[95] Owners also used some silver bars to make objects such as frames for paintings and mirrors, cutlery, and other domestic products. More silver was used to make the ritual objects used in the celebration of the Catholic liturgy. Some silver certainly escaped taxation as contraband, and production figures may be incomplete.

The records of the Pachuca treasury indicate the increasing wealth that came from the region (see Table 2). There were many ups and downs in the amount of silver sent to Mexico City in bars before 1751. After this date the value of the silver bars began to grow, exceeding 82,000 marcos (656,000 pesos) a year. The records of the treasury provide some figures, although we do not have specific figures for Regla until after 1761.

Thanks to historians Bernd Hausberger and Francisco Canterla, we know that between 1761 and 1766 the percentage of silver that Terreros registered in the treasury was between 57 and 76 percent of the total production of the region. The total percentage of silver produced in his mines may have been even higher, because workers had the right to sell their share of the ore to other refiners who registered the silver under their own names. From 1760 to 1767, Terreros sent between 67,000 and 86,000 marcos to Mexico City. Terreros's share of total remissions from the region reached a high of 69 percent in 1763 and 1764, dropping to 59 percent in 1767 and to almost nothing in 1768. This decline was the consequence of five different work stoppages in the mines and refining haciendas.[96]

Extensive tunneling and timbering gave Terreros access to rich silver-bearing ores, but these still had to be transformed into silver bars. The production of silver from raw ore took place in industrial refining facilities called *haciendas de beneficio de metales* or *hacienda de minas*. Water, ore, and chemicals used in extracting silver from base metals—mercury, copper pyrites, lead, and salt—were mixed together in large open areas called patios. It was these low-walled mixing areas that gave the process the name of patio process. Workers or mules stirred this mixture of chemicals into a claylike substance by walking through it. The mixture was allowed to dry and then was burned in a kiln where the silver separated from the mercury.[97]

Every miner of consequence sought to control the refining process by building or renting his own mills. Competition also came from independent refiners who served smaller mine owners as well as from mine workers who sometimes received a part of their pay in unrefined ore, a practice known as *partido*. These workers then sold their partido ore to the independent refiners or refined it themselves by constructing small furnaces equipped with bellows that smelted the ore to dislodge silver.

As early as their first partnership, Bustamante and Terreros had begun to refine their own ore in the rented refining haciendas of Ixtula and San Miguel. After Terreros purchased the San Miguel refinery from another miner around 1757, he expanded it and built an aqueduct that brought water to the open yards or patios. About 1753, Terreros also bought a site previously used for refining from the son of another local miner, Isidro Escorcia. It was in this hacienda,

Table 2 Silver Registered in the Pachuca Treasury between 1743–1767

(In Marcos, for an approximate value in pesos multiply each figure by eight)

1743	38,549
1744	69,139
1745	Missing
1746	Missing
1747	64,943
1748	58,610
1749	80,027
1750	Missing
1751	94,142
1752	96,842
1753	93,218
1754	104,327
1755	Missing
1756	Missing
1757	117,239
1758	86,612
1759	82,410
1760	132,045
1761	137,615
1762	110,272
1763	122,178
1764	145,740
1765	146,127
1766	129,607
1767	146,755

Source: Canterla, *Vida y obra,* 40.

originally called El Salto, that he began to construct on a vast scale and at the cost of nearly a half-million pesos the hacienda that eventually became Santa María Regla.[98] The viceroy proclaimed "that it appears impossible that one individual could have undertaken to construct, pay for, and put all his passion into such prodigious, never before created works."[99] Nineteenth-century travelers still marveled at this building:

This stupendous work of Mexican miners in former days . . . is said to have cost many millions of dollars. . . . It has an air of vastness and desolation and at the same time of grandeur, that shows well amidst a war of the elements. Down in a deep *barranca* [gorge], encircled by basaltic cliffs, it lies: a mighty pile of building, which seems as if it might have been constructed by some philosophical giant or necromancer. . . .

All is on a gigantic scale: the immense vaulted storehouses for the silver ore; the great smelting furnaces and covered buildings where we saw the process of amalgamation [with mercury] going on; the water wheel—in short, all the necessary machinery for the smelting and amalgamation of the metal. [We saw] the great cascade, with its rows of basaltic columns. . . .The columns look as though they might have been the work of those, who on the plains of Shinar, began to build the city and the tower whose top was to reach to heaven.[100]

Contemporaries asserted that Pedro Terreros himself had planned this great hacienda. It still stands. Modern visitors remain impressed by the extent of the buildings, with windowless, cavernous rooms that later owners adapted for filming adventure and mystery movies and even to produce mushrooms. (See Figures 5, 6, 7, and 8.)

The scallop shell (*romero*), the symbol of a pilgrim, decorates the outside of the chapel. It will be remembered that Romero is one of Pedro Terreros's last names. The scallop shell also decorated buildings at San Miguel and might have meant to Terreros the successful conclusion of a long journey dedicated to spiritual as well as material ends.

It was in this hacienda, currently known as Santa María Regla, but previously called La Regla, that Pedro Terreros employed on a large scale the older method of reducing the ore to silver by smelting. While this older method was less efficient because more silver was lost, it was also cheaper because it required less labor and livestock and did not use expensive chemicals like mercury. It required only furnaces, charcoal, and bellows to fan the flames. Over time, Terreros began to increase his use of smelting.[101]

Another of Terreros's great haciendas, that of San Miguel Regla, where he often lived between 1766 and 1781, and where his daughters also resided for some of their young lives, has been a hotel since at least 1956. Visitors can still see the aqueduct of "piers and arches which carried the water to the circular, shallow, open tanks." The tanks are under the lake at San Miguel, but the kiln chimneys are visible.[102]

One of Terreros's major accomplishments remains his extensive acquisition of property. In 1762, Pedro Terreros owned a total of seven refining haciendas.[103] In 1780 he purchased the largest agricultural hacienda between Pachuca and Tulancingo at the death of his former partner in the mining company, Tomás Tello. Terreros also converted the region around Huasca, some 20 miles northeast of

Fig. 5. Kilns at San Miguel Regla. Photograph by Marco Hernández.

Pachuca into the District of the Reglas (Comarca de las Reglas). At the end of the twentieth century, the name and portrait of the count of Regla have come to dominate the public spaces of San Miguel Regla, and many commercial establishments have appropriated forms of his name and title. Of another refining hacienda, San Antonio Regla, which Terreros began to construct and use after 1760, only a chimney survives, emerging from a small muddy lake. This hacienda fell victim to a different phase of industrialization when the electric power company transformed the site, probably sometime in the 1940s.

Other miners and refiners offered competition by continuing to mine for silver-bearing ores in Real del Monte and Pachuca. Especially challenging was a company headed by Manuel Moya, financed first by Mexico City's wealthiest merchant, the count of Jala, and then by another group of investors. This company competed with Terreros but ultimately failed to make a significant profit. Juan de Barandarián, one of the partners with Terreros in the original Banco de la Compañía, worked in Pachuca from 1734, spending fourteen years and seven months exploiting the Santa Brígida vein in Real del Monte. He benefited from investments made by Manuel Aldaco, a powerful silver banker, but he and others such as Marcelo de Anza eventually left the region.[104] Even so, Regla never enjoyed a complete monopoly of silver production in the Real del Monte region.

Unlike other investor-merchants, Terreros confined his interests to one mining region, with the exception of some investments in the relatively close-by mines of tin and silver in Zimapán.[105] He never invested in wealthy and more distant areas such as Guanajuato, Zacatecas, Bolaños, or Catorce.

Fig. 6. Waterfall at Santa María Regla.
Photograph by Marco Hernández.

Fig. 7. View of Santa
María Regla. Photograph
by Marco Hernández.

Fig. 8. View of Santa María Regla.
Photograph by Marco Hernández.

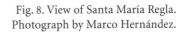

CONCLUSION

How did Pedro Terreros, a younger son of an impoverished family from a marginal region in Spain, become a man of great wealth and power in one of the most vital industries in all the Spanish Empire? His position was achieved in part as a result of good fortune. The deaths of his brother, uncle, and his later business partners, Bustamante and Valleameno, when he was still a very young man provided Terreros with the opportunity to gain success in Querétaro and then in Real del Monte. He eventually became chief owner in the region's richest mines. Luck, however, was only one reason for his success. That other merchants, such as his friend Domingo López de Carvajal, invested in his enterprises suggests that Terreros also inspired confidence among his contemporaries. In 1770, Terreros wrote that López de Carvajal had invested more than 600,000 pesos in Terreros's mines.[106]

Pedro Terreros rarely experimented with new technologies. Although his Mexico City representative had informed him of a device to drain mines using a single operator, he chose not to employ it.[107] His investment in mines relied largely on traditional methods, such as tunneling, timbering, and drainage, and in the rationalization of the refining process. He did utilize gunpowder to open shafts and to dislodge silver-bearing rocks by blasting, but this was a cheap, if often dangerous, innovation.

Fortune, friends, and wise investments only partly explain his success. His great talent, attention to detail, incredible hard work, and tenacity—that were frequently referred to in his contemporaries' correspondence—also contributed to making him the dominant force in the mines of Pachuca and Real del Monte. A fearless man, always convinced of the rightness of his actions, he succeeded in overcoming a lack of investment capital in the mines. By uniting in his own person the role of aviador, miner, and refiner, he wielded greater strength and influence than did any of his precursors. Together with his use of his uncle's estate, Pedro Terreros's skill as a merchant and financier was the basis for amassing the necessary capital to invest in the mines.

Although Terreros sometimes worried about when he would receive *avíos*, the coins he needed to meet his payrolls and other expenses, from his partners and mercantile businesses, he often had money to lend to borrowers who had property to use as collateral. His willingness to furnish money to miners who needed to buy mercury, or for any of the other endless expenses of the industry, gave him the strength and power to complement his skill in warding off competitors. His sometime use of the "bellicose habits of the Spanish nation," as might be indicated in the occasional display of temper, and his invasion of his rival's mine, contributed to his success.[108] He also seems to have possessed personal charm and a personality that inspired trust and confidence. The completion of the drainage adit at Real del Monte, the building of large refining mills, the construction of an aqueduct to carry water to the refining mill of

San Miguel Regla, all demonstrate his ability to attain success by overcoming obstacles.

In evaluating the ideas and plans that facilitated Terreros's achievements, the question arises whether his often rough treatment of other miners was an essential element in his ascent. Terreros appeared to believe that small entrepreneurs hindered the mining industry, and he hoped to monopolize the mines by eliminating them. He (and the colonial government as well) believed that small mine owners inhibited the mining industry since they could not contribute significantly to draining the mines or overcoming other impediments. Numerous mine owners also meant that different entrances to many mines existed, which in turn facilitated loss of valuable ore through theft and a consequent reduction in taxation.

Throughout the eighteenth century, in nearly all the mining communities that survived until the latter part of the century, the cost of draining old mines and discovering new ones increased. The government and businessmen tried to resolve the problems by creating larger enterprises, concentrating capital, and placing management of mines and refining haciendas under the control of a single individual or a closely connected group. Combining the bulk of the silver mines and refining haciendas under single ownership had a venerable tradition in Mexico, as the law permitted miners to pay a lower rate of taxation on the silver they brought to the treasury while independent refiners paid double the amount of taxes on the silver they produced. Pedro Terreros proved to be more successful in the long run, or perhaps more predatory, in achieving this vertical integration of the mining industry than were his predecessors. By 1766, Pedro Terreros owned much property and had achieved substantial wealth. Despite these achievements, however, endemic labor problems surfaced almost from the beginning of his time in Real del Monte, developing into near catastrophe both for him personally and for his mining enterprises.

CHAPTER 4

The "Honorable Men" who Worked the Mines

The workers harbor in their hearts a perpetual mortal hatred
for mine owners and press-gangs. These men, in turn, aware of the
workers' vices and customs, live in constant fear.

— José Antonio Areche, 1770, quoted in Danks,
"Revolts of 1766 and 1767"

José Antonio Areche, the chief crown attorney, investigated mine workers' rebellions in the Pachuca region. His report and evidence presented in workers' own words indicates that the men who worked the mines viewed their employers, especially Pedro Terreros, as arrogant, cruel, and high-handed. Mainly mestizo and mulatto, free workers felt that they were unrecognized and unappreciated partners in an enterprise that involved risks to their lives and health whenever they descended into the mines. Exposed to danger from collapsing walls, sudden floods, and fires, working in icy water amid smells of excrement, breathing clouds of metallic dust, the workers considered themselves to be courageous, fearless, pugnacious, faithful comrades to one another, imbued with "individual bravery and collective valor." Although they identified themselves as family men, they were also fond of gambling and dancing. It was thus that the workers described themselves and their lives in testimony in investigations following work stoppages, mass actions, and riots in 1766 and 1767.[1]

Mine owners and members of the elite had a negative view of the workers whom they characterized as lazy, insolent, rebellious, and full of vice. It was not uncommon for owners to characterize their own employees as diabolically clever thieves, intent only on robbing the owners of their tools, candles, and the richest pieces of silver ore. They also viewed them as dangerous and prone to riot. In a statement that reflects Pedro Terreros's opinions, although filtered through the words of a royal official:

> This class of person, with their malicious judgments nourished from
> the cradle with vicious customs peculiar to their miserable upbringing,
> do not aspire to any glory other than that of acquiring goods in order to
> flee or to get drunk. Nor are they governed by any reason other than that
> of their own interest, and if the means of achieving this is denied them,
> no matter how irrational and unjust their desires, they believe them-
> selves to be oppressed and aggrieved. From this rises their refusal to work

in construction [*obras muertas*], because it is useless to them however important it might be to the mines and to the owners.[2]

Even the jurist, Francisco Javier Gamboa, generally believed to be sympathetic to the workers, opined that "workers caused greater damage [to the mines] than epidemics or war," and found them to be "insolent and obsessed with money." Members of the elite viewed impressed Indian workers, less inclined to steal or to riot, as "lazy and inept."[3]

The enmity between mine owner and worker became acute in Pachuca and Real del Monte, and open conflict between them erupted several times during the forty years that Pedro Terreros invested in and worked these mines. Terreros was a slave owner and also had a license that allowed him to obtain forced labor from Indian villages. Terreros also supplemented his workforce by actively employing press-gangs (*recojedores* or *sacagentes*) who obtained free men—Indians, mestizos, mulattos, as well as poor whites—to labor in the mines by capturing them and bringing them forcibly to work. He employed these techniques, which were common among mine owners in central Mexico. The principal way in which his labor policy differed from that of other eighteenth-century mine owners was in his continual use of slave labor when it was declining elsewhere in New Spain. Any attempt to increase production in the mines made his need for workers even more acute. His labor policy played a crucial role in his success, and it was also the one that revealed some of the darkest aspects of his character. He knew that manpower was the key ingredient in making mining profitable and was relentless in the task of getting workers. Labor for him was a means to increase production, and he showed little concern for the human needs of workers.

When the Pachuca region lacked a single large owner and unguarded mines provided opportunities for worker entrepreneurs, mine workers enjoyed some autonomy. But with the arrival of an aggressive owner like Terreros, they became subject to a stricter labor discipline and to the often relentless activities of press-gangs. All this led to accumulated resentment and anger on the part of the workers. The distinction between free and forced labor became especially difficult to draw during the years when Terreros controlled the Real del Monte mines.

By the end of the eighteenth century, free mine workers dominated the labor force in Mexico. Between 1741, when Pedro Terreros entered the mining region of Pachuca and Real del Monte as an investor and entrepreneur, and the end of the eighteenth century, the composition of the labor force shifted from partial dependence on unfree labor—occasional chattel slavery, and forced labor of Indian villagers—to free labor. Press-gangs operated in Indian villages as well as in Pachuca and Real del Monte and supplemented the supply of free labor. Forced labor, while by the eighteenth century an auxiliary to a free labor force, remained central to Pedro Terreros's ideas about operating his mines and refining haciendas.

For mine owners, finding the men (and some women) willing to risk their lives and health to extract silver ore at a price the owners were willing to pay proved difficult, so they frequently resorted to forced labor.

Workers were attracted to mine owners who paid them high wages and were willing to provide them with a share of the ore.⁴ But as the mines became deeper, the danger of floods greater, and the costs of extraction higher, the necessity for forced labor grew since it was so expensive to pay for free labor. In fact, for undercapitalized mine owners, acquiring the money for wages ranked with the lack of capital for investment in the fixed works of mining as a constant problem. Constructing tunnels, shafts, and drainage canals also depended on an abundance of cheap labor and often did not produce silver-bearing ore.

The use of slave labor, one traditional way of solving this problem, had been employed from the very beginning of commercial mining in the Indies. By the 1740s, slavery had almost disappeared in most silver mines, because of the rise in population.⁵ Pedro Terreros vastly increased the use of slaves in the mines. Nonetheless, free workers had become the most important category of men working underground. They usually received a wage of 4 to 6 reales a day, high wages for the workers of New Spain. Agricultural and unskilled urban laborers were more likely to receive about 2 reales. Many workers received some limited noncash compensation. Highly skilled workers, such as the pickmen (*barreteros*), who dug out the ore and applied the explosives, may have earned up to 12 reales a day, leading to the general impression that mine workers received excellent pay.

In 1748, Bustamante analyzed the difficulties facing mine owners. His conclusions, while perhaps reflecting his partner's views as well as his own, identified the chief difficulty in the mines as the workers. He observed that the workers who received partido (a share of the ore they mined and one method of extra cash compensation) believed that "the metal the owner receives is given as though it were charity, while the metal that the workers steal is owed to them in justice because of their labor."⁶ With their share of the ore and what they could conceal of rich pieces of ore called *mogrollos*, often these men felt no necessity to work the required three shifts a week. Hence, a common feature of every mining town was press-gangs, often armed with whips, who seized men defined as idle or vagabonds and forced them to work. This kind of forced labor had a long tradition throughout Europe, as monarchs sought to insure an adequate supply of oarsmen to man their galleys. Vagrancy ordinances were used as a legal fiction.⁷

The use of enslaved and forced Indian labor was one way for miners to circumvent the shortage of cash caused by the increased costs of mining. Terreros had difficulties with each category of worker: slaves, forced, and free laborers. At the root of these difficulties was his desire to spend as little as possible for labor. Terreros simply did not value the contribution of the mine workers, whether Indians, *castas* (men and women of mixed origin), blacks, or manual workers of any ethnic category. He appeared to view them as mere instruments for the implementation of the great work that would benefit the towns of Pachuca and Real del Monte, the nation, the king, and himself.

Terreros conceived of himself as a philanthropist who produced silver for the king and who brought prosperity to the community. The aid he gave to the local religious institutions convinced him of a symbiotic relationship between the mining industry and the community, but blinded him to the needs of the men whose labor made possible his philanthropy. He perhaps perceived himself as the patriarch in charge of the fate of all those who occupied the lower places in the hierarchical structure of society. Even the worker's pay could be viewed as an act of charity on his part, since it took resources from his other philanthropies.

Sometime after 1756, he became the largest employer in the Pachuca region, paying up to 3,000 pesos a week in wages. In four of the mines where he employed mainly free workers, there were as many as 956 men per shift and in each week there were fourteen shifts.[8] Having enough coins to meet this substantial payroll presented problems; his correspondence reflects at least once a worry about lack of *avíos*, by which he might have meant coin to meet payrolls.[9] It is difficult to determine whether he suffered from a general lack of liquidity or whether he lacked the actual coins.

The government played a leading role in providing and regulating labor from Indian villages to the mine operators. Based on the concept of a moral economy, which suggested that royal officials mediate between employers and workers, officials regulated the amount that should be paid, and how many hours and days they should work; the government also licensed press-gangs to individual mine owners. In the end, official rhetoric favored the workers, proclaiming that they must be well-treated and given work suitable to their abilities. The crown also ordered that mine owners must "fulfill the royal laws that are so full of piety and clemency." As an official pointed out in 1724, "The good intentions often fail because a shortage of laborers will reduce mine owners to poverty."[10] But as the government dictated wages, attempted to control press-gangs, and issued pious pleas for good treatment, the insatiable hunger of the Spanish crown for silver meant that officials tended to decide in favor of the employer. Workers still believed, however, that the viceroy, as representative of the king, would intervene on their behalf. Pedro Terreros argued that the government had failed to provide him with sufficient workers at a low wage and the right to determine the length of imprisonment or the kind of punishment for various offenses. He further complained that royal officials inflicted only "mild punishments" on rebellious and obstreperous laborers.[11]

SLAVERY

The beginnings of slavery in Mexico and the extraction of precious metals are intimately connected. In the sixteenth century the crown, seeking to end the enslavement of the Indian population, instituted the policy of importing Africans to replace Indian slaves.[12] Between 1741 and 1781, the years in which Pedro Terreros invested and worked in Real del Monte, slavery disappeared in other mining regions. This was partly the result of a growing mestizo and mulatto population and partly because miners with bonanza mines became willing to pay wages and share the ore with the workers under the partido system. But Terreros insisted on retaining chattel slaves as mine labor.[13]

Pedro Terreros had a long history as a slave owner. Beginning with the purchase of one slave from his still meager earnings as an apprentice merchant, he initiated the acquisition of slaves in 1741 when he started to invest in the silver mines. Starting with slaves purchased in Querétaro, with several coming from the estate of his uncle, he continued purchasing slaves from his cousin, the heir to his uncle's estate, through 1744. He purchased these slaves for 150 pesos each, although they were evaluated at 200 pesos.[14]

It would appear that he entered the Pachuca region as a slave-owner as well as an investor, and slaves formed an essential part of his labor force. Much of the information that we have about him during the 1740s, when he was still a merchant, concerns slave dealing. In March 1744 he paid 1,313 pesos to purchase nine slaves from the owner of a textile mill (*obraje*). This purchase of a large number of slaves and their transportation to the mines even attracted the attention of the authorities in Mexico City and formed part of a debate about the cost of slaves and whether it was better to use slaves instead of men and women who had committed crimes and were sentenced to terms in obrajes.[15] In Mexico City, in October and November 1743, Terreros purchased five or six slaves for prices from 120 to 150 pesos. Sellers ranged from recent widows seeking to realize cash from property they had inherited from their husbands, to owners of obrajes who were suffering financial losses or trying to rid themselves of difficult workers.[16] Almost all of his purchases were of creole or Mexican-born slaves.

In later years, Terreros employed agents to procure slaves, including his mother-in-law, his representatives in Mexico City, and Pedro Villaverde, the administrator of Jesuit haciendas.[17] In 1768, shortly after the Real del Monte strikes, he purchased a number of slaves that were sent to him in Pachuca from Mexico City.[18] Another notice that we have of his acquisition of slaves occurred as late as 1771, when he bought four slaves from an obraje in San Angel.[19] Two years before his death, he still operated at least one of his mines with slave labor.

Costs of slaves able to work in the mines (males between the age of twenty and fifty, but mostly in their twenties) varied between 100 and 200 pesos, with the price of most slaves 150 pesos and below. For one slave, a blacksmith, Terreros paid 500 pesos.[20] Terreros paid the cost of branding, 4 reales for transport between Mexico City and the mines (probably more from Querétaro), and 6 pesos for alcabalas, or sales taxes. Slave prices may have been declining, as in 1761, one man purchased his freedom from Terreros for 117 pesos.[21]

That relations between former owners and slaves could be close is suggested by the requirements that former owners occasionally imposed on the purchasers. Families selling slaves sometimes exacted a restriction on whether a slave could be used in the mines, would be employed as a coachman, or that the wife of a slave would be provided with a job as a cook. Terreros surely found these restrictions burdensome, and whether he observed them is unknown.

In one case, a slave claimed that he himself had placed conditions on his work in the mines, alleging that when he was purchased in Querétaro along with other slaves in an obraje, he had come voluntarily to work in the mines in 1744 in order to collect partido (a share of the ore) and buy his freedom. In 1749, this same slave, Tomás Antonio Guzmán, had found a lawyer—under a statute providing for a *procurador de pobres* (lawyer for the poor)—to represent him before the crown about both mistreatment and lack of partido. Identifying Terreros as "owner of the mine La Rica, who purchased slaves in obrajes and led them to work in the mines," Guzmán and another slave asserted that they were tolerating incredible labors with the hope of obtaining their freedom. They accused Terreros of "giving them many blows, with which they were wounded and marked, they were cruelly whipped, and kept continually nude and hungry." Their wives, who were not slaves, had accompanied them to the mines and had worked for the owners for 3 reales a week, grinding corn and making gruel for long hours.

Terreros and his partner Bustamante, who spoke for him, claimed that Terreros's good name had been injured and denied the charges. Bustamante observed that Terreros was a vecino (citizen) of Querétaro and resident in Mexico City in 1749 and that he had bought slaves but did not supervise them. Terreros tried to clear his name and reputation by having his friends testify to the good treatment that his slaves received. In a society that accepted brutality, Terreros's special efforts to deny that he personally beat a slave indicates that such behavior on the part of leading citizens damaged their reputations. However, it might also indicate that Terreros was trying to avoid paying a fine. Whether in fact he did beat the slave rather than assigning this task to one of his employees cannot be determined.

In another aspect of the defense of the two partners, Bustamante added that in the mines he always used free labor and that he did not use press-gangs to coerce labor into his employment. It may have been true in 1749 that Bustamante, still the active partner, did not choose, or did not have permission to employ press-gangs to round up unwilling workers. This situation changed when Terreros began to run the mines; he had permission to employ two men who worked as a team to round up workers. Bustamante asserted that slaves had never had the right to partido, or a share of the ore, which Antonio Guzmán apparently had counted on in order to buy his freedom. Pedro Terreros agreed to let the two slaves find another master if the new master would repay their purchase price.[22]

The experience with Antonio Guzmán failed to stop Pedro Terreros from purchasing and employing slaves. They provided a reliable workforce and subject only to the heavy mortality suffered by all who labored in the mines. It proved a fortunate investment, because they kept one of his mines operating after the Real del Monte work stoppages by free labor in 1766 threatened his other mines.

Possibly because Terreros initiated his career in the mines by trading in slaves, he lacked the experience to deal with workers who enjoyed more protection from powerful institutions, such as the church, the state, and, above all, their own communities. Whatever the reason, in a very early stage in his career Pedro Terreros began to have difficulty in dealing with the men who worked for him.

INDIAN LABOR

Indian communities owed obligatory labor to Spanish enterprises, but Spanish and creole landowners and miners seeking to use this labor had to obtain royal permission, which specified the number of workers, how long they must serve, and how they should be treated. For the Pachuca mining region, starting in 1576 and continuing at least until 1779, viceroys had granted numerous requests from miners for forced labor from Indian villages.[23] The original license to the Veta Vizcaína had granted the general right to require men from the surrounding indigenous communities to work in the mines, but specific permission had to be requested from Mexico City.[24]

Bustamante and Terreros may have received forced laborers from the villages surrounding Pachuca between 1739 and 1754.[25] But in 1754, Terreros alone as owner of the Veta Vizcaína received permission to activate the terms of the original grant, and a viceregal decree ordered the villages surrounding Pachuca to send to the mines groups of fifteen men for two weeks, although the men could be forced to remain for another tour of duty if no replacements arrived. Failure to comply with this order would result in a fine of 500 pesos for the villages.[26] The men would receive 2½ reales a day, less than the 4 reales customarily paid to free workers. More important, these men did not chose labor in the mines and they received no partido to compensate for the difficulties and dangers of mine work. During the two-week *tanda*, or turn of their labor, they suffered harsher conditions approximating those of slaves and could not leave their place of work.

The 1754 order failed to produce the required number of workers, and Actopán, one of the largest Indian communities, had sent no men. In January 1757, the countess of Miravalle, Terreros's mother-in-law, arranged a meeting with Viceroy Amarillas and his wife to argue his case, reporting to them on the progress of the work in the mines and her son-in-law's need for labor. She expected and probably received a favorable response.[27]

Through his mother-in-law, Terreros arranged a loan to the Indian alcalde mayor (the principal municipal official) of Actopán. These Indian officials had the task of collecting tribute owed by villagers. This man perhaps had absconded with money already collected and might have been faced with jail and confiscation of his property. He borrowed the money from Terreros and in return agreed to send the men. By February, work gangs from Actopán began to go to Terreros's mines.

Several events conspired to exacerbate the situation at Actopán. One was that when Terreros's mines flooded in March, he called for increased work crews. This coincided with the initiation of the agricultural cycle when Indians began preparing and plowing their land. Several men who had been sent to Terreros's mines escaped with reports of insufferable conditions, and these reports were coupled with the fact that some of their wages went to repay the loan made to the alcalde mayor. In April 1757, rioting and rebellion broke out in the town. The authorities in Mexico City sent twenty-five reluctant militia to quell the uprising and enlisted priests to calm the populace while at the same time carrying out an investigation. They also jailed four Indian men and one woman.

Nonetheless, the Indians of Actopán had not protested in vain. The government, threatened with rebellion that it did not have the soldiers to suppress, sent Domingo Trespalacios, a judge from the audiencia (high court) in Mexico City to calm matters and to continue the flow of repartimiento workers. In his investigation the complaints of mistreatment included excessive physical punishments such as the beating death of an Indian at the hands of his boss, insufficient and unusual food, such as a kind of biscuit rather than corn tortillas, and the forced subtraction of money for Masses and the burial of the dead as well as for repayment of loans, all of which made wages scant. Indians also pointed out that being employed in the refining haciendas exposed them to mercury, which caused serious illness, and the work required more specialization and training than they possessed. Pedro Terreros asserted that the work was easy, and the officials in Pachuca testified that the Indians were "stupid and incompetent."[28]

Beyond the opposition of the Indians themselves, the labor draft for the mines stirred up other local antagonists. Officials in Tulancingo along with creole and peninsular farmers, as well as other non-Indian members of the community, demanded that the levy be cancelled since the large numbers of unemployed in Pachuca and Real del Monte could be hired as laborers. One of these men testified, "Pedro Romero de Terreros does not lack workers because of a shortage of labor, he lacks workers because the pay is so bad." Another witness in the investigation testified, "Don Pedro needs more workers because he treats the ones he has so badly."[29]

Trespalacios ordered a reduction in the number of Indian men who would be sent to the mines and decided to punish only one person for the rebellion. He also inquired into the numbers of men from Actopán who already worked as free labor in the mines in order to reduce the quantity of Indians who could be compelled to work under the repartimiento system. This assumed that Actopán had already contributed to the mines. Although the mine owners did not know the origin of the men who came to work in the mines, two historians studying this dispute have concluded that the government heeded the Indian protests and reduced the labor service. Trespalacios repeated once again, as officials had in 1722, that repartimiento Indians must be succored, could not be locked up nor mistreated, should be paid every Saturday, should have their work adapted to their skills, and should not be taken violently to the mines by press-gangs.[30] While it proved impossible to discover the village origins of each worker in the records of the mine owners, enough formerly ethnic Indians from the surrounding villages appeared as workers in the mines of Terreros that the forced labor drafts from Actopán should have been mitigated.[31]

While Trespalacios soothed the Indians with his injunctions about good treatment, at the same time he also organized groups of men to work in the mines. In response to a letter from Pedro Terreros, the audiencia judge also promised the mine owner that he would send him fifteen men the next day, twenty-five the following day, and as soon as the men had sown their crops, fifty more would be sent from surrounding villages.[32]

Pedro Terreros, discontented that another mine owner who did not have the right to forced Indian labor had received fifty men while Terreros had received none, wrote to complain to Trespalacios. On May 1, 1757, Trespalacios answered by stating that workers had the right to chose where they would labor, suggesting that Pedro Terreros was reputed to have inferior working conditions.[33] Nonetheless, Trespalacios promised him even more men three weeks later, after the men had put in their crops.

At the same time that Terreros was demanding and receiving this labor, his press-gang continued rounding up men. On June 4, 1757, when Pedro Terreros had gone to Mexico City, these men seized a group of Actopán Indians who had emerged from confession at the Franciscan college in Pachuca. The Indians had refused to submit and fought back. Trespalacios wrote to the guardian of the college, demanding to know how this could happen. The guardian protested that somebody had opened a gate to let the press-gang into the grounds of the friary. The guardian sent Trespalacios's letter on to Pedro Terreros.[34]

Between 1762 and 1764, Terreros again requested and received permission to have forced labor from the surrounding villages.[35] He sought this privilege shortly after the completion of the adit because he needed new canals to dispose of the water and to connect two of his mines. He required additional refinery workers because a flood in his principal refining hacienda had broken down the walls.[36] He succeeded in obtaining only thirty-one workers from this forced labor draft, a small percentage of the estimated one thousand workers he employed—far less than he wanted.[37]

Successful resistance in Actopán as well as other Indian communities made

the use of repartimiento labor somewhat more difficult than Pedro Terreros
had anticipated. These communities had assistance from other local groups who
opposed Terreros. Landowners also suffered from a shortage of labor to work
their fields, and others who depended on the labor of Indian villagers proved
reluctant to support repartimiento for the mines, insisting that there were abundant workers in Real del Monte, whose wages and partido supported shopkeep-
ers, independent refiners, and perhaps also churches and convents. Clearly convinced that Terreros had the money to pay wages, they opposed forced labor
and did not support him in 1757 and probably objected to his later efforts. Nevertheless, all participants in the dispute agreed that work in the mines was a
public responsibility, because it provided an engine of support for the Spanish
crown. Beyond their patriotic duties, they also profited from the prosperity of the
mines and suggested by implication that Terreros should receive fewer profits
and that they should receive more.

In dealing with forced Indian labor, Pedro Terreros appeared indifferent to
the fate of the workers. In a note he signed, written after the first rebellion on
May 29, 1757, he ordered that according to a "superior order in all the jurisdic-
tions, the people must be taken who are needed for the labor in my mines."[38] It
is possible that in his own mind and in those of his contemporaries, Pedro
Terreros considered Indian labor as disposable as machinery and perhaps shared
the view of his mother-in-law when she wrote sympathizing with him "that
what happened with the workers is that they are forced to perform hard work
when what they desire is softness and ease."[39] The individual fate of mine workers
provoked contempt and an implication of cowardice among many of the elite.
Dealing with the Indian communities, facing rebellion, and lacking local support,
all hardened Terreros in his attitudes and perhaps made him identify even
more with the role of "Persecuted David," a successful man envied by others,
especially by those who were jealous of his success and perhaps denied him the
possibilities for future profits for himself, the community, and the crown.

Slavery was becoming far less common in colonial Mexico in the last half of the
eighteenth century, yet Pedro Terreros continued to use it. Meanwhile, the right to
the forced labor of Indians persisted as a privilege until the end of the colonial
period. Two years before Terreros's death in 1779, the workers from Pachuquilla,
the neighboring community to Pachuca, protested their forced labor in the mines
because Pedro Terreros had slaves working in another mine who should have
been used instead of free Indians.[40] This complaint demonstrates the continual
use of two different kinds of forced labor, one involving complete ownership
and the other only temporary exploitation. Throughout the colonial period in both
Mexico and Peru, the most valuable right of mine owners, far more precious
than their licenses and property, was the privilege of enjoying the forced labor
of Indians, who were always paid less than free workers.

Other mine owners, as well as Terreros, possessed the right to enter Indian communities and take men against their will to work in the mines. In one of the best documented cases, José Borda, the famed wealthy entrepreneur of Taxco and patron of one of the jewels of colonial architecture, had many protests against forced service in his mines.[41] Since these protests remained peaceful and legal and caused no documented rebellions, Borda never accumulated the negative publicity that Terreros received. It was the escalation of problems with free workers that caused Terreros difficulties in the eighteenth century and made his reputation suffer in the twentieth century.

FREE LABOR, PARTIDO, AND RECOGEDORES

Neither slaves nor Indians met the insatiable need for labor, nor could forced labor resolve the perennial shortages resulting from mine owners' unwillingness or inability to pay high wages. As the Mexican population grew in the eighteenth century, when a mining bonanza appeared, men flocked to the newly prosperous center to find work. Despite the perceived abundance of workers, a scarcity soon emerged, often accompanied by the end of the bonanza. When the pay proved inadequate, labor shortages began. Scarcity of workers also resulted from injuries that resulted from mine collapses, falls from ladders, mercury poisoning, working waist deep in water, and other menaces of life in the mines.

Both the government and mine owners perceived that mining towns and surrounding communities, such as Actopán, abounded in able-bodied men who sought to escape labor drafts in favor of better-paid work. Terreros had the right to use press-gangs to supply his mines and refining haciendas with workers. But even so, lack of labor frustrated Terreros's grand plans for mines and refining. He wrote that he needed twenty times as much labor as he was able to hire.[42] This inability to find labor might have been caused by his reputation of maltreating workers. As in the case of the Indians, when men had the right to chose, they elected to work for other mine owners. In one case several years earlier, Terreros had tried forcibly to remove men from another mine in order to oblige them to work for him, thus provoking a protest in the mines. He still continued to supplement his regular free labor gangs with the roundup of so-called vagrants both in the streets of Pachuca and Real del Monte, as well as in the Indian communities.

The brutal behavior of press-gangs was a constant grievance. They lassoed, beat, and dragged men off to the mines. Men resisted this treatment and responded to violence with violence. Pedro Terreros once remarked that he had never heard of a mine worker killed by a recojedor, but he knew of many cases in which the recojedores had lost their lives. We might add that their brutality provoked the violence.[43]

When free workers descended into the mines, they received a wage and some categories of workers secured additional remuneration in the form of a share of the ore they had extracted. After they had filled a specified number of sacks of ore with their quota, called their *tequio*, the contents of the next sacks were divided in half with the owner. Workers could process this ore themselves, or sell it to an independent refiner. Since they collected the ore, they could choose the richest ore; thus, they valued partido more than their pay.[44]

When mine owners who had the cash to pay wages tried to rid themselves of these "worker partners" by ending the custom of ore sharing, protests resulted. In the mining community of Santa Eulalia in northern Mexico, "workers routinely responded [to the deprivation of partido] by walking off their job until the customary benefits were restored."[45] In Chihuahua, however, by midcentury, mine owners and government had succeeded in eliminating partido. Not every owner could afford to pay wages, but in Real del Monte, they all paid partido, and in the cases where no wages were paid, the workers shared half of all the ore they produced. It became the goal of Pedro Terreros to end partido, although the militancy of the workers in the Real del Monte mines would make this impossible for him.[46]

WORK STOPPAGES OF 1766-67

On August 15, 1766, in one of the many rebellions that occurred between 1766 and 1768 in the Atlantic world in the aftermath of the Seven Years' War, the workers in Pedro Terreros's mines laid down their tools and refused to return to work.[47] This work stoppage culminated decades of conflict over the use of press-gangs, low wages, and which of the workers had the right to partido. This strike against Pedro Terreros in 1766 might also be considered a part of the wave of protests that ranged from the Esquilache rebellion in Madrid in early 1766, the beginnings of rebellion in the English North American colonies with the Stamp Act protests, and the Mexican rebellions in Guanajuato against the excise tax and in San Luis Potosí and in Michoacán over local issues and protests about the expulsion of the Jesuits. Each of these uprisings stemmed from local grievances fueled by anger over increased taxation and reforms in the system of government that sought to strengthen royal control over the American colonies. In the case of Spain, it would increase the flow of silver, enabling Spain to exercise once again a leading role in European politics.[48]

It was also the continuation of a tradition of labor militancy in the Pachuca-Real del Monte mining region. The first recorded incident occurred when Pedro Terreros imported miners from Guanajuato between 1753 and 1755, which led to the death of four men. In the early nineteenth century, British mining companies hesitated about investing in Real del Monte because its workers were famed for their combative character. As late as 1985, miners in Pachuca engaged in an innovative labor protest by demonstrating dressed only in hard hats, boots, and belts.[49]

The militancy of the workers in Real del Monte and their ability to close the mines derived in part from geography that permitted several thousand workers to have extensive contacts with each other and gave them an organizational strength lacking in other mining regions where the mines were more dispersed and workers more closely connected to their employers, administrators, and work captains. In other areas, such as Zacatecas, they often lived in close proximity to owners and their agents, celebrating fiestas, having relations of *compadrazgo* (godparenthood) with them and depending on them for protection. In Real del Monte, the workers lived dispersed throughout the mountains and valleys. When "a disequilibrium occurred between the organization of work and the aspirations of the workers," it was easy for the workers to react strongly "against the innovations of colonial administration or by private mining enterprises."[50]

Apparently the beginning of the work stoppage came not from Terreros's suppression of partido, which was an idea that he later advocated and clung to after the end of the work stoppages and rebellions, but from changes in the ways in which the partido was measured in addition to alterations in assessing workers' pay.

When the work stoppages of 1766 began, Pedro Terreros had been absent from the region for nearly a year, leaving his business in the care of Marcelo González, one of the most hated administrators. During the months that Terreros was away from Pachuca, several measures inflamed grievances of the workers. These measures included a perceived increase in the size of the sacks to be filled that constituted their basic work task, a cut in the pay of some mine workers, and an increase in the money subtracted for medical care, for sharpening tools, and for alms for religious services. Except for the increase in the size of the sacks, which were later tested twice by royal officials and found to be the same irregular size as they had always been, all of these complaints had merit. Another grievance surfaced concerning the fact that only slave labor worked the mine of La Palma, which was in bonanza, indicating once again how strongly workers believed in their rights to a share in the best ore. Perhaps the most serious complaint concerned the pay of the men called peons, who had had their pay reduced from 4 to 3 reales, either because they were also to receive partido or because, as Terreros claimed, the 4-reales pay had been granted them only until the completion of the adit. The men also objected to the brutal methods of the press-gangs. One of the scholars who has investigated these events suggested that one of the precipitating events was the grant by the authorities of the right for the other large miner in the region to use press-gangs, thus putting miners at risk of being forced to work when they had just finished their shift in another mine.[51]

On July 28, 1766, seventy-three men presented a petition detailing their grievances. The local priest in Real del Monte may have helped them to prepare the document. Their petition prompted a response from the viceroy, who requested that the press-gangs proceed in a gentler and fairer way. Unrest continued for a number of days, exacerbated by the imprisonment of four of the leaders who had presented the petition and by the workers' suspicion that the viceroy had granted their requests, but they had been denied knowledge of the fact by the officials in Pachuca who did not accurately read the viceroy's response.

Local authorities advised Terreros to return to the mining region. He did so, but went to his refining hacienda of San Miguel rather than to Real del Monte, because of illness. Until the outbreak of violence on August 15, perhaps affected by the recent death of his wife, he appeared to be ignorant of the seriousness of the situation.

Scholars viewing the unfolding events, documented in numerous investigations carried out during the succeeding four years, have chosen to emphasize or to accept different versions of the next episode, but the certainty is that the miners refused to work. Without the men to keep the mines drained, within a few days the waters would flood them and ruin Terreros, a number of other owners, and impoverish the community.

Pedro Terreros agreed to negotiate with the workers on August 14, 1766. Two thousand men allegedly converged on the mine of San Cayetano, the place chosen to hold the meeting. Four men were chosen to speak with Terreros. The issue of partido was raised in this meeting; Terreros began by asserting that under the system of partido, he got the poor ore and the workers the good ore. The workers agreed that this charge might be true, but declined ultimate responsibility because they were often instructed to dig in places where only poor ore existed. To compensate for this, if they were to make any money, they had to take the best ore. The two sides agreed that more capable captains, those who decided where men would extract ore, should be selected. (Later the question of the employment of captains caused still another work stoppage.) Moreover, favoritism was rife, because the captains of the teams selected their friends to work in the most promising places.

The two sides changed their venue to another mine, where Pedro Terreros accused the workers of stealing his tools, which he could find in every pawn shop in Pachuca. The workers inquired why they had not been prosecuted, and he responded that he was a good Christian. A more accurate answer might have been the difficulty of finding the culprits. Terreros suffered from the petty thievery endemic in many industrial enterprises. In the last issue that the participants discussed in these negotiations, we hear the voice of Pedro Terreros justifying his actions by the 3,000 pesos in wages that he paid each week, which he saw as a contribution to the region.

At the end of the negotiations, the issue of partido appeared to have been resolved to the satisfaction of the two sides. Pedro Terreros asked the workers not to cheat him by taking the best ore, and if the workers would agree to that, he allegedly said, "Take out as much partido as you wish, not just two sacks of it, but half a mine, and I will divide it with you without contradiction." Terreros then described his many complaints against the workers, including the money that he had lost years earlier when they rioted and refused to permit men from Guanajuato to work in his mines. He also accused them of preventing Indian village workers from entering the mines.[52] The negotiations left unresolved the question of the wages to be paid to the peons, the men who carried the heavy sacks of ore or water from the mines, whose wages had been reduced.

The next day, August 15 (the Assumption of the Virgin, the feast day of the city of Pachuca), all the tension and discord surfaced once again, revealing that there were still vast differences between the two sides on the division of partido, the actions of press-gangs, and, above all, Terreros's decision to continue paying the less-skilled peons 3 rather than 4 reales a day. Perhaps, although this is not absolutely clear, these men were to continue to receive partido. Even though officials told Terreros to pay 4 reales to the peons, he refused to do so, insisting that he had agreed to that amount of money for only a limited time.

While nearly 3,000 workers returned to work in the mines, the atmosphere was inflamed. Neither Terreros nor his administrators appeared cognizant of this vast disaffection among the workers, nor that, as Viceroy Antonio Bucareli put it years later, the "brake of obedience had been broken," and the habits of deference and respect of the plebeians for the upper class had temporarily disappeared.[53]

Accounts differ about the events that occurred late in the afternoon of August 15. According to Friar Melchor Velasco, whose account was sent to Mexico City immediately, Terreros and two other men, the alcalde mayor and one of Terreros's employees, were returning from an inspection in the mines, and then stopped to hear Mass in an interior chapel when a crowd of men suddenly attacked them. If it had been an act of valor for Terreros to have negotiated alone with the workers the day before, it was foolhardy to attend Mass, protected only by the brilliant uniform of the alcalde mayor, which the owner and administrator believed to be sufficient, within a mine where many disaffected men worked.

The workers had been angered by a series of events that occurred during the day—the reduction in pay of the peons, the capture of men by press-gangs, and a special act of retaliation by Terreros's administrators against two of the strike leaders. When the alcalde mayor, a young man recently arrived from Spain, tried to frighten the workers by drawing his sword, the workers used the customary weapons, the abundant stones within the mine, and began flinging them at Terreros, the alcalde mayor, and a mine administrator. When stones began to rain down on the three men, the alcalde mayor and the mine employee were severely wounded, and later died, but Terreros escaped physically unscathed. He hid, buried up to his neck in horse fodder. Then, dressed as always when in the mines in sober black clothes, he joined a procession organized by the parish priest of Real del Monte with the canopy for the Blessed Sacrament, covered with a cloak given him by the parish priest. He remained in the church until midnight and then galloped off to his refining hacienda of San Miguel.[54]

For many years, his actions were governed by the memory of August 15, 1766, when he nearly lost his life in the eruption of worker violence. He remained in self-imposed exile for the next eight years. His feelings of distrust and rejection might have been increased by mourning over the death of his wife.

For the next several days in Pachuca, the workers controlled the city. They released prisoners from the municipal jail and the friars and priests minimally oversaw the workers.[55] The viceroy also sent troops, but depended more on the negotiating skills of Francisco Javier Gamboa, the jurist who had written the mining ordinances in 1762, and who had also ruled against Terreros in an earlier dispute with the marqués del Valleameno, one of the other miners in Real del Monte. Gamboa carried out the investigation under the direction of the new viceroy, the marqués de Croix. Gamboa's instructions from the viceroy included the statement:

> In these kingdoms, kindness is unknown. For the benefit of this one man, [Terreros?] the wretched workers are trampled upon, violated and tyrannized. The men are content with their low wages and the few benefits that the law allows them, and do not aspire to greater riches. You [Gamboa] and everybody else know the disorder and almost tyrannical despotism with which the mine workers are treated in this kingdom.[56]

Viceroy Croix, from the north of Spain, began his term of office with little sympathy to the upper-class creole residents of Mexico. He has been described as "authoritarian and inflexible." He might have been instructed by the crown and the Council of the Indies to weaken the powers of local elites.[57]

Following the viceroy's instructions, Gamboa appeared sympathetic to the workers. He heard their complaints with interest and understanding during the extensive investigation and trial that he carried out between August and October 1766, although he also secretly suggested that more workers might be arrested through trickery so that no additional protest would be provoked.[58] But as soon as Gamboa left the region later in the fall of 1766, unrest broke out again. There was another riot over partido and a rebellion at the refining mill of La Regla, which began with a dispute over the stealing of a cloak and broke out into a work stoppage when a foreman began to beat a suspected worker. The man was humiliated in the presence of other workers. A woman began the work stoppage by accusing the men of cowardice and the laborers refused to continue working.

Another work stoppage occurred at Regla's Dolores mine in October; this time over the selection of captains. At issue was whether workers had the right to select the man who would decide where to find the best silver ore. In November and December demonstrations occurred against the recojedores of the Morán mine, the other principal mining enterprise in Real del Monte. Then, apparently, the protests ended for an extended period, reoccurring some years later under different conditions and over different issues.[59]

Troops were sent to Real del Monte in 1766–68 and paid for by Pedro Terreros, but the numbers of soldiers were small, the numbers of workers were great, and men and women could hide in the mountainous terrain and escape arrest. Sentences given to workers included exile and service in presidios. Pedro Terreros believed that the men had received only mild punishments and feared that within a few years they would return to murder him.[60]

THE AFTERMATH

For Pedro Terreros, the events of 1766–67 seemed to transform a successful career into a near disaster. In the workers' rebellion, he had barely escaped death. He might also have felt that Gamboa's investigation failed to do justice to him, leaving him as the scapegoat and perpetrator, both at that time and again in the middle and late twentieth centuries, for work stoppages, riots, and rebellions, even for those that had been directed against the other principal miner in the region. Terreros certainly believed that Croix refused to imprison and punish severely the men who had been responsible for two murders and the attempt on his own life.[61]

The events in 1766 further intensified Terreros's vision that his efforts were unappreciated by royal officials and the crown. Since 1748, he had been reminding the colonial government in Spain of his merits, as a mine owner and philanthropist, and he had received only token recognition. His requests for a title, for an entail, for the right to cast silver on his own haciendas, and for the ownership of the mine of San Vicente had all been rejected, several of them various times. His victory over the Valleameno interest had been gained through the attrition of his opponent and his own willingness to resolve the issue by force, rather than through royal favor.

As a result of his fears that workers intended to kill him, he determined to work only those mines that he could operate with slave labor and forced Indian levies and naturally selected those that were in bonanza. He may also have accumulated from previous years a substantial backlog of ore to be refined, making his decision to curtail production from the Veta Vizcaína of limited consequence to royal revenues and to his own accumulation of wealth.[62] He kept a skeleton force to prevent flooding in his other mines and to forestall claims to his title to the Veta Vizcaína.[63]

It is certain that the local economy suffered because of Terreros's curtailment of production. Payrolls declined as free miners no longer found employment in the principal mines in Real del Monte and the 3,000 pesos that Terreros had previously paid in wages no longer circulated through the community. If we add to this our knowledge that the other mine owners were operating on the basis of partido, the lack of ready daily cash might have afflicted the region. Limited production in the Veta Vizcaína might also have damaged nearby landowners who had supplied the mines with hides, mules, grain, and other commodities.

But good fortune began to shine on Terreros in the years after the Real del Monte work stoppages. The appearance of a report favorable to Pedro Terreros, which had been delayed for two years, reflected the fact that Viceroy Croix and the *visitador* (crown investigator), José de Gálvez, also feared workers' violence, thus confirming Terreros's own apprehensions. His success as well as his limited but still productive mines were made all the more evident by the failures of the mines of Manuel Moya, the owner of the Morán mine, who was the other principal owner in Real del Monte. These facts, contained in letters from the viceroy and Gálvez, underlined the importance of Terreros's contribution to the silver industry, and convinced the king that Terreros should be granted his title of nobility. The king had personally delayed this favor for the last ten years.[64] From 1768 on, Pedro Terreros was called the count of Regla. It was with this title that he signed his name and that he has become known both to his contemporaries and to posterity.

The reign of the viceroy, marqués de Croix (1766–71), coincided in part with the great reform inspection of José de Gálvez, who in 1767 had carried out the expulsion of the Jesuits in Mexico, ruthlessly repressed other rebellions from 1767–70, organized the tobacco monopoly, and established new internal boundaries and provinces in the colony. One of his tasks was to increase mining production, but he had not yet succeeded in doing so. The marqués de Croix mended his relationship to Regla and received a loan of 400,000 pesos sometime before his departure in 1771.[65] Gálvez had worked with two principal mining leaders, Manuel Aldaco and José Borda, who recommended that the price of mercury be lowered. He had tried, between 1769 and 1771, to get Regla to participate in these meetings. But Regla refused, offering as an excuse that he feared his enemies might harm him, and that the men who had tried to kill him were still determined to do so. Another reason might be that Regla rarely spent his time on public service.[66]

Despite a new title and other privileges, the favorable report on the work stoppages and riots of 1766–67 written by the alcalde mayor of Tulancingo, who echoed Regla's opinions and speech, and the seconding of that report by the crown attorney José Antonio Areche and the visitador José de Gálvez, Regla still refused to open his six or seven closed mines. No conciliation would work until Regla's demands that more men be punished more severely for the work stoppages and violence were met.[67] The fact that in 1770, the workers accused of participating in the 1766 events had served their sentence and had permission to return to Real del Monte must have further aroused Regla's suspicions.[68]

Increasing silver production by reforming the mining industry constituted one of the chief goals of the new viceregal administration of Antonio de Bucareli (1771–79). Despite Bucareli's commitment to this reform, his point of view was essentially a conservative one. He opposed drastic changes in the mining industry, such as the abolition of partido, but undertook the "pacification " of the region, noting:

> The brake of obedience has been broken, and the populace [*vulgo*] should be reduced to their former subjugation [*subjeción*], especially the inhabitants of the mining towns, who are degenerate by their upbringing and by their habits. They are proud and daring because they consider themselves irreplaceable and because they are united in order to sustain themselves in any dispute. It can be verified that with slight motives, the riots will be repeated. Although there are troops stationed in Pachuca, a place located at the base of the mountains, and although for some time there has not been any visible disturbance, this is a suspicious calm, and the count of Regla and his administrators, believing that the laborers could be aroused on any pretext, live in mutual suspicion with the workers.[69]

Despite the denial of any efforts to suppress partido in Real del Monte during the viceregency of Bucareli, Regla received many concessions that he considered essential to improving public safety. He secured his own commissioner in Real del Monte in cases of disputes, thus avoiding the judges in Pachuca that he perceived as unfriendly, and assuring him a more favorable hearing in the local courts. On April 7, 1775, the crown appointed Fernando Ruben de Celis as deputy judge (*juez comisionado*) for Real del Monte. The count of Regla also asserted that the men who had been responsible for the events of 1766–67 still lurked in the shadows of the mining camp, because their sentences of exile had expired. Believing that these men waited only to harm or kill him, Regla insisted that he would come to Mexico City to confer with Bucareli only in disguise, a notion dismissed as unnecessary by the viceroy.[70]

The count did travel to Mexico City to discuss the question of partido. He continued his opposition to the custom of partido, alleging that it could lead to destruction of the pillars holding up the underground caverns, that it caused disputes, that the mine owners suffered from inability to profit from the richer veins, and, above all, that he had no need to pay partido because he could afford to pay wages.

Bucareli, however, remained adamant on the subject of continuing partido, pointing out that while Regla had millions of pesos in his estate, other mine owners lacked these resources and that the payment of partido encouraged "four men to work as though they were six." In one of the few favorable statements about workers from a member of the elite, the viceroy wrote that "it is not just to presume that all workers are perverse; there are many honorable men with large families."[71]

Viceroy Bucareli, in this dispute as in so many others, decided on the side of tradition. Behind this appeal to tradition lay a variety of interests represented by powerful groups who sought to retain partido. These included mining entrepreneurs who had no money to pay wages and needed the workers as partners, independent refiners whose source of ore was partido, and local merchants and taverners who benefited from the increased money available. The crown's desire to encourage investment in the mines to all who could be persuaded to gamble in this fashion combined with local pressures to defeat Regla on this issue, and Bucareli, perhaps fearing new worker protests, ordered that mine owners continue to pay partido to workers in Real del Monte. One of Regla's chief aims, the suppression of partido, did not occur during his lifetime.

In assessing Regla's relations with mine workers, one wonders if his treatment of them was a necessary ingredient in his success. Had he been more generous to his workers and not several times sought to reduce their wages, and had he been more sympathetic to their needs, would he still have become one of the two wealthiest men in eighteenth-century Mexico? It would seem that his habit of commanding, of watching every expense, and of paying the least amount possible for most services made possible his spectacular career. Although Regla did not succeed in suppressing partido in his own lifetime, by the end of the eighteenth century, it had disappeared. In the question of partido, as in Regla's desire to eliminate competitors in the mines, the future rested with him rather than with the workers. Nineteenth-century industrialists did not wish to make workers their partners and sought to control the production of ore from mines through its transformation into silver.

In a broader vision of Regla's career, he appeared far more skilled at managing money than managing men; this seems to be true for all men outside his immediate circle of employees and colleagues. His poor relations with workers and the agitation of 1766–67 had many effects, among which was his partial withdrawal from the outside world. In many ways, the workers' strikes of 1766–67 became the defining experience of his life. In fact, this experience may have lessened his satisfaction in receiving his first title, and in the mid-twentieth century, it may have undermined his reputation as a philanthropist.

CHAPTER 5

Marriage and Family: 1756–1766

> It is a truth universally acknowledged, that a single man in
> possession of a good fortune must be in want of a wife.
> —Jane Austen, *Pride and Prejudice*

The fictional account of Jane Austen's heroines and the real-life events occurring in Mexico City in 1756 share a plot—that of a wealthy man marrying an impoverished young woman. But this superficial resemblance masks differences between the story told by Jane Austen and the customs in the Spanish colonies in the mid-eighteenth century.

In Mexico, men from families with inherited wealth tended to marry young in order to preserve properties in the family line. In contrast, those with large capital, such as peninsular merchants, if they could not marry their employer's daughter, widow, or other relative, often remained single during their youth and sought young wives of good family or wealth, only when they became middle-aged. Some of these men had half-forgotten wives in Spain and could not remarry; others remained single while young women of "good family" in Mexico languished for lack of appropriate husbands.[1] Some bachelors did marry late in life, after they had amassed substantial resources, contracting alliances with much younger women who could be expected to produce many children. As a Spanish-born older man marrying a creole younger woman, Pedro Terreros replicated patterns followed by merchants elsewhere in Hispanic America.[2] Marriages between the economic elite and the landholding aristocracy tended the minimize the differences between creole and peninsular.[3]

THE BRIDE AND WIFE

Pedro Terreros lived more than a quarter of a century in Mexico without taking a wife. What made him decide to undertake the Christian duty of matrimony? Had he remained single, the church and above all his favorite group within the church, the Franciscans, might have gained from his bachelor status and lack of heirs by receiving gifts during his life and the bulk of his estate at his death. But he decided differently. If he had worked the silver mines as a work of charity, intending the profits for the Franciscans, he might have become fearful that their vows of poverty and rules against administering property and handling money would result in abandonment of the mines. He needed a family to enhance his social and political position, to enlarge his kinship network, and to advance and perpetuate his ambitions as a patriarch. A single man such as Pedro Terreros, lacking influential relatives in Mexico City, might suffer serious defeats in the competitive atmosphere in the upper social levels of the capital city. Or perhaps he simply fell in love. In the Mexico City marriage market, he must, in any case, have been the most eligible of bachelors despite his forty-six years.

The winner of this prize in the matrimonial contest, María Antonia Trebuestos y Dávalos, age twenty-three in 1756, the youngest daughter of the third countess of Miravalle, came from old stock of conquistador origin. Her sixteenth-century ancestor, Alonso Dávalos, one of the original settlers of northwestern New Spain, derived his land and power from the area of Compostela, the ancient capital of the region of New Galicia in the area west of present-day Guadalajara. María Antonia also counted Leonor Cortés Moctezuma, descendant of Aztec kings, among her forebears.[4] The extended family had flourished as owners of land and livestock for more than a century and a half. Shortly before 1700, they began to marry their daughters to Spanish-born men of apparent influence and to seek a noble title. Ironically, they became impoverished at the same time that they gained the noble title of the count of Miravalle. Combining María Antonia Trebuestos's youth, social position, and respected genealogy with Pedro Terreros's wealth, experience, talent, and continuing prospects set the stage for a "good marriage." It would provide the money to revive the title of the counts of Miravalle–her mother's title—and guarantee the establishment and continuation of the genetic line of the Terreros family of Querétaro. A "good marriage" in the high society of eighteenth-century Mexico balanced a young woman with noble ancestors and a mother of proven fertility with a man of wealth able to sustain an affluent lifestyle. In this union the bride did not bring her husband a monetary dowry, only her name and family prestige.

Of María Antonia's life before her marriage to Pedro Terreros, we know only that she was born on the hacienda of San Lorenzo in San Cristóbal de Ixcuintla in Sentispac, in the audiencia of New Galicia in northwestern Mexico, and that she was the youngest of eight children. Straitened circumstances account for the family residence in such a remote place. Visiting one's own haciendas for extended periods and consuming food and services produced by the labor of men and women living on these haciendas helped make ends meet for land-rich but money-poor families.

When María Antonia was less than two years old, her father died. A year and a half later, her mother moved the family to Mexico City. She did this both to escape creditors and because a woman alone with her children in the country could be threatened by powerful men. In an urban area, however, with relatives nearby, the laws protecting women could be enforced. She also needed to oversee her other properties. Not only was María Antonia's mother a countess, but also she had inherited two positions on a profitable tax agency called the Santa Cruzada, which collected a head tax on all residents of New Spain from the viceroy to Indian villagers and slaves. But the inheritance of the Miravalle titles could only be enjoyed after the mother paid her debts, settled lawsuits, and found money to pay the taxes, called *lanzas* and *media-anatas*, imposed by the crown when a noble title changed hands. The difficulties increased in 1751 when the crown began the process of expropriating her familial positions at the Santa Cruzada. The threatened loss of these two inherited positions made the family's economic situation even more precarious. Financial insecurity of the kind suffered by the nobility persisted throughout María Antonia's childhood.

One of María Antonia's four older sisters, Angela, later to play an important role in her sister's and brother-in-law's life, had made a financially weak marriage and then was widowed; another sister entered a convent, although there was no money to buy the cell or to complete paying the dowry. Two sisters remained unmarried at home. None of the three sons had married as young men, probably because such a change in their civil status would mean the loss of the chaplaincies that provided them with a small income. The salvation of the family rested with the youngest child and her ability to marry a capable Spanish merchant or government official with sufficient wealth.[5]

This coup was achieved through the wedding of Pedro Terreros with María Antonia in 1756. We have no idea how they met or how the marriage was arranged. During their ten years of marriage, which ended with her death, he finished the major projects of his mining career, such as the adit and the completion of refining mills, and he and his wife purchased and furnished the house that would consolidate the presence of his family in Mexico City. María Antonia lived up to the promise of her mother and paternal grandmother by producing many healthy offspring of both sexes. It was, indeed, a marriage in which the social expectations of the partners would be fulfilled. The union of an older man and a young woman was not always a marriage of convenience. Genuine affection, as in this case, soon appeared.

What do we know of María Antonia's personality? We know that she fell deeply in love with her husband, which can be seen in her letters to him. She urged him not to look for "another treasure in Pachuca," because she would be content to "live only on chile and tortillas" if her husband were with her.[6] She wished that she might be "capable of taking away your cares, but I am a poor useless creature; all I have is good will [*voluntad*]."[7] Two months later, she wrote, "Soi tu negrita que te adolita," in which she makes up a word "adolita" so that there is a rhyme; it translates into English as "I am your little slave who adores you."[8] On another occasion she observed "that my head is all in a whirl and it hurts me," indicating in this context that she did not think highly of herself, although it could be one of her complaints about her aches and pains."[9] While she appears in these early letters as a dependent woman, in the later letters of her mother, and in letters to Pedro Terreros from three of his colleagues she is viewed differently. In these letters, she emerges as an authoritative leader of the household (albeit a secondary one).[10]

María Antonia's great attraction and affection for her husband seems evident. What was his vision of her? In a letter Pedro Terreros wrote to his offspring, which was read at his funeral, he refers to his wife's "discrete character, virtuous soul, and pious, moderate, and benign heart."[11] These words, written years after her death, may reflect eighteenth-century notions of the ideal behavior of women rather than any serious assessment by Pedro Terreros of his wife. However, it is hard to imagine that his wife would have written to him with such affection if he had ignored her strong feelings of attachment to him. His regard for her opinion might be reflected in letters written by two of his colleagues to him, which could be interpreted as showing Pedro Terreros deferring to her judgment. The correspondence of one colleague in Mexico City charged with finding and decorating the house refers frequently to his desire to please "My Lady," that is, María Antonia. After her death, Terreros continued to adorn her bedroom by adding symbols of her recently acquired rank of countess, which she could only enjoy posthumously.

The wedding itself exhibited an aspect of his personality. The elaborate wedding ceremonies celebrated him, but they also celebrated her. As part of the wedding, Pedro Terreros ordered his notary to issue a document, called an *arras,* that would provide his wife with 50,000 pesos for her to enjoy if he would die before her.[12] The arras is normally part of the dowry document, in which the wife's family provides goods and money to support the couple, and the husband, through the arras, promises that his wife will enjoy 10 percent of the wealth that he had at the time of their wedding. It also symbolically means that he "is entering on a commitment to her family."[13] This arras stands alone, as María Antonia had no dowry. It was not an addition to the dowry, but a promised gift from the groom to the bride. This was an unusual, if not unique, marital arrangement.[14] The wedding and the accompanying arras were such notable items that the contemporary chronicler, José María Castro Santa Anna, devoted several pages of his *Diario* to recounting them. In his account of the arras, the actual amount is doubled, as he stated that Pedro Terreros had agreed to provide his wife with 100,000 pesos. Like the chronicler's description of the wedding, the exaggerated sum was designed to impress the audience with the wealth and generosity of the groom. So the arras served the needs of both bride and groom.

THE WEDDING

Wedding ceremonies in the eighteenth-century could be as elaborate as those described below, or as simple as an exchange of vows between a man and a woman with a priest and witnesses, following the custom in Spain of "an informal wedding ceremony."[15] One example of such a ceremony was the marriage in Mexico City in 1744 of Pedro Terreros's cousin by marriage, Jacinto Rodríguez Suasnabar y Sosa, to a daughter of the leading family in Querétaro, and in a presumably simple ceremony without the presence of the groom, as the marriage was by proxy.[16] Other examples of simplicity were exemplified in the wedding of the twenty-year-old daughter of a wealthy noble family, the Fagoagas, to an elderly municipal official of a provincial town. The Fagoaga family wedding observance took place after seven in the evening in the house of a relative. There was no nuptial Mass and no church ceremony, only an exchange of vows, and the signature of witnesses in the presence of a priest.[17] How common this simple ceremony was at the time is demonstrated by Castro Santa Anna, who chronicled numerous instances of similar ceremonies, all taking place at seven in the evening.

In contrast, Pedro Terreros and perhaps the Miravalle family as well chose to make their two-day wedding celebration a major event in Mexico City; the wedding challenged, though did not exceed, the ceremonies for the reception of viceroys or the celebration of major holy days. This wedding, and the accompanying household effects, clothing, and jewels cost Terreros more than 50,000 pesos, almost 20,000 pesos more than he later spent purchasing his principal dwelling place in Mexico City, and the countess of Miravalle claimed to have spent more than 16,000 pesos on the wedding and the decorations.[18]

The event began at 7 A.M. on the feast day of Saint Peter, June 29, 1756, Pedro Terreros's saint's day as well as his forty-sixth birthday. Archbishop Manuel Rubio Salinas y Haro left the cathedral accompanied by "numerous people of distinction and titles." The procession made its way to the house on the Calle de Espíritu Santo, where the Miravalles lived.[19] The wedding service, which included a Mass at which the archbishop officiated, took place in the family's private chapel. After the formal ceremony, the bridal party and assembled guests returned to the cathedral to attend a service dedicated to Saint Peter. Adding to the emphasis on this saint, Luis de Torres Tuñón, a prebend of the cathedral delivered the homily. We might speculate that he chose as his text the statement from the New Testament Gospel of Matthew, which tells of the changing of the name of one of the apostles from Simon, meaning sand, to Peter, meaning rock. Or perhaps the priest spoke about the rocks of silver ore from which this latter-day Peter had created his fortune. He may also have praised the generosity with which this Spanish Peter, resident in New Spain, had endowed and would continue to endow the church.

Another procession brought the company back to the Miravalle house for the first of several formal banquets. In the afternoon, the wedding party circled the Alameda, a promenade site of the aristocracy. The carriages, chaises, sedan chair, and even the mules (which alone cost 600 pesos) shone. The next day, a slightly more private observance of the *tornaboda*, or the celebration on the day after the wedding, included feasts and a procession to the Alameda. (See Map 4.) Probably the newly married couple rode in the coach and liveries that Pedro Terreros had just given to his bride.

Guests at the feasts no doubt noticed that the bride wore splendid jewelry. In a country where "no man above the rank of beggar [*lépero*] married without presenting his bride with at least a pair of diamond earrings or a pearl necklace with a diamond clasp," the wife of a wealthy man had to display remarkable jewels.[20] Perhaps an array of jewelry and other gifts had been placed on exhibit in the bride's mother's house, just as modern brides display their wedding gifts. The jewelry, given by Terreros as a gift, was valued at 26,001 pesos, slightly more than half the value of Pedro Terreros's contribution to the wedding expenses. This jewelry represented a practical investment that could be converted into cash and depreciated less than clothing, bed coverings, mules, and carriages, which Terreros also included in accounts of wedding expenses.[21]

Clothing, another feature listed in dowry and estate inventories and of utmost importance in public processions, was the second most costly expense of the wedding, amounting to 26 percent of the total, or 13,261 pesos. Some of this clothing was for Pedro Terreros, whose wedding suit alone cost 2,200 pesos. He chose a fabric of green and gold that was lined with three yards of silk, shot through with gold and silver thread.

A significant gift of clothing, probably for María Antonia, was two lengths of cloth for a *rebozo*, or long shawl. Given the absence of any other expensive women's clothing in the accounting prepared for Pedro Terreros, we can assume that the countess of Miravalle supplied María Antonia's wedding gown. In contrast to usual custom, Pedro Terreros furnished clothing for his three brothers-in-law and purchased lengths of fabric to clothe others, perhaps his sisters-in-law and the witnesses or wedding sponsors. The tailor, Francisco de Pedraza, received 4,748 pesos. Of the many people who provided goods or materials for this wedding, his was the only name mentioned in the accounts, suggesting that the position of tailor was an especially coveted one, above that of jeweler, carriage maker, or cook.

The countess of Miravalle, in whose house the ceremony and feasts had taken place, claimed in a codicil to her will that she had spent more than 16,000 pesos on the decorations for the festivities and in supplying her daughter with clothing, jewelry, and housewares; and she had not requested a receipt of her expenses from her son-in-law because his contribution had been so much greater. Added together, the total cost of this wedding reached nearly 66,000 pesos—far more than a relatively well-off priest would make in an active lifetime.

In addition to the array of material possessions and sumptuous entertainment appropriate to the occasion were three charitable contributions undertaken by Terreros to celebrate his marriage. They signified to his relatives and to friends among the Franciscan friars that his marriage did not end his generosity to religious causes. Two of these spiritual contributions consisted of paying dowries and entrance fees for two nuns in existing convents, and more impressive still, to founding a new convent with thirty-two nuns. The third contribution, establishing a mission in Texas, should provide the church with a host of new converts.

MARRIED LIFE

At the time of his wedding in 1756, Pedro Terreros described himself as a vecino, or householder, of Querétaro with another residence in Mexico City and as a miner registered in Pachuca.[22] In fact, he really lived in the Pachuca region. His commitment to living near his mines and refining haciendas had occurred before 1751 when a widowed cousin from Querétaro, Ana Terreros y Sosa, left her two daughters behind and came to keep house for him.[23]

Unlike some wealthy miners, Pedro Terreros intended to have his wife live with him in Pachuca. After the elaborate wedding ceremony in late June, sometime in the late summer or early fall of 1756, the couple departed from Mexico City for Pachuca. María Antonia remained in Pachuca until March 1757. Following custom, she returned to her mother's house for the birth of her first child. Her next two children were also born in her mother's house. For the birth of one of her children, the stay extended to six months. Except for these sojourns, she lived in Pachuca and its environs until 1765.

Family visits between Mexico City and Pachuca occurred frequently. The countess of Miravalle traveled the road between the two cities many times, and her daughters, María Antonia and Angela, also undertook this trip at least twice a year. When the women visited, it was an elaborate trip. Anticipating one of her journeys in 1759, María Antonia wrote her husband on September 27 that she planned to leave Mexico City on Saint Francis's day, October 4, and that she would need ten mules and four good coachmen. She also mentioned that their two daughters, Micaela and Juana, accompanied by their nursemaids, would travel in the *forlón*, or carriage, perhaps the same one that Pedro Terreros had purchased for their wedding.[24]

Such visits included a gathering of servants and coaches before dawn in preparation for the departure of the family. The assemblage took place in the courtyard of the house in Pachuca or in the central patio of the Miravalle house in Mexico City. Before the sun rose, as many as four coaches drawn by mules or horses had congregated and liveried servants packed the family's traveling cases, along with mail, gifts, household effects, and food. The roads were so bad that the carriage in which María Antonia was traveling overturned at least once.[25] The cavalcade from Mexico City passed to the north, journeying through thousands of acres that comprised the Jesuit hacienda of Santa Lucía, which would become the property of Pedro Terreros twenty years later. By nightfall, they reached the hacienda of La Bata, property of Terreros's trusted servant, Pedro Villaverde. Here they spent the night and changed horses and mules. Occasionally, the trip consumed two whole days; at other times; they approached their destination as early as one in the afternoon of the second day. Pedro Terreros and his servants traveled this path on horseback in less time.

A Terreros house in Pachuca, where three of the Romero de Terreros children were probably born, still stands. It is surrounded now by nineteenth- and early-twentieth-century structures and serves as an elementary school. The house is large and set back from the street, having a sizable open area in the front. From the street, the house appears to be only one story, but when one enters the house, the second floor is obvious. The interior boasts an enormous patio with room for mule trains and carriages, and on each of four sides there are six columns that support the second story. The house in Pachuca is larger than the one Pedro Terreros purchased in 1764 in Mexico City, although the house may have been modified by the second count of Regla. (See Figure 9.)

Our knowledge of Pedro and María Antonia's life together comes from surviving letters to Pedro from his mother-in-law and from his wife. Unfortunately, none of Pedro's letters to them has survived, despite the fact that he was an indefatigable letter writer. But some notion of his opinions can be gleaned from their responses. The countess's letters are lengthier and more informative than those of her daughter, but the bulk of them are businesslike. María Antonia's letters to Pedro were written during her stays in Mexico for her first and third pregnancies; only a few remain from her second pregnancy. Between December 1756, when the countess had just returned from a visit in Pachuca, and 1765 when the family moved to Mexico City, we have knowledge about María Antonia's health and the birth of children. Only rarely do we learn about the development of the children, such as weaning one of the babies at eighteen months or the fact that the oldest child was learning to talk or to read.[26] Purchases of commodities and gifts, celebrations, politics, and health dominate the correspondence. Pedro Terreros was concerned about María Antonia's health during her always difficult pregnancies when she resided in Mexico City, and he wrote to her mother about her health when she lived in Pachuca. María Antonia endured the frequent ills of pregnancies—swollen feet, vomiting, and continual nausea. She also suffered through lengthy and incapacitating headaches, toothaches, and limb pain.

The countess of Miravalle's first preserved letter was written to her son-in-law in December 1756, when María Antonia must have been about three or four months' pregnant. The letter informs us that the countess "was sorrowful that my dear daughter was indisposed. I hope that if it becomes a cause for concern, you would advise me."[27] Less than a month later, María Antonia suffered from *flución*, a term referring to an abnormal flowing of blood and excrements, a common ailment of her pregnancies and one that was often described in eighteenth-century medical writings.[28] A day or two later, María Antonia enjoyed excellent health for a short time. She apparently missed her mother very much, and the countess's letters begin to suggest that she return for the birth of the first child. Her strong suggestions that the trip to Mexico City be sooner rather than later were strengthened by the advice of the new professor of medicine at the university, Vicente Díaz. He advised the countess that María Antonia should be bled from the ankle before seven months of pregnancy.[29] This recommendation, combined with María Antonia's desire to be with her mother, brought her to Mexico City by the end of March.

The letters written by María Antonia and her mother from Mexico City in the months before the birth of her first baby show how much she missed her husband. Addressing him as her "padrecito," often an affectionate term for husband, she wished that she could help him escape from his cares, and that he would come and be with her.[30] Another letter recorded that she was always thinking of him and wondering what she could do to amuse herself without him. In a darker moment, she writes that her health is so bad that she hopes "to see my padrecito before dying." The day before her first baby is born, she writes, "If you should take up your pen and write to me and cannot form your letters, my dearest, you will not be blamed if you knew the heavy burden I bear with continual nausea and anguish day and night without any relief."[31] Her complaints about his absence during her first pregnancy range from simple longing to accusations of neglect. Her mother wrote to him apologizing for her daughter's letters, asserting "that the passion that she feels does not yield to reason, and as love is a child and Cupid wears a blindfold, it is necessary to put up with her impertinences."[32] It seems that the countess feared that passionate love, not tempered by reason, would be unwelcome at the house of Pedro Terreros, that stern and successful merchant and miner.

Unfortunately, we do not know how Pedro Terreros responded; but we do know that he did not arrive in time for the birth of his first child. We might wonder if he tolerated María Antonia's "impertinences" in a loving fashion, appreciating her strong attachment to him. Did he enjoy having a dependent, childlike, fearful wife who clung to him? Did he sympathize with her fears? Or was he concerned that his wife would be unable to sustain the burdens of managing a large and wealthy house? These duties would grow beyond the capacity or authority of Doña Ana, the relative who had cared for Pedro Terreros's bachelor establishment. In this eighteenth-century family, the debates over these questions, if they occurred at all, were not documented in their letters.

Terreros's absence might be explained by the demands of the mines. In April and May 1757, he suffered perhaps one of the most serious crises of his mining career. The Indians of Actopán, on whom he had counted for heavy and unremunerated labor, had rebelled at the same time that his mines were threatened

Fig. 9. Regla's house in Pachuca. Photograph by Marco Hernández.

with destruction from flooding.[33] Perhaps he judged that being in Mexico City with his wife during her first confinement was less essential than his attention to these disasters that threatened to ruin him.

Terreros's mother-in-law, while troubled by the potential of flooded mines, also feared that her daughter might die. Her anxiety might have been based on a fear that there was more danger in a first pregnancy, as well as on the on the fact if María Antonia died without a living child, the legal ties between the cash-poor Miravalles and her wealthy son-in-law would be severed. We know that the law specified that in a marriage with no offspring because of the death of the wife, the Miravalles would have no right to any of Terreros's wealth.[34] Because the countess had not secured a notarized receipt for her share of the wedding expenses, Pedro Terreros would have had no obligation to return any money to the family. The Miravalles would be bereft of the opportunity that this marriage had provided them for the infusion of liquid wealth into their family. We will never know if the countess considered all these possibilities in the first days of May 1757. We know only that María Antonia's health gave her great anxiety.

During her last weeks of pregnancy, María Antonia suffered many ailments. Relieved only by baths and drinks prescribed by the doctor, she found comfort in the Virgin of Sorrows (*de los dolores*), her favorite evocation of the Virgin and an ever-present theme in her letters and activities. Given the amount of physical and emotional suffering caused by her continuous pregnancies, the devotion to the figure of this Virgin was an appropriate choice.

The letters also reflected positive matters, as mother and daughter planned for the birth of the baby. They made and ordered clothes, providing "all that is necessary and decent." The countess sought a wet nurse and interviewed a Spaniard, Antonio Trejo, whose daughter was only one month from giving birth and whose baby would be cared for by her mother. The potential nurse remained unnamed. The countess asked Pedro Terreros for his decision. Perhaps he was the one who then decided that María Antonia should nurse the baby.[35]

The first of María Antonia's nine babies was born early in the morning of May 9, 1757. The countess lost no time in writing to Pedro Terreros. At 3 a.m. she reported that the "baby girl is fat and that both mother and daughter are healthy." No regrets over the birth of a girl appear in the letters. In fact, Pedro's cousin, Friar Alonso Giraldo de Terreros, wrote nine months later from the mission San Sabá in Texas that he hoped that his niece (common usage in Mexico to name a cousin of another generation as niece or nephew, or uncle or aunt) would have her own entailed estate (mayorazgo) filled with property, a wish that would be granted many years later through her own efforts.[36]

Yielding to the pleas of his wife, Pedro Terreros visited Mexico City sometime between May 19 and 26, the day after his daughter's baptism on May 18, 1757. Among other names, their daughter was called Micaela—a name shared by both the countess and her daughter. Like all Pedro's and María Antonia's daughters, she also bore the name of María. A hint of the baptismal feast that celebrated María Micaela's initiation into both the Christian community and noble society of Mexico City can be judged from the detail that each coachman received one peso—perhaps more than he would earn in several days—for his services in delivering people to the celebration. Pedro Terreros observed generously the custom of providing for servants and local residents at ceremonies and celebrations.[37]

Between May and August 1757, María Antonia continued to live in her mother's house. Her health improved only marginally, and she complained in one letter, "having been in Purgatory, I am now relieved of my bodily pains for my birthday." She worried about the baby, called *la indita*, and cut off writing a letter when the baby wanted milk.[38]

On a more serious note, she wrote, "baby is better, but I am saddened by the painful news that the doctor says that I cannot continue to nurse her because dizziness [*vaguidos*] is causing me not to have enough milk. The remedy which they gave me caused me stomach pains, and the doctor says that the only cure is not to nurse her."[39] In a later letter she asks for her husband's decision apparently on whether to try to continue to nurse the baby.

Although María Antonia wrote of her inability to nurse the baby as a small disappointment, it had larger consequences in terms of her fertility. Pregnancy may be inhibited either because a couple refrains from sexual intercourse during the lactation period, as the church commanded, or sometimes because a woman does not ovulate until she ceases to nurse the baby. So María Antonia's fertility increased by not nursing her baby. She became pregnant more than ten times in the next nine years, despite three or four visits to Mexico City lasting between four and six months. In fact, her mother began to write that "María Antonia está como siempre," that is, María Antonia "is as always" with the word pregnant omitted.

To find a wet nurse for the first baby, now that they knew it would be essential, the countess interviewed not an ethnically white or Spanish person, but a series of Indian women. The choice of a wet nurse is referred to only once again several years later. On September 29, 1759, María Antonia delayed her trip to Pachuca because an Indian wet nurse had left and she wanted to be sure that the milk of the next one would agree with the baby.

One mysterious aspect of María Antonia's life emerged while she remained in Mexico City. Her mother wrote to Pedro Terreros on June 16, 1757, urging him to return to Mexico City to quench gossip because his wife continued to leave the house and attended Mass at three churches in one day. Why this activity should be seen as scandalous is uncertain. The forty days' prohibition against women entering a church after childbirth had not yet quite passed.[40] Possibly, attendance at Mass was viewed as dangerous because it might involve walking in the streets of Mexico City. Fear of gossip about attending the public celebration of Mass might have encouraged María Antonia to retreat into private worship or to resort to superstition. She may have been seeking cures for her ill health and protection for her baby, as she requested a Medal of San Gerónimo, or Saint Jerome, to protect the baby against witches.[41]

Most of María Antonia's letters document visits from others, and it appears that she did occasionally leave the house once gossip had driven her from attending church. An aunt, who was a nun, wrote asking that María Antonia and her mother visit her in the convent. She may also have seen the archbishop in his palace in Tacubaya, and she once attended on the Viceroy and Vicereine Amarillas in their palace.[42] Most of her reports of contacts with friends and family outside the domestic group document visits in her mother's house, from her husband's cousin from Querétaro, the inquisitor, and various other aunts and cousins. This contrasted with the behavior of her mother, the countess of Miravalle, who left the house frequently.

By August 1757, María Antonia and her new baby, Micaela, had departed for Pachuca. Her desire that her husband not seek "another fortune" in Pachuca and instead return to be with her in Mexico City was not to be fulfilled for many years. The whole pattern of Pedro Terreros's life dictated his presence in the silver mines. No sooner did she return to Pachuca than she became pregnant again. Of this pregnancy we know almost nothing; very little of the Miravalle correspondence for the latter part of 1757 and the first part of 1758 has survived. This

child, Juana María, was born May 15 or 16, 1758, only a bit more than nine months
after the return of María Antonia to Pachuca. She was baptized a week after her
birth; her godfather was her best-connected uncle, Joachín.[43] María Antonia
remained in Mexico City through the beginning of July and then returned with
her two baby girls to Pachuca. The predictable effects of the reunion of the couple
was that María Antonia again became pregnant, and a year and six weeks later a
third daughter was born in Mexico City. It became obvious that Pedro Terreros's
wife was emulating the fertility of her mother, who gave birth to seven children
who survived to adulthood. During this third pregnancy, around April 1759,
she repeated the pattern of returning to Mexico City. This time, her husband
accompanied her on the trip, staying longer than usual in Mexico City.

The weeks before the birth of this third child were filled with more than the
previous discomforts. María Antonia could not sleep because of her anxieties
and pains, and she became more tired every day, perhaps because of anemia.
She reminded her husband on May 9 that she was writing on Micaela's birthday
and that he was to light candles to Our Lady of Sorrows. She was bled, and to the
usual discomforts of pregnancy were added those of a toothache.[44]

The couple's third daughter was born on June 20, 1759. The baptismal ceremony
occurred six days later. The countess wrote that they had named the child María
Antonia and added the additional names of Josefa, Manuela, and Micaela. Josefa
was a common name, Manuela was a Terreros family name, and Micaela was a
repetition of the name given to the oldest daughter. The youngest Miravalle son,
Vicente, was the godfather, and the priest who baptized the child was a member of
the countess's paternal family of Dávalos, indicating the importance of María
Antonia's connections in strengthening kinship bonds within the family.

María Antonia's sentiments of love and her desire to write affectionate letters
continued. She mentioned the sadness of celebrating St. Francis's day without
her spouse and wondered how she could amuse herself without him. At the
same time, her letters became more business-like, perhaps the result of greater
maturity (as her mother might have wished), the rhythms of marriage, or the
strains of producing three babies within three years. Her independence grew,
but she still expected her mother to inform her husband of practical details,
such as who would be the godparents and what name would be given the child.

Sometime in October 1759, after the end of the rainy season, María Antonia
returned to Pachuca. She did not come back to her mother's for the birth of her
next three children. Her last two children were born in the house that Pedro
Terreros had purchased in Mexico City in 1765. The visits for the birth of the first
three children were extended ones; future visits were only for Easter or Christmas in the company of her husband. In any event, no further letters of hers have
been preserved, and possibly none were ever written.

For María Antonia's fourth pregnancy her mother finally agreed to be there for the birth, and she wrote asking Pedro when María Antonia had the *falta*, that is, her last menstrual period, so that the countess could arrange for the midwife (*partera*), general servant (*tenedora*), and wet nurse to accompany her. In August 1760 she arrived in Pachuca for the birth of the fourth granddaughter, who would bear the Miravalle family name of (María) Ignacia. The countess again stood as baptismal sponsor, as she had for her oldest granddaughter, Micaela. In a prescient comment, María Antonia wrote either in 1757 or 1758 that she was looking for the skin of an animal so that it would not be so easy to have daughters.[45] It is difficult to imagine what ritual would require an animal skin, and how she might believe that this would influence the sex of her unborn children. What is notable is the implication that after only one female infant, she feared the birth of additional daughters rather than sons.

With the birth of the fourth daughter, it began to appear that Pedro Terreros might be confronted with the fertility pattern faced by his uncle, Juan Vázquez Terreros, who had four or five daughters and only very late in life fathered a son. The four older daughters of Pedro Romero de Terreros, born in 1757, 1758, 1759, and 1760, often had difficult lives and produced no offspring. The oldest daughter, Micaela, did indeed inherit an entail, but she lived in solitude and suffered painful relations with her siblings, perhaps because of her personality or resentment over the size of her inheritance. The second daughter, Juana, died before reaching the age of four, and Antonia, the third daughter, squandered her inheritance and died as a young woman. The details of Ignacia's life are still to be discovered.[46]

When Pedro and María Antonia were expecting their fifth child the countess, perhaps expecting another daughter, wrote asking if they would excuse her from the journey, only inquiring if she could choose the midwife.[47] Justo, the oldest Miravalle son, invited to be godparent, refused because he lacked money to provide a great feast.

This reluctance disappeared when the fifth child proved to be a son, and Pedro Terreros hosted an elaborate reception in Pachuca. The countess changed her mind about traveling when she learned that her daughter had given birth to a boy and made the journey for the baptismal service to stand as godparent for the third time.

Pedro and María Antonia's first son, born on August 30, 1761, was baptized on September 6 with the names of Pedro Ramón Mariano Joseph Francisco Miguel; he was generally known in later life as Pedro Ramón. The name Ramón was selected because the feast day of San Ramón fell on the date of his birth. Mariano represented the male form of the adherence to the use of Mary in the names given to boys as well as girls. Francisco may signify the devotion of his father to Franciscan causes, and this name was also given to his two other sons. As for Miguel, it also represented the interest in eighteenth-century Mexico in the life and deeds of Saint Michael, the warrior archangel.

Friar Gaspar Gómez—apostolic preacher, former professor in sacred theology, and ex-guardian of the College of Propaganda Fide of San Fernando of Mexico, one of the most important theologians and Franciscans in Mexico— traveled to Pachuca to perform the baptism. The countess even received a letter from the new viceroy, the marqués de Cruillas, which congratulated her because her daughter had given birth to a son.[48] One legend, repeated by the nineteenth-century observer Madame Calderón de la Barca, reports that for the baptism of this son the guests walked to the church on ingots of silver and that all the important people from Mexico City were invited to attend.[49] It appears unlikely that Pedro Terreros paved the streets with silver, although his daughters did wear shoes made of gold cloth.

In fact, the baptism of Pedro Ramón was the first of three celebrations hosted and paid for by Pedro Terreros held in Pachuca. The second was the ceremony to mark the completion of the adit, which drained the mines and would produce great wealth for Pedro Terreros, the Kingdom of New Spain, and the Spanish Empire. The third, the grandest of all, the celebration in honor of the coronation of Charles III, was an observance mandated by the Spanish crown. High officials attended each of these events.

Around 1761, the growing family in Pachuca adopted one aspect of upper-class familial practice. Large elite families needed more than one woman in the family to run the household and to oversee the care of the children. In María Antonia's case (as in the case of other women whose role was to have many children), the physical strain of constant childbearing consumed much of her energy. So Angela Labandero, the widowed oldest daughter of the countess, went to live in Pachuca with the Terreros family. Angela Labandero had three children of her own, and her two daughters remained in Mexico City in the household of the countess. In return for this sacrifice, Pedro Terreros paid the tuition of her son in seminary. Among other advantages of this plan, her son could inherit a Miravalle family chaplaincy.[50]

Angela Labandero had a dependent position within her brother-in-law and sister's house. It would appear that when she wanted to return to Mexico City to see her children, she requested permission from Pedro Terreros through her mother.[51] Her willingness to return to Pachuca was attested to by her mother in several letters, but she may have been unhappy about leaving her own family.[52] Despite the presence of her older daughter in the Terreros household, the countess continued offering medical advice, expressing her concern over the illness of her grandson, and informing her son-in-law that she would write to María Antonia about how to experiment with remedies.[53] The countess prided herself on her knowledge of pharmacopeia and treatment of illnesses, boasting to Pedro Terreros that even the interim viceroy, Francisco Antonio Cajigal, arriving from Havana in 1760, had heard of her medical skill.[54] Perhaps her advice was as effective as she boasted it was, since María Antonia had nine full-term pregnancies and only one of the children died.

The family, and above all Pedro Terreros, had no way of predicting whether his only son would survive, and shortly after his birth María Antonia conceived again. A series of pregnancies followed, some of them not reaching full term. The countess gave advice about bathing, telling her daughter when to use the Aztec sweat bath, called a *temascal*, especially recommended in the case of a miscarriage. One wonders if this adobe brick structure formed part of the household appurtenances of the family in Pachuca, or if María Antonia visited an Indian village to use it.

María Antonia fell into melancholia during her sixth pregnancy, and her mother urged her to amuse herself. The countess wrote to her son-in-law that it was important that the depression be lifted, and that she would leave for Pachuca within two weeks. By July 29, 1762, she still could not come; and on August 2, Pedro Villaverde, the owner of the hacienda of La Bata where the family customarily stayed in their trips between Mexico City and Pachuca, sent word that another baby boy had been born. Pedro Terreros himself wrote on August 8. She answered her son-in-law that she had been praying at both the sanctuary of Guadalupe and the cathedral, apparently with good result given the birth of a boy. She urged him to baptize the baby quickly, making him a Christian. Her advice was followed, and the second son was named Francisco, doubtless reflecting the attention Pedro Terreros both received from and dedicated to the Franciscans. In a rare moment of optimism, the countess concluded by telling Terreros that the only way in which the family's good fortune could be completed was the termination of the adit, which did indeed happen before the end of the year.[55]

Unfortunately, María Antonia's health did not improve, and December 1762 found her in Mexico City while her sister Angela remained with the children in Pachuca. Her mother kept her in Mexico City, first for the celebration of the Virgin of Guadalupe (December 12) and then for Christmas. She had her bled, her health improved, and then her customary bout of flución, returned again.[56]

After spending Christmas with her mother, María Antonia returned to Pachuca and immediately became pregnant. On February 3, 1763, her mother responded to the news (transmitted by her son-in-law) with advice that she not stay in bed and vomit if she felt nauseous. By the end of February, she had lost the baby, not apparently her first miscarriage, and her mother urged her to bathe herself as if she were pregnant in the Aztec sweat bath.[57] When María Antonia became pregnant once again, the medical word from her mother was to avoid bathing herself until the pregnancy was well advanced and also to avoid exercise. At some point her mother considered the successful conclusion of a pregnancy desirable; at another point, she advised her daughter to avoid further conception. On July 14, she wrote to her son-in-law that "it is necessary she not become pregnant again and that she recognize her cycles."[58]

Although dominated by concerns over health, the correspondence of the countess with the family in Pachuca covered many business matters and described the clothing that she sent to the family from Mexico City. The range of items arriving in Pachuca included food, stockings, shoes, a canopy to be placed over the images of saints, a monochord (a one-stringed instrument), dolls for the girls, and toys made of a sugar and almond paste called *alfenique*.

In the early years, the only grandchild who emerged with a distinct personality was the oldest, María Micaela. The countess of Miravalle welcomed her first words and celebrated the fact that Pedro Terreros now "has somebody to call him daddy [*tata*]." She rejoiced that Micaela had learned to read. For her two oldest granddaughters, Micaela and Juana, she hoped that "God would raise them to be saints."[59] This was a wish not to be granted her: one of them died when still a child and at best could become but a little angel (*angelito*); the other one, who would inherit the entail, would find that the possession and administration of wealth could conflict with a profession of sainthood. Perhaps Micaela's later efforts to bring the relics of Saint Columba to Mexico originated in her grandmother's pious hopes for her.[60]

Some months after expressing her aspirations for her two granddaughters, the countess asked Pedro Terreros if María Micaela could come to live with her.[61] Since the countess had been raised in the households of both her maternal and paternal grandmothers, she sought to establish the same relationship with her granddaughter when María Micaela was nearly two and a half.[62] Pedro and María Antonia apparently rejected this suggestion—possibly because they did not wish to be deprived of the company of their oldest daughter, or alternatively because Pedro Terreros lacked confidence in the capacities and customs of the creole elite of which his mother-in-law formed a part. The countess of Miravalle continued to be a successful administrator of her family haciendas as well as a skilled political operator. The grandmother could have instructed Micaela in the administration of haciendas and businesses, skills that Micaela painfully acquired as an adult, so the plan had merit.

In 1765, María Antonia moved to Mexico City where she had two more children, María Dolores in 1765 (bearing the name of her favorite virgin, Dolores), and in May 1766 José María, whose birth resulted in the mother's death. The eight surviving children, including three sons, assured the continuation of the family name of Pedro Terreros. (The Appendix provides a list of birth and death dates for the children of Pedro Terreros.)

María Antonia's death at the age of thirty-two occurred not quite ten years after her wedding, on June 2, 1766, twenty-three days after the birth of her last son. What might have been expected with these painful and continual pregnancies had finally occurred. She was buried in the vault of her Miravalle ancestors in the seventeenth-century church of the Merced, long favored by the family as a recipient of charitable gifts. No special burial place existed for the less prestigious Terreros family.

Her husband spent 6,219 pesos on her funeral—a great deal less than he had spent on their wedding. But in doing so he followed his inclination as well as a tendency for members of the elite to request modest funerals, with fewer mourners, alms, and smaller processions. This modest funeral expenditure was compensated for by the 14,750 pesos he paid for 57,500 Masses to be said for her soul, a fitting tribute to a woman who had been very religious and had even provoked a rebuke from her mother for continual attendance at Masses! He also continued giving the limosnas, or donations, requested by his wife.[63]

CONCLUSION

What can be surmised about the ten years of matrimony of Pedro and María Antonia? During the course of her marriage, she passed from a young suffering woman very much in love to an experienced matriarch of her household. She made decisions on the spending of money and on the appearance of the house, and who controlled the kitchen of an enormous household, receiving continual gifts of the meat from young lambs. Once she had to decide on the disposition of the meat from a large slaughtering operation.[64] As her mother's letters make clear, she underwent continual physical suffering and occasional emotional travails. Her religious devotions rarely faltered.

Pedro Terreros's desire for many heirs, expected from a man of his class, can be added to the possibility that he had a strong affection and sexual attraction to his young wife. No sooner did his wife return from her visits to her mother than she became pregnant. We do not know if Pedro Terreros had intimate ties with women before his marriage; we know only that he certainly did fulfill the matrimonial debt required of married couples by the church—that they multiply and make the earth fruitful.[65] In following this pattern, the history of his marriage and that of his former partner, José Alejandro Bustamante, followed a similar course. Bustamante's wife produced eight children in less than ten years and probably also died in childbirth.[66] The records of other families of similar status reveal a pattern of older men marrying younger women who repeatedly became pregnant.[67] María Antonia's marital life also mirrors that of her mother, who experienced at least nine pregnancies in fourteen years of marriage. Underlying this pattern is the church's doctrine about the matrimonial debit, which mandated that sexual intercourse was a duty of each partner. The church urged abstention from intimate contact between husband and wife while a mother nursed her baby, for forty days after the birth of a child, and on special holy days.[68] But none of these numerous prohibitions stood in the way of the production of a large offspring, or *prole*, as the countess of Miravalle referred to her grandchildren.

Letters written to Pedro Romero de Terreros provide information not previously available about the role of the father in upper-class families. In Pedro Terreros's case at least, he was consulted about the most intimate decisions concerning his family's health and welfare: when and how the children should be weaned, what they should be fed, and what medicines they should be given. He reported to his mother-in-law about everything from his wife's depression to her toothaches. Finally, he was expected to be around his children enough so that they could call him by an affectionate diminutive such as daddy (tata). The godparents, in this case the countess of Miravalle and her sons, as was customary, determined the names the children would be given and which of her offspring would be the baptismal sponsors.

How representative was the behavior of this family? Sometimes, the family's actions confirm what we already know, for instance that godparents were chosen only from the immediate family. Even when the official chronicler recorded that Luis Marrugat, a business associate of Pedro Terreros, and his wife had hosted the baptismal feast and were godparents, in the parish register only the names of Miravalle relatives appear.

Since we do not possess Pedro Terreros's written responses, this vision of family life assumes a lopsided aspect, with feminine elements predominating. The character and even the actions of the patriarch often recede into the distance after he impregnated his wife, except when he is consulted about whether his wife should nurse their first child. In addition, many stresses and strains of family life cannot be specified. The often angry, imperious, single-minded, overwhelmingly ambitious man, as he was known to his colleagues and to his workers, seems to behave to the contrary in his domestic role. In fact, Terreros appeared to be exceptionally generous to his family.

In his occasional dislike of creole society, as well as in his patterns of marriage and production of children, Pedro Terreros followed the customs of peninsulares whose pretensions to nobility and to the preservation of their names could be satisfied only by making money and undertaking good marriages with young women of child-bearing age preferably with wealth or respected names. However, through marriage he had also set his roots in the society whose customs he sometimes deplored.

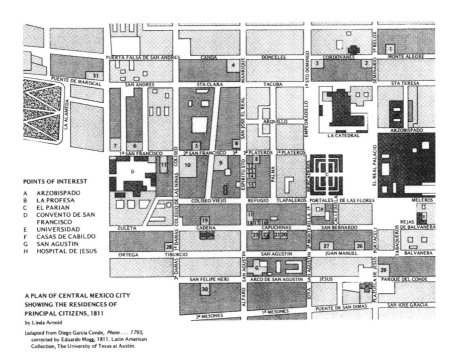

POINTS OF INTEREST

A ARZOBISPADO
B LA PROFESA
C EL PARIAN
D CONVENTO DE SAN FRANCISCO
E UNIVERSIDAD
F CASAS DE CABILDO
G SAN AGUSTIN
H HOSPITAL DE JESUS

A PLAN OF CENTRAL MEXICO CITY
SHOWING THE RESIDENCES OF
PRINCIPAL CITIZENS, 1811
by Linda Arnold

(adapted from Diego Garcia Conde, *Plano . . . 1793,*
corrected by Eduardo Mogg, 1811. Latin American
Collection, The University of Texas at Austin.)

RESIDENCES

1 MARQUES DE SALVATIERRA*
2 MARQUES DEL APARTADO house
3 GABRIEL DE YERMO*
4 CONDE DE HERAS SOTO house
5 CONDE DE ALAMO*
6 CONDE DEL VALLE DE ORIZABA (HOUSE OF TILES)*
7 MARQUES DE GUARDIOLA house
8 MARQUES DE AGUAYO*
9 MARQUES DE PRADO ALEGRE house
10 BORDA house
11 CONDE DE VALPARAISO, MARQUES DE JARAL houses (HOTEL ITURBIDE, 1ª SAN FRANCISCO)
12 JOSE JOAQUIN DE ITURBIDE
13 CONDESA DE MIRAVALLE*
14 MARQUES DE VIVANCO*
15 CONDE DEL PENASCO house
16 JOSE MARIANO FAGOAGA*
17 MARQUESA-VIUDA DEL APARTADO*
18 CONDE DE PEREZ GALVEZ*
19 JOSE JUAN DE FAGOAGA*
20 MARTIN ANGEL MICHAUS*
21 CONDE DE JALA house
22 MARQUES DE INGUANZO*
23 CONDE DE HERAS SOTO*
24 FERMIN DE APEZECHEA*
25 MARQUESA DE SELVANEVADA*
26 CONDE DE BASSOCO
27 CONDE DE LA TORRE DE COSIO house, CONDE DE LA CORTINA*
28 MARQUES DE ULUAPA*
29 CONDE DE SANTIAGO CALIMAYA*
30 CONDE DE REGLA*
31 MARISCAL DE CASTILLA

* denotes in residence in 1811

Map 5. Central Mexico City. Courtesy of Linda Arnold.

CHAPTER 6

A House for the Count of Regla: 1764–1781

The custom of building a home in the city was very European.
Wealthy landowners and silver miners were not content to remain
on their estates. Wishing to participate in the political, economic
and social whirl of the capital . . .they built for themselves large,
lavish town houses. This type of noble residence was known in Rome
as palazzo, or in Paris as hotel, in Vienna as palais or Stadhaus, in
London as town house. In Mexico City, it was called palacio. By
the end of the Viceregency that city alone boasted almost forty. All
had one thing in common—monumentality. Many still exist.
—Mullen, Architecture and its Sculpture

At the end of 1763, Pedro Terreros was close to the pinnacle of his career. He had completed the adit to drain the underground workings, modernized the great refining haciendas, later to be called San Miguel, San Antonio, and Santa María Regla, cleared titles to his mines, and had begun the purchase of agricultural haciendas. He had also attained social recognition. A military order had accepted him as a member, and the king had granted him the honor of *gracia de gentilhombre de cámara con entrada*, the honorary right of entrance into the king's dressing room.[1] His sponsorship of the celebration of the coronation of Charles III in Pachuca was carried out successfully, and prominent people in the kingdom had attended the baptismal ceremony of his son in 1761. A flourishing family life had been crowned by his wife's creation of five healthy children, two of them sons. On the international scene, the Seven Years' War had ended in early 1763 and brought about the prospect of future peace and prosperity.

But difficulties still persisted. He had not yet received his title of count of Regla. He was further plagued by lingering doubts about his ownership of the mine of San Vicente and of shortages of labor, merchandise, and mercury. He may have concluded that resolution of these problems could be facilitated by maintaining a presence in the capital in Mexico City. Moreover, his wife had never been as happy in Pachuca as in Mexico City in the company of her family, acquaintances, and notable clerics. The highest honors might come to her, as to her husband, in Mexico City. Perhaps this move also signaled a decision by Terreros to spend less time in his mines and more in Mexico City pursuing other aspects of his affairs.

A determination to establish a residence in the city of Mexico came by January 1764. The fact that María Antonia and the children had not been able to return to Mexico City for Christmas because of the illness of Pedro, the oldest son, influenced their decision. The acquisition of a house also coincided with the purchase of agricultural haciendas. In 1764, he bought the haciendas of San Pedro de las Vaquerías and San Francisco for 129,500 pesos, which began to provide him with income.[2]

The accumulation of real estate, whether agricultural properties or the purchase of the house in Mexico City, are connected through the person of Luis Marrugat, a Catalan merchant resident in Mexico City, who had recently taken charge of Pedro Terreros's Mexico City affairs. Marrugat purchased mercury, mining equipment, and countless other commodities, including slaves for Terreros.

Mexico City, known as the "City of Palaces," contained numbers of palatial structures that served families as a place to live and a place to do business.[3] These houses, all constructed or reconstructed during the eighteenth-century period of prosperity for mercantile and mining elites, symbolized the power and financial success of families, and a house came to be synonymous with a family and its enterprises.[4]

THE PURCHASE

The first indication of his intention to establish a family seat in Mexico City came from the countess of Miravalle. In January 1764, she protested Terreros's decision to buy a house, since they could stay with her. But soon she assented to the project of finding or building a house, writing, "My house is at your disposal and from here you can look for a place built to your taste. There are lots of old houses which have been constructed by convents of nuns."[5]

In March 1764, the narrative shifts from Miravalle's letters to those of Luis Marrugat. The Catalan proposed that Terreros and his wife build a new house. He argued that the three houses that were for sale had many disadvantages and suggested a building site that belonged to an entail and that had the benefit of the finest water (*merced de agua primorosa*) and enough space to construct other houses. Marrugat's advice that Pedro Terreros should become an urban real estate entrepreneur, a path that would make so many fortunes in the next two centuries, had the additional advantage of providing the Catalan with a lot of remunerated work. Rejecting the extravagant and time-consuming idea of building a new house favored by both his mother-in-law and his colleague, and desiring a house immediately, Terreros moved to buy one of the three houses available on the market in February and March 1764.[6] It is an interesting comment on the Mexico City real estate market at this time in 1763 and 1764 that of the three suitable houses for sale to a wealthy buyer, two of them belonged, or had belonged recently, to convents, and one was being auctioned as part of the estate of someone recently deceased.

Marrugat advised against buying one of these houses because it did not have an *entresuelo*, which was "a great domestic convenience." The entresuelo, a level story or floor between the first and second stories, separated the family's business from its domestic affairs. In most large houses, the ground floor consisted of storerooms, offices, and commercial space, and would have large open areas for parking coaches and other vehicles and for the receipt of merchandise. The second story consisted of the family's living quarters. In the entresuelo, administrators might work and live; collateral family members might also reside on this floor. It also could be a residence for those servants who connected the family to the business.[7] The entresuelo shielded the family from the noise of the coming and going of carts, horses, and messengers and defined the class status of the administrators and servants who lived there as a higher category than domestics who might live on the ground floor, on the roof, or in hallways. Hence, these old noble houses had three floors.

Probably Terreros agreed with Marrugat about the advantage of an entresuelo, because he selected a house with a very large and complete one that included windows onto the street. The other factors that influenced his decision are not known. Did the fact that the house had previously belonged to the marqués del Villa de Villar de Aguila—the very person who had sponsored the construction of the aqueduct in Querétaro and that the twenty-eight-year-old Pedro Terreros might have admired a quarter of a century earlier—play a part? Although the house had been sold by the family, the marqués's coat of arms still decorated the entrance door. Perhaps, in the end, Marrugat convinced Pedro Terreros that he could buy this particular house for less money than either of the other two. Located at one end of the old central district, on the corner of the street of San Felipe Neri (now the Republic of El Salvador Street), with the church of San Agustín across the street, and the Jesuit church of the Third Order of San Felipe Neri almost adjacent to the house, it was surrounded by religious institutions. In its location it bore a similarity to Terreros's uncle's house in Querétaro, as well as many other palatial residences in eighteenth-century Latin American cities. (See Figure 10.)

Based on Marrugat's letters about the purchase of the house, it appears that a potential purchaser may not have been permitted to view the interior of the house. Hence Marrugat depended on the good will of the current tenant, who provided a good report and permitted Marrugat to view the patio and notice the high columns. A high government official also assured Marrugat that the house was a good one. The house had been sold four or five years previously to the nuns of the convent of San Bernardo for 40,000 pesos, and they had been able to rent it for only 800 or 1,000 pesos annually, so they were anxious to sell. Marrugat informed Terreros that the house could be purchased for about 26,000 pesos, ignoring the fact that the nuns would be reluctant to lose 14,000 pesos.

Fig. 10. Regla's house on
San Felipe Neri Street,
Mexico City. Photograph
by Juan Romero de Terreros.

Nevertheless, the nuns knew that there were few, if any, people in Mexico City
with that much cash.

Marrugat narrated the negotiations to buy the house with military metaphors.
Recounting the "battle" that he waged, he described every step, imagining
strongholds that he conquered with his *mesicanos* (a term for pesos), as though
the pesos represented soldiers and the house a castle to be conquered before Holy
Week. If they did not succeed by that date, it would disappear until another
season of combat, as the nuns would rent again if it were not sold.

On a Sunday evening the nuns met and voted to sell the house for 32,000
pesos; they also demanded that Terreros pay the alcabala or sales tax. Marrugat,
who had told Terreros he could purchase the house for 26,000, described the be-
sieging of the "castle" with his 30,000 mesicanos, referring to the top price that he
was prepared to offer. Then he tried several more sieges and found that the

> enemy made a strong stand over the castle of the alcabala and were repuls-
> ing us with great strength. In order to capture [the house] it was neces-
> sary to bring up 1,800 mesicanos, and I was defending myself with 30,000

and finally, in order to begin to conquer, I had to offer reinforcements. I attacked with a bold move, and I will notify you quickly with a favorable response.[8]

Pedro Terreros, initially unwilling to pay more than the original sum quoted him by Marrugat, nonetheless had to offer 32,000 pesos. He did not have that amount of liquid cash on hand, so Marrugat devised schemes to raise it. One scheme was that 10,000 pesos would be gained through the sale of livestock from the hacienda of San Francisco Vaquerías, giving him enough additional money to pay for the house. The sticking point was who should pay the alcabala.

By the end of the first week in April 1764, the archbishop of Mexico, the same one who had married Pedro and María Antonia eight years earlier, and who had referred to Terreros as the "father of the destitute and faithful supporter of religion," and who was also responsible for the welfare of the convent, accused Marrugat and Terreros of taking advantage of the nuns, and suggested that their payment of the alcabala should be undertaken as an act of charity. Terreros refused. The archbishop asked Marrugat where he came from in Spain. When Marrugat told him "Cataluña," the archbishop, laughing, spoke to him in Catalan. Marrugat reported his happiness in "speaking with such a humane and modest man."[9] As a result, the nuns received their 32,000 pesos, and Terreros apparently paid the tax. So all the investiture of fortresses and attacks with armies of Mexican pesos was resolved by a friendly ethnic contact, with Terreros paying a much larger than anticipated price. Terreros, as an Andalucían, might have felt dissatisfied because ten days later he still had not returned the signed contract.

The house purchase was further delayed because the nuns had included other properties belonging to the convent in the title documents. Marrugat asked that they straighten out the papers and send him only the title of the house on San Felipe Neri Street (see Map 6). However, the papers were in disarray, and the nun in charge of accounts, the Madre Contadora, was old and unable to prepare them. To organize the house title, the convent needed to admit a young nun with good eyesight to act as clerk. A young woman had already been identified, but lacked a dowry, an essential prerequisite for admission to a convent. The archbishop agreed to admit her for a 2,000-peso dowry, at least 1,000 pesos less than the norm. The last round of negotiations was carried out when Terreros arrived in Mexico City just before Holy Week in 1764. In the end, the deal was made, possibly, as Marrugat wrote, so that "My Lady, María Antonia might have the pleasure of reading the purchase papers." This is a hint of how fervently she desired a house in Mexico City.

After Pedro Terreros bought the house, new and still more serious problems emerged with his unseen purchase. When Marrugat visited the house he discovered a nightmare. The walls surrounding the house were so high that the sun would enter the house only in the spring.[10] Because of the high altitude of Mexico City, 7,800 feet, the temperature remains chilly, except at midday, from June when the rainy season begins through a generally dry winter until March, when the weather turns warm and dry. Purchasers or builders of homes in Mexico City used to consider the orientation of the house to provide maximum sun as an important factor in providing comfort and light.

Marrugat, trying to explain the deficiencies of the house to his employer, accused the majordomo of the convent of bad faith for having failed to inform him about the lack of light. The majordomo in turn accused Marrugat by saying that "only a Catalan could have done me the damage that you have done."[11] Perhaps the majordomo believed that the archbishop and Marrugat, both being Catalans, had conspired in some way against him and the convent. The lack of light and sun surely afflicted the spirits and health of María Antonia. Whoever was at fault, the unexpectedly dark and cold house serves as a metaphor for the difficulties and sad times that lay ahead for the family established by Pedro Terreros and María Antonia Trebuestos.

PREPARING AND FURNISHING THE HOUSE

Between Easter and Christmas 1764, Marrugat prepared the house, purchased furnishings, wall coverings, and household goods. He recorded his labors in letters to Pedro Terreros; his information together with 1782 inventories of the house supplement our knowledge of his work and of how the family used the space they had recently acquired. These sources provide an index of tastes and ideas about domestic activities and of how it was hoped the house would impress visitors. They also serve as a key to the personalities of Pedro Terreros, María Antonia Trebuestos, and Luis Marrugat. They illuminate aristocratic customs and family life, although, as always, these documents tell us much less than we would like to know.

The effort and money expended in decorating and furnishing the house was enormous. One wonders how Terreros lacked the cash to purchase the house, and still spent so liberally for furnishings. Some of the money, cast in silver bars rather than in coined pesos, could have served as payment to workers such as silversmiths. As a miner, Pedro Terreros had access to silver bars. It would appear that the ways and finances of the very rich in eighteenth-century Mexico were indeed strange and inexplicable.

Marrugat supplied very few details about construction work on the house. There were few monetary decisions for which he would have had to consult Terreros, having only to pay workers their low wages. Terreros had solely to decide whether the *vigas*, or beams, in the main living room should be removed. On the advice of the *maestro*, the construction foreman of a crew of up to twenty-five carpenters and masons, Marrugat recommended they leave them because they would hide

---

PLANO 2

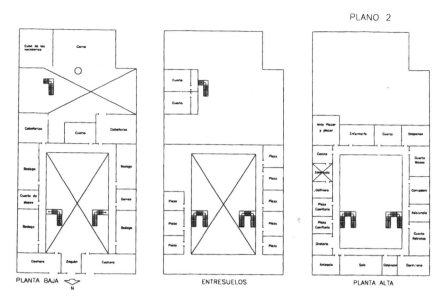

PLANTA BAJA   ENTRESUELOS   PLANTA ALTA

Map 6. Plan of the House on San Felipe Neri Street at the time of its construction in 1743 by the marqués del Villa de Villar de Aguila. Courtesy of Verónica Zarate and from the AGN, Vínculos, vol. 153. Drawing by E. Toscano.

the almost inevitable leaks. If they should select a clear ceiling that might have been decorated with painted figures and flowers, the beams would interrupt the designs. Besides, the painting on the ceiling would be ruined by roof leaks. Given the elaborate European style of the furnishings, one might opine that a beamed ceiling would clash.[12] We know that Pedro Terreros chose a painted ceiling for the family chapel, but whether he kept the beams and did not paint the ceiling in the main *sala* (room) is uncertain. Apparently little was left to Marrugat's discretion, because he even had to request permission to remove the coat of arms of the marqués de Villa de Villar de Aquila from the front door.

Marrugat hoped to have the house ready for family occupancy before Christmas. Strangely, international politics both hindered and helped him. The Seven Years' War had cut supplies to the colonies, thus merchant warehouses lacked goods. The annual fleets, which provisioned Mexico with European goods, would not leave Spain until January 1765, after the expected moving date.[13] However, instead of the fleet, the royal official, the count of Ricla, who had recently been appointed to govern Havana, had arrived in the Indies with a large collection of luxury goods that he intended to sell to wealthy citizens in Havana, Mexico City, and perhaps Central America. As part of the emoluments of his office, an official of this stature had the right to trade in merchandise and could easily calculate that the colonial market had been starved. Thus his merchandise carried a heavy price tag, and Marrugat made purchases from him selectively.

There were alternative sources of supply. Goods could be bought at auctions, from the estates of those recently deceased, or from certain newly arrived ships. A chronic shortage of currency made it possible to purchase goods at low prices through auctions. In fact, in 1782, after the death of Pedro Terreros, when his executors wished to have a low evaluation of certain goods, they hired an auctioneer. Similarly, when Marrugat had described the price of one of the houses for sale from an estate in Mexico City, before they settled on the house on San Felipe Neri, he gave three evaluations—the lowest being that of the auctioneer. Marrugat attended numerous auctions and wrote to Terreros about his experiences looking for mirrors, Turkish rugs, mahogany writing desks, and chairs.

What furnishings and fabrics did Marrugat seek to buy? One of the biggest expenses was for fabric of different kinds—but all of the same color, *carmesí rojo*—crimson fabric of a red tone rather than a purplish one, which would be placed in the frames (*bastidores*) in the corridors, on the walls of public rooms, and on the floors. Fabric was used in the eighteenth century instead of wallpaper. In this house it also served for carpets. A red velvet carpet covered the floor, and red damask curtains with borders of silver thread adorned the windows. If the red fabric did not provide an atmosphere of warmth, it certainly reflected opulence. Was Marrugat seeking to use this red color to provide warmth to a cold house in which the sun rarely entered?

Mirrors, another way in which light, if not warmth, might be captured, ranked first on the list of objects that Marrugat sought at auctions. From an estate inventory prepared for an auction, he found seven mirrors with crystal frames evaluated at 2,200 pesos and he offered 1,300 pesos.[14] Seven additional mirrors had already acquired silver frames, no longer crystal ones, leading to the conclusion that the ambience of wealth had greater importance than the reflected light of crystal frames. Putting frames around mirrors assumed importance for Marrugat, who worried about the quality of the silver frames to be prepared, so much so that he advised Terreros that the designs for the frames must not be done capriciously. Marrugat employed a silversmith who had made a charcoal drawing of the frames, gave the artisan five silver bars to use in fashioning frames not only for mirrors, but for screens, religious paintings, and even paintings on copper.[15] The process of making frames for mirrors, screens, and religious objects continued after the family had occupied the house for many months.

The most numerous items purchased by Marrugat were *taburetes*, leather-backed chairs without arms. Marrugat sought these chairs in variable sizes and complained about the interpretations of small and large in the furniture collection from which he intended to buy them. The bulk of the chairs that Marrugat purchased were to be placed in the two salas extending along the entire front of the house.[16]

Marrugat also purchased furniture for Pedro and María Antonia's bedrooms. As was customary in upper-class eighteenth-century households, the fact that each of them had a separate bedroom did not prevent sexual relations; in fact, they had two more children. Marrugat arranged for María Antonia's bed to be brought over from her mother's house since it was deemed sufficiently elegant to fit into the new house. Another bedroom contained two beds painted green, which were probably among the beds that Marrugat had had a carpenter make for the children.[17]

The furnishing of the house, which continued for a longer period than the six months Marrugat needed to prepare for the family, reflects the grandiosity of Pedro Terreros. María Antonia's death in 1766 did not put an end to the acquisition of silver goods, fabrics, and rugs ,which continued for years. The material luxury represented by the household goods symbolized the lifestyle expected of a family of Regla's status. By 1768, Pedro Terreros's social status was augmented when he finally achieved his much desired title and became the count of Regla.

ARRANGING THE HOUSE: 1765-1782

After the death of María Antonia and the strike in Real del Monte, Regla exiled himself to his refining hacienda of San Miguel. But it seems probable that the children continued to live in Mexico City for some time, with Regla returning to Mexico City rarely until about 1774. In fact, between 1765 and the death of Regla in 1781, we have scant information about the house and its usage. Our chief source of information about the family—the letters of the countess of Miravalle—almost disappear after the family moved to Mexico City in 1765.

At Regla's death, despite his establishment of three entails, the law required that the unentailed property be divided among the remaining heirs. The nine men undertaking the inventory went through the house room by room three times. Two immense rooms, the salas or salons, covered the part of the house facing the street of San Felipe Neri. The largest room, called at different times the *sala principal* (the great room), or the *salón de dosal* (canopy salon), or the *salón de sitial* (receiving room with a seat of honor for princes and kings), measured approximately 50-feet long and 29-feet wide. Crimson velvet carpet covered the receiving room. A portrait of the king, along with a chair and table for his occupancy, adorned the room; few men had the right to display such symbols of royalty. Ten sheets of metal carried large engravings or paintings of the life of Christ and the Virgin; there were also screens, Chinese vases, two candelabra, and two-dozen chairs with red-damask seats.

For the second large public room, called the *sala de estrado*, Marrugat had purchased small chairs. The *estrado* was a raised, movable platform in one part of a room that served as a special place for women, who sat on cushions. As an indication of how customs were changing, a house furnished some thirty years earlier would probably have had fewer chairs and more pillows. By the late eighteenth century, the custom of having women sit on cushions was being replaced by the practice of having them sit on chairs. The inventories of 1782 indicate that there was still a platform in the principal sala. Customarily, the estrado had a Turkish rug, and Marrugat had difficulty in finding one for a modest price. One, available from an estate sale, cost 580 pesos; other rugs called *de la tierra,* meaning made in Mexico, or also called San Migueleños (meaning perhaps that they were woven in the wool collecting town of San Miguel el Grande) and cost only 100 and 150 pesos. The chairs for the estrado are smaller than those destined for other parts of the room, but how much smaller remains as much of a riddle for us as for Marrugat.[18] The purchase of thirty-six chairs demonstrates that the family intended to carry on an active social life, an expectation never fulfilled because of the death of María Antonia, the strike of 1766, and Pedro Terreros's decision to live at his refining hacienda of San Miguel Regla.

A richly adorned chapel was discussed in the greatest detail by a Regla descendant and art historian in his description of his ancestor's house. It was carpeted with crimson damask and filled with "paintings, niches, crucifixes, proof of membership in confraternities [*patentes de hermandades*], relics, silver floral arrangements [*ramilletes*]," and a central candelabra with sixteen branches.[19] More light could be produced in this room than in others. It also had a painting of the sky with both sun and moon as though they shone at the same time—a typical baroque exaggeration.

No room was without its religious remembrances. One repeated image is that of San Miguel, the archangel, depicted as a soldier in eighteenth-century Mexico. He also had defeated Satan and was visualized as a soldier conquering evil. He is often depicted with a scale that weighed the good and evil one did in life, playing the role of judge.

If Pedro Terreros wished to remember and memorialize the warrior, María Antonia's favorite evocation was the Virgin of Sorrows, or Dolores, who appears in statues and paintings. The contrast between the personalities of this couple is depicted graphically by their preferred chosen figurative representations; one of war and the other of grief.

Adjacent to the chapel were elaborate bedrooms belonging to the count and countess of Regla. The bedroom of María Antonia contained moldings of carved and gilded wood and a bed with decorated columns and curtains of scarlet damask. This bedroom had mahogany chests (*roperos*) for clothing or linens and, above all, a raised platform covered with Italian damask. The eleven chairs scattered throughout the room indicate that it served as a social center, as well as a place to sleep. Religious objects, including paintings and statues of the Virgins of Guadalupe and Loreto and of Christ crucified, were also plentiful.

The dressing room (*tocador*), identified as belonging to María Antonia, contained the posthumously conferred coat-of-arms of the countess of Regla placed on a wall. It was embossed, painted, and framed with chiseled silver and measured about 9-feet high and 5-feet wide. The existence of the coat of arms needs some explanation. María Antonia did not live long enough to become the countess of Regla; she died two years before Pedro Terreros received the title, so it appears that he continued to decorate this room after her death, not an unreasonable idea for a man who had ordered 50,000 Masses for her soul. Yellow Chinese damask hung from the balconies and decorated the floor. In addition to an elaborate dressing table with basins, mirrors, and table, the room contained a *papelera,* or writing desk, another indication that María Antonia did conduct some household business here, and a statue of Saint Peter, perhaps an indication of her affection for her husband. The room also contained a clavichord and small stools. On the walls were four *pantallas,* or screens, and a mirror with chiseled silver frame.[20] We might speculate that María Antonia played a musical instrument and that she preferred the color yellow to that of crimson.

The bedroom of the count of Regla had a curtained bed, a painting of Saint Peter (a notable remembrance of his namesake), and six smaller paintings of other saints. Just as María Antonia had a dressing room adjacent to her bedroom, so Regla had an office (*despacho*) next to his. The office was furnished with a mahogany desk, a clock (there are several very elegant ones in various places in the house), three tables, a couch, two large cedar chests for holding valuable silver bars and papers, and twenty-two chairs made of marbled wood with damask seats.[21] He could conduct business with a sizable group of people, if the need arose.

There were a series of other bedrooms in the house, but the inventories are not specific about their contents. For example, there is no information about the furniture in the children's rooms. Much of the practical household furniture might have been transferred to the refining hacienda of San Miguel when the children ceased to live in Mexico City. With the exception of a few women's stockings, ribbons, and handkerchiefs that were listed as belonging to the countess of Regla, there is little indication of women's presence in the house. It might be surmised that between about 1775 and 1781, only the count, and not his daughters, visited Mexico City. At some point Regla had moved his clothing from the bedroom and occupied one of the two large public rooms in the front of the house. The clothing that Regla kept in the Mexico City house consisted of ornate and highly decorated outfits, including three pairs of trousers to match waistcoats and vests. Since he could hardly have expected to wear out the trousers of ceremonial garments, perhaps the extra pairs were in anticipation of other accidents. I did not detect any simple black suits of the kind that the scientist Antonio de Ulloa reported that the count of Regla had worn in 1777 at the refining hacienda of San Miguel.

The dining room, as observed by his descendant, was "the simplest and least luxurious of the whole house."[22] Perhaps he referred to the fact that instead of silver-framed mirrors, gilded statues, moldings, and damask valances, the dining room had as a wall decoration ten strips of Chinese wallpaper with gilded frames, which could have been very expensive and a mark of wealth and status. Other furnishings included a cedar cabinet, eighteen chairs, and a table, not to mention enough plates, trays, and bowls to feed three hundred people. The silver center-piece on the table was valued at 11,736 pesos; when taken apart in 1782, it filled four trunks. This collection of tableware, less extensive than those in the estates of other wealthy families, was probably accumulated to celebrate public and family events. Perhaps the baptism of José María and the funeral of María Antonia, only a month apart, required the collection of this amount of tableware in order to feed celebrants and mourners. Or these materials may have been collected for the ceremony of the coronation of Charles III in Pachuca in 1763. Like all the objects in the house, the extensive collection of tableware is one more example of the elaborate display essential to maintaining one's position.

The entresuelo, so prized by Marrugat that he had made such a point of recommending it as one of the chief assets of this house, is described as having windows on the street and also windows that looked out on the patio. The ground floor contained store-rooms and only two ancient carriages according to one of the three inventories of the house, but according to another inventory, the coaches and other vehicles used to transport the family were more elegant. If the family spent much time in Mexico City, they might be expected to take outings on the Alameda, go to Mass at more distant churches, and attend baptisms, weddings, and funerals.

In the corridor hung four maps of the world, a map of Barcelona (perhaps a gift from the Catalan, Marrugat), and a globe, but even in hallways there were representations of the Virgin. Of the sixteen books found in the corridor, only seven were obviously religious, different from the book collection of Regla's uncle inventoried more than forty years earlier. Regla's nonreligious books included Gamboa's commentaries on the mining ordinances, with which Regla had had some disagreements, and works by the countess of Miravalle's cousin and audiencia judge, Joaquín de Rivadeneira, whom she had tried to arrange to be the judge in the case of Terreros against Valleameno in 1758.

The division between sacred and secular is mine; the books were listed at random in the inventories. Books from the estate of Pedro's uncle, such as the copies of David Perseguido, seem not to have gone to the house in Mexico City, although we must remember that there were goods in the houses in Pachuca, Real del Monte, and in San Miguel Regla, where the family definitely lived, which cannot be found in any existing inventory. Perhaps Terreros had sold them, or left them in the property belonging to his cousin, Juan Manuel, the heir to the Querétaro house.

For a man who chose to donate a library of books to the Franciscan friary in Pachuca, but which he asserted was lost at sea, this collection of books is meager.[23] It is also surprising that when the friar delivered the homily at Regla's funeral, he declared, in speaking of Pedro Terreros's early years in Querétaro, that the most valuable property was religious books.

When the count of Regla had set up his entails, he had promised to provide 300,000 pesos in property to each of his daughters who would not inherit an entail. The value of the property to be given to the daughters was artificially inflated, so that it would reach 300,000 pesos, while the property in the entails was assigned a low value. The men assigned to protect the interests of the daughters protested in vain. It might be speculated that these procedures did not promote family harmony in later years.

THE FAMILY AND THE HOUSE AFTER
THE DEATH OF MARÍA ANTONIA

The major blow to the family was the death, at the age of thirty-two, of María Antonia. In 1766, after many years of ill health and difficult pregnancies, she died in the house on San Felipe Neri Street without ever having had the opportunity to make her mark in the theater of politics and social life of Mexico City. Despite her many illnesses, the family might have assumed that she would continue to withstand the physical punishments of her pregnancies. Her mother and four older sisters lived long lives, and numbers of her female relatives also reached mature ages. However, she lived to enjoy only a year and a half in the house on San Felipe Neri Street, during which time she gave birth to two children. Based on her earlier experiences, it is likely that these last two pregnancies brought her pain and suffering. But at least in 1765–66, Pedro Terreros spent a good deal of time in Mexico City with his wife. He thereby fulfilled her desires, expressed so poignantly in 1757, that if he truly loved her, he would be with her at the time of her ill-health and be present in the house when the last two children were born. For the fifty-six-year-old Terreros, it must have been a tragedy to lose his young wife.

During his time in Mexico City, Terreros had left his unpopular administrator, Marcelo González, in charge of his mines. Petitions for the redress of grievances and the walkout of August 1766 occurred soon after the death of María Antonia. After nearly losing his life, Terreros took refuge in his refining hacienda of San Miguel and for nearly eight years he continued to live there, but the children remained in the house on San Felipe Neri Street. In 1768 the bookkeeper, Eliseo Vergara, prepared a large sheet with the accounts. According to Vergara's record, Pedro Terreros paid a modest 20 to 27 pesos a month for the food for a household of seven children and their caretakers who are not enumerated in the account.[24]

How much contact the children had with their father after the death of their mother is a mystery. The family's relationships with their Miravalle grandmother, aunts, uncles, and cousins after the death of their mother continued. We do know that Regla lent his mother-in-law 14,000 pesos on two different occasions, the last in 1769.[25] Some of that money may have gone to help her purchase a more elevated government post for her son, Joaquín. This debt was carried forward to the second generation, and it seems probable that the debt could never be paid, because many of the original members of the family became poor. The count of Regla also appointed his youngest brother-in-law, Vicente Trebuestos, as the paid director of the Monte de Piedad in 1775; Trebuestos remained in that position for more than ten years after Regla's death.

As another indication of continuing relationships with their maternal relatives, María Antonia, the second oldest surviving daughter of Regla, left money in her will to establish a chantry fund for four Miravalle cousins. Her brother, Pedro Ramón, the second count of Regla, set up the funds and these four men were attached to his household and served in his chapel in the house on San Felipe Neri Street. These charities were ecclesiastical endowments, which were established by families to say perpetual Masses for the repose of souls of deceased family members and provided employment to the men ordained to perform this task.[26]

In 1782, after Regla's death, Pedro Villaverde, the administrator of the Jesuit haciendas, hacienda owner, employee, and close companion to the count of Regla, sought redress for what he considered his inadequate compensation for his work for the family. He wrote that among other unpaid duties, he had supplied horses and mules for frequent journeys between Mexico City and Pachuca, Real del Monte, and San Miguel. The oldest daughter, María Micaela, officially in charge of settling her father's estate, responded to this demand, stating that they had traveled that road many times during the lifetime of her mother, but after her death, they no longer made those trips.[27] Not wishing to pay Villaverde's claims, she could have been denying journeys that actually had been made. But it is also possible that if Regla believed that men were lying in wait to kill him, he might not have wanted to risk the safety of his children by having them travel between Mexico City and San Miguel.

We may conclude that the children, in their early years, grew up without much physical contact with their father, while they stayed in the house at San Felipe Neri and he remained at San Miguel. They could have lived with him after their infancy. At the time of Regla's death in 1781, his sons lived in Spain, where they had been sent in 1775 to be educated as noblemen. The youngest son, José María, was then nine years old.

Regla's daughters, ages seventeen through twenty-four, lived with him at the residence of the refining hacienda of San Miguel Regla. But before his death, he had written a letter to his sons and daughters that was to be read in his presence before his death. In this letter he told them he was repeating what he had told them many times, that they were to live in union as though he were still with them, and that they were to love one another as he had loved them, repeating the words of Christ to his disciples. He urged them to support his charities, especially the Monte de Piedad, to give to the poor. They were to practice moderation, honor, charity, and respect for their superiors. While he said that he had spent much time reminding them of these principles, he also pointed out in the letter that none of them had yet "taken state," that is, married or undertaken a religious vocation, a task usually arranged by parents. There is no surviving manuscript copy of the letter, but it appeared attached to the printed copy of the eulogy read at his funeral.[28]

San Miguel, where Terreros's daughters spent the years before their father's death, still has extensive buildings of the refining hacienda and residence, which now sits just at the outskirts of the town of Huasca. It became one of the first old haciendas to be made into a hotel and resort in the late 1940s. The portrait of the count of Regla decorates many of the public rooms of the hotel. Despite renovations and the addition of amenities required by modern-day standards of comfort, the rooms in the house are cold and sunless, even in April when the weather should be at its warmest. Hence, the rooms in which the count of Regla and his daughters lived in San Miguel Regla suffered from the same deficiency as the house in Mexico City: a lack of sun.

FATE OF THE HOUSE ON SAN FELIPE NERI

While the hacienda of San Miguel Regla has profited from the enormous expansion of the tourist industry, a less happy fate has befallen the house in Mexico City in the nearly two hundred and fifty years since the count of Regla purchased it. The family lived there for two generations. The third count of Regla, Pedro José María Romero de Terreros, abandoned the house before his death in 1845 (under pressure from his sons) and followed most of the other members of the upper class out of the central district of the city. In an effort by the secular state to bury the religious associations of the colonial period, the city fathers changed the names of the downtown streets to the names of Latin American nations. The Republic of El Salvador became the new street name of San Felipe Neri, and the National Library of Mexico came to be housed in the old Augustinian Friary across the street. The area continued to be commercial. When Regla purchased the house in 1764, amidst all the religious buildings there had been a printer carrying on his trade on the ground floor of the house. In 1977, as in 1998, this space was occupied by a stationery store, as though the house had partly returned to its old usages. The street continues to be in a busy, if depressed, business district.

Sometime before the end of the nineteenth century, the house passed into the hands of the son-in-law of a member of the fourth generation of the Reglas, the Rincón Gallardo family, and among the many later owners of the house was José Landero, the heir of one of the last mining families in Pachuca and Real del Monte. Eventually the house became the property of the National Banking and

Insurance Commission (Comision Nacional Bancaria y de Seguros). In the course of years, the name of the house changed from "Casa del Conde de Regla" to "Casa de Plata," or House of Silver, a perfectly appropriate substitute. A plaque erected sometime around 1936 reads: "This was the house of D. Pedro Romero de Terreros, Count of Regla, Founder of the Monte de Piedad."

The facade maintains its original finish of *tezontle*, a form of ocher-red volcanic stone used to dress many buildings in the eighteenth century, combined with carved stone of a harder consistency.[29] Two modern floors have been added, and in 1984 nine tenants lived in the building. When the authorities sought to remove the original door, of fine workmanship, the tenants saved this historic object by protesting that the house would be left without a street door to protect them from incursions. If not for the tenants, the original door might have been found decorating an elegant modern house in another section of Mexico City.

Two studies of the house in the late twentieth century differ on some details. One claims that the entire interior was gutted and that only the walls and the facade remain; another finds much of the original material still preserved. The two experts represent another example of the opposing views generated about the most famous owner of this house.

What cannot be disputed, however, is the extraordinary luxury displayed in the house when it belonged to the first count of Regla. Manuel Romero de Terreros, writing in 1913, observed that the sumptuous luxury of the great houses of the eighteenth century could hardly be compared with those to be found in the early years of the twentieth century. A modern historian can hardly fail to wonder at the man who could spend so much money on a house and its furnishings, and still find himself reluctant to pay workers the often customary wage of 4 reales a day. But Regla was not unique. Other successful entrepreneurs exhibited the same combination of stinginess toward others in their business contacts and of lavishness in houses, clothes, and other material goods.[30]

CHAPTER 7

Charities: Spiritual Dimensions of Material Wealth

> Hard work and good fortune gave him [Regla] great wealth,
> whose quantity he never knew, because in his indifference [or selfless-
> ness], he never kept a balance sheet, he earned and spent with an
> open hand without keeping accounts, letting God fill his coffers, and
> so God did; Regla, in just recompense, put everything that he owned
> at the disposition of God.
>
> — Marroquí, *Ciudad de México*

Pedro Terreros, count of Regla, lived his life in the certainty that God had given to him a substantial fortune so that he might in turn benefit as well as worship God. Along with Regla's reputation as a man who could turn base metal into silver and who exploited his workers resides his fame as a man of charity. His most substantial donation dedicated to helping artisans and the middle class is the Monte de Piedad, which he founded in 1775. He saw affinities among his roles as a silver miner in which he provided employment and prosperity for Pachuca and Real del Monte, donations to support the Virgin of Guadalupe's cult, missions to convert the Apache Indians, funds to construct a battleship, and dowries to enable women be become nuns. In the conservative tradition of his time, he also gave money for Masses for the repose of the souls of the dead, and this included all members of his family.

Juan Vázquez Terreros, Pedro Romero de Terreros's uncle, exemplified the charitable practices of late-seventeenth and early-eighteenth-century Mexico, and this influenced his nephew's behavior. The figure of Friar Alonso Giraldo Terreros, Pedro's cousin, whose activities and career played a dominant role in one phase of Pedro Terreros's emergence as a public figure and dispenser of charity, also inspired donations. The charitable aspirations of José Alejandro Bustamante, in contributions to convents and nuns, too figure in this story of Pedro Terreros's justification for his life and work.

Two ideas that circulated in eighteenth-century Mexico asserted that the possession of wealth brought with it social obligations to help the less fortunate. It was commonly believed that generous charitable donations won the believer a place in heaven. The life and actions of Pedro Terreros demonstrated what a significant effect these ideas could have. Arising from the ideology of the Judeo-Christian world, the belief that charitable works contributed to attaining a place in heaven encouraged the donation of wealth to the needy or to ecclesiastical institutions. The Catholic Church performed such tasks as the establishment and administration of most educational institutions, hospitals, missions, and convents, and the conduct of liturgy, charity, and religion usually overlapped. But charity also existed outside church institutions and included feeding the hungry, clothing the poor, dowering the bride, and caring for the sick.

The Siete Partidas, the Spanish medieval law code, commanded that in the distribution of alms and charity one's family members should receive preference over others, "not so that the relatives would become rich, but so that they can live without having any reason to do evil. It is better that they be aided by their relatives so that they do not shamefully seek alms from others:"[1] In other words, charity began at home. Pedro Terreros followed these injunctions that permeated his society, and in this respect, as well as in many others, he mirrored the charitable goals of his time. In discussing his charities, it is difficult to distinguish family obligations from favors to the larger society; nor perhaps should one. Men of wealth coveted posts as administrators of pious funds or as leaders of confraternities, which conferred the honor of precedence in public processions, as well as the pleasure of dispensing gifts to outsiders and favoring one's own family members. Pedro Terreros's contemporaries assumed these posts, for example acting as administrators of dowry funds. But the miner of Real del Monte, although not shy, had an introverted character, a dislike of crowds, and a workaholic disposition that did not seek this kind of personal recognition. He worked hard at his mines and at his own philanthropies, but he refused to become directly involved in municipal jobs and in the public service positions that his partners undertook. Terreros accepted such appointments, essential in the life of a patriarch, but he employed deputies to undertake the actual work. He did, however, take seriously the injunction to contribute to charities, both under his own name and later in life anonymously.

In determining how families or individuals could contribute to various ecclesiastical institutions, and at the same time assist their family members, the church had provided for the establishment of special *obras pías*, through which donors could have their money invested in urban real estate, agriculture, or trade. The interest from these investments supported individual chaplains, usually priests, or contributed to dowry funds, which supplied money for women to enter convents or to marry a more well-to-do man that would have been possible without such assistance. Institutions such as convents, missions, and schools run by the religious orders, principally the Jesuits and Franciscans, sought support from those of wealth with no direct heirs, whether wealthy bachelors, unmarried men and women, or widows. Since early medieval times, the church had depended heavily on such donors. But in the Hispanic world, they were even more important because of the laws enjoining that when parents made their wills, four-fifths of the estate had to be divided among their legitimate children, although they could also give generously to religious and charitable organizations.

One notable aspect of Terreros's charities concerns the preference for Franciscan organizations and his identification with that order. At the beginning of his career, a Franciscan allegedly introduced him to Bustamante and encouraged him to invest in the mines, and at the end of his life, another Franciscan, a specialist in accounts, spent nearly two years working on the settlement of his estate.[2] His funeral sermon was preached by a Franciscan and for much of his life he served the order, and they in turn served him. Friars solicited contributions and brought into their circle wealthy lay people. Because Franciscan rules forbade friars from handling money, they depended on pious lay people to undertake these tasks. Terreros became the syndic (*síndico*), treasurer, and administrator of the colegio of Santa Cruz of Querétaro, the first institution established to train and support missionaries in Mexico.[3] He served there almost until the time of his death, naming a relative to act as his deputy when he no longer lived in Querétaro. He emphasized his assistance to the missionary colleges, and in his will he instructed his executors to bury him in the chapel of whichever missionary colegio lay nearest to his death place. For Pedro Terreros, Franciscan institutions were an obvious choice, as their churches, colleges, and missions dominated the ecclesiastical landscape of Querétaro and Pachuca, the two cities where he lived. All four of his female first cousins entered the Franciscan convent of Santa Clara in Querétaro, and his cousin, Fr. Alonso Giraldo de Terreros, entered the Franciscan order in 1721.

FAMILY CHARITIES IN SPAIN AND MEXICO

After the record of his baptism in Cortegana, Spain, one of the few early surviving references to Pedro Romero de Terreros finds him, at age nineteen, in the city of Veracruz, Mexico, delivering silver liturgical objects to be shipped to the confraternity in the parish church in Cortegana, gifts from his brother and his uncle.[4] In 1733 and 1735, the years of his uncle Juan Vázquez's final testament and his death, he made other donations to his hometown in Spain; the most noteworthy was a donation of 4,000 pesos to establish a chantry (*capellanía*), a church fund for reciting Masses for the repose of family member's souls for one of Pedro Terreros's numerous brothers. This suggests that the nephew persuaded the uncle to remember Cortegana when he drew up his will. Both gifts illustrated the Spanish ideas of charity, which placed the highest value on enhancing the spiritual and material well-being of the church and one's own family. It should also be remembered that some of the bequests in the will of his cousin, the nun María Teresa Terreros, were paid late or not at all, because the conflict between the needs of business and those of charitable organizations became palpable.

Pedro Terreros's gifts to family members in both Spain and Mexico adhere to the dictates of the law on the subject of kinship obligations. Whether his motivation came from a disinterested vision of assistance to his family, by the desire to save his soul (as his friend and colleague, Domingo López de Carvajal, suggested would happen), by a need to display his wealth to a community where he had been poor, or to assure his family of a higher place in the social order, we cannot be certain. But given Pedro Terreros's success in Mexico, he certainly did not want any family members to disgrace him by begging for alms. Money from Mexico improved his Spanish family's condition through a pension for his father, chaplaincies for two of his brothers, material assistance to a third brother, a dowry for a niece, the daughter of his sister, and perhaps a small entail. Unfortunately, none of these gifts improved family relations among the brothers, as reported by López de Carvajal. But the bulk of his charities and the requests for money came from relatives in Mexico. Frequent supplications from family members, notably nuns in convents in Mexico City and Querétaro, included requests for money for housing or chocolate, for a visit from his wife and mother-in-law, and, above all, plaintive pleas for letters from him. These letters imply that Terreros was sympathetic to their requests and suggest that the nuns wrote to him to maintain relations with an influential man who became so vital to their well-being.

For a significant family relationship that describes best how charity was supposed to work, we turn to Terreros's cousin in Querétaro, Juan Vázquez Terreros y Suasnabar, the only son of his uncle Juan Vázquez and who was either twelve or fourteen when Pedro arrived in New Spain between 1728 and 1730. His letters to Pedro, available from 1752 to 1765, are addressed to his "cousin, cogodparent, and My Dear Sir" (*Primo, Compadre, muy Señor Mío*), a mixture of familiarity and distance. Juan Vázquez Terreros seemed to be employed in undertaking tasks for his cousin, such as the collection of debts and perhaps the purchase of haciendas. Another connection was Juan's son, Pedro, to whom Pedro Terreros had been a godfather in 1742 and whose education he supported. "Pedrito" progressed in his studies and according to a report "he was virtuous with infinite gifts in making himself loved and distinguished among all those of his school." He studied Virgil, Horace, and Cicero. With this proof of his pleasant personality, diligence, and moral obligation to support a godchild, Pedro Terreros and his wife set up a chaplaincy valued at 4,000 pesos for him.[5] Another reason for this chaplaincy might have been that his father, Pedro Terreros's first cousin, Juan Vázquez Terreros y Suasnabar, demonstrated his financial irresponsibility by borrowing money from the Jesuits that he could not repay. Pedro Terreros rescued his cousin and a year later, in 1764, decided to set up the chaplaincy that protected Pedrito from the unchecked spending of his father.[6]

Although chantries were a popular foundation throughout the Hispanic world, Terreros established only one. They were not, in other words, significant for him. Nonetheless, like other wealthy eighteenth-century women and men, he created one as a way of caring for Pedrito. For example, José de la Borda, a wealthy contemporary of Terreros, placed 60,000 pesos in a chantry to support his son when the latter entered the clergy.[7] The marqués de Rivascacho invested

16,000 pesos in four chantries, one each for his brother, godson, and two cousins. And the second count of Jala became a priest after the death of his wife, at least partly because he wanted to enjoy the income from a chantry.[8]

Terreros's interest in the education of young men for the clergy included others who were not his biological relatives; he rewarded the sons of those who had assisted him. He paid for the education of his wife's nephew, José Labandero, whose mother, Angela, lived with and helped to care for his family in Pachuca, and for the advanced education of one of the sons of Pedro Villaverde, his principal supplier of agricultural commodities, an employee, and closest friend in the creole community. José Joaquín Villaverde received his doctorate with the assistance of Terreros.[9]

A woman who identified herself as an "Indian Capuchin" clarifies the public expectations from a wealthy man such as Pedro Terreros. She asked Terreros to assist her sister to enter a convent, adding that she knew Terreros to be a charitable man without needing a town crier to tell her so. She described him as the fundamental rock for those who wished to become brides of Christ and as "the helping hand to female orphans" (*ámparo de huérfanas*) and "the father of the poor." She also implied that he might have helped the letter writer to enter the *beaterio* of Santa Rosa. It is possible that in the late 1740s and early 1750s, he had helped an Indian woman and perhaps her sister as well. Terreros agreed to provide at least one dowry for a woman who was not white, although later some of his donations to nuns specified that he wished the money to go to white women.[10]

DOWRIES FOR NUNS AND A CONVENT

Many wealthy individuals in colonial Mexico preferred charities dedicated to women, and among the most frequent recipients of these impulses were female convents.[11] Becoming the patron of a convent represented the highest honor that could be bestowed by fellow citizens, the king, and nuns themselves. It is difficult for modern readers to imagine the size and prestige of female convents, as well as other ecclesiastical institutions in New Spain. Like young men dreaming of making fortunes, when Pedro Terreros and José Alejandro Bustamante signed a business contract in 1743 in Querétaro, they promised to found female religious institutions in three different cities of Mexico.[12] Both men had reasons to be concerned about nunneries. Pedro Terreros had four female cousins in the convent of Santa Clara, but Bustamante might have had a stronger motivation. His parents had written their will in 1717 and had advantaged one of their daughters, promising her a third of their property, rather than an equal share with her siblings, if she did not become a nun.[13] This amount clearly diminished the amount that Bustamante inherited, and one wonders if he resented his sister's good fortune. Several of Bustamante's daughters became nuns after Bustamante's death and at the expense of Pedro Terreros, since he provided the funds for them to enter convents. Did Terreros follow the instructions of Bustamante in dowering his daughters? Was that an unwritten part of their agreement, or was it friendship or Pedro Terreros's moral obligation to his compadre?

The first time Pedro Terreros appeared as a noted public figure in Mexico City was during a ceremony held to celebrate the entry of young women to convents for which he had provided the dowries. One of the main charitable outlets during the course of his lifetime was the contribution of between 144,000 and 190,000 pesos to provide dowries for fifty-eight young women to enter convents in Mexico City and Querétaro. The entry fee or dowry for each applicant to profess fluctuated between 3,000 and 4,000 pesos, plus certain initial costs, which varied according to the convent and the size of the entrance celebration. On one occasion—May 30, 1753—five novices entered the convents of Santa Clara and Santa Isabel at the expense of Pedro Terreros. Within a few days, three more girls would profess with his assistance. He provided 48,000 pesos for these dowries, or 6,000 pesos for each novice, which was double the required minimum. Two of the young women who received dowries from him were the daughters of José Alejandro Bustamante, for whom he had some responsibility as godfather.

The payment of dowries to enable girls to enter convents had a twofold purpose: social and spiritual. Pedro Terreros specified that the girls had to come from white Christian families, and that their parents lacked resources to provide dowries for them. Entry into a convent prevented the girls from marrying into a lower social class, helped to preserve the social order, provided for their future without indefinitely burdening other members of the family, and enabled them to pursue a vocation as a nun. In many convents in New Spain, the donors constructed houses or apartments for the nuns, often consisting of a living room, bedrooms, bath, and kitchen for the nuns. Female members of one family lived together, accompanied by servants, cloistered within the convent walls.

The second of Pedro Terreros's provisions in establishing these endowments was that prayers be said for him and for members of his family. In this emphasis on the remembrance of his soul, Pedro Terreros shared a concern with his contemporaries. Many Mexican wills provided for the founding of chantries, or chaplaincies, which furnished an income for a clergyman to say Masses for the soul of the founder, exactly like the chantry that Pedro Terreros had set up for his godson. Lest it seem that the money given for Masses and prayers subordinated the interests of the living to those of the dead, it should be pointed out that money given for endowing convents and chaplaincies often served social or economic purposes. The money for the chaplaincy was invested by the church in mortgages, whose return in interest was used to support clergy and nuns. These obras pías fell within the scope of charitable donations by supporting socially defined contemporary needs.[14] However, in the opinion of late-eighteenth-century and nineteenth-century reformers, these obras pías sustained a bloated and overextended church.

In 1756, Pedro Terreros carried out the letter of the contract signed with Bustamante thirteen years earlier and offered to found in Mexico City a convent of the strict order of the Franciscans.[15] For the new nunnery, he had obtained a site next to the San Fernando Colegio de Propaganda Fide. The friars donated the site to him on July 5, 1756. Beginning in February 1754, he had given 1,000 pesos every two weeks for the construction and decoration of the church of San Fernando. In November 1756, he gave 10,000–11,000 pesos for the principal altar.[16] Terreros family members had served as guardians in the colegio, and these connections surely facilitated the transfer of land.

Property in hand, and with assistance from Viceroy Amarillas, Terreros elaborated the rules for the new convent. He proposed that it be modeled on the Reales Descalzas of Madrid and the convent for Indian nuns known as Corpus Christi, which was the last Franciscan convent to be established in Mexico City more than forty years earlier. Although Corpus Christi accepted only noble Indian novices, Pedro Terreros stated that this new convent should admit only white Christian girls of good family.[17] Patronage, or the right to appoint candidates for entry into the convent, was to remain in the hands of the Terreros family—with the additional proviso that one place must always be left vacant in case some woman of particular distinction wished to enter the convent, someone who was not necessarily a family member. Terreros expressed the need for the convent, arguing that there was no Franciscan convent of the strict order in Mexico so that a woman desiring to follow the austere rules of the *discalced*, or strict order of the nuns who were followers of Santa Clara, could only enter a Capuchin convent.

The application for permission to establish the convent to be submitted to the Council of the Indies emphasized ideas from the 1743 contract with Bustamante, but with modifications. Modeled on a Madrid convent, the central idea was that Spanish women (that is, white women) should practice deprivation of material goods equal to that of the Indian nuns. Terreros asserted that the lack of dowries kept many Spanish women from becoming nuns. In his convent, they would only need "a humble habit and a poor bed. . . .and the costs for their austere and penitent life and parsimonious refectory" would be supplied by alms given by donors. Whether Pedro Terreros intended the rules of this strict convent to be an implied rebuke to the wealthy convents of Querétaro and Mexico City, or whether he needed to stretch the 100,000 pesos he had available or had decided to spend, can only be surmised. Perhaps he owed this conception to his and Bustamante's ideas of fifteen years earlier, when they had promised to establish convents with the profits from their mines.

Far from being pleased or receptive the provincial, or head, of the Franciscan province of the Mexico City region rejected the gift, producing an overwhelming number of reasons for this denial. These included expenses for which no provision had been made, such as the lack of a stipend for preaching a sermon, the distance that a friar would have to travel to San Fernando from the Friary of San Francisco in order to perform the Mass, and necessary repairs, clothing, and medicines. The provincial noted, with perhaps some bitterness, "that even though [the nuns] had taken the vow of poverty, they should not be condemned to misery and penury." Although Pedro Terreros in his final statement had agreed to provide up to 200, 000 pesos for the expenses of building the convent and the church, and the dowries for thirty-three nuns, he had also insisted that they be a mendicant community and that the alms they collected be voluntary. Since nuns lived in enclosed communities, which they could not leave to beg for contributions in the streets, they depended on the income from their dowries and alms from donors to support them. The friars believed that the alms would be insufficient and would cut into the money available for other mendicant communities. In the year 1756, all the Franciscan convents in Mexico were in deep financial trouble, so the idea of another underfinanced institution troubled the Provincial.[18]

In addition, the question of who would enter the convent caused the Franciscan father concern on two counts: the difficulty of finding and keeping women able to maintain the strict regimen of prayers and fasting required by the strict order of Clares, and the control of patronage by the Terreros family, which could easily conflict with the needs of the convent. After all, he noted, even Viceroy Vizarrón had not received the privilege of patronage when he had established Corpus Christi. He coupled his rejection of the new convent with a suggestion that Pedro Terreros use the money to provide dowries for women in existing institutions, for whom there was abundant space, but who lacked the necessary funds. Apparently Terreros followed this advice, because he continued to give money to nuns and to convents throughout his life, according to one claim almost equaling the amount that he had pledged for the new convent.

It is possible that Pedro Terreros suffered some disappointment over this refusal and that he did not wish this convent to be established. As a significant patron of the Franciscans, it takes a leap of imagination to believe that they would lightly deny him this privilege immediately after he had proposed it without some sort of prior agreement from him. For a man who felt that he had enemies, there is an absence of complaints about this brisk rejection, but the fact that his idea had been dismissed may have festered for years in his imagination. It is possible that he already had the idea of establishing a different kind of institution in Mexico.

An explanation for this rejection might be supplied by a curious document in the family archives, written in nineteenth-century script, promising that Bustamante and Terreros would establish Montes de Piedad, institutions that, Franciscan in their origins, provided for nonprofit pawning of personal possessions. Only after the Montes de Piedad had been inaugurated would the partners establish convents. This is an even more grandiose and inflated plan than that conceived in Querétaro in 1743. It might be surmised that Pedro Terreros intended

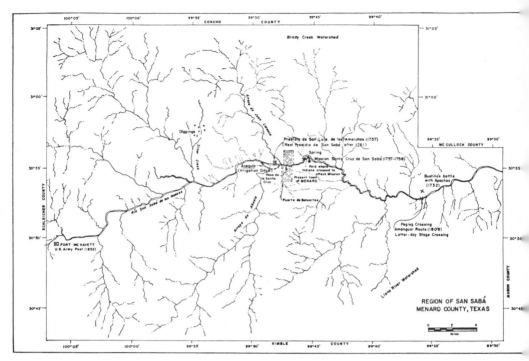

Map 7. Region of San Sabá: Menard County, Texas. Courtesy of Robert Weddle.

that the offer of the gift of a convent should be rejected, and that by offering to establish a convent, Terreros discharged his solemn promise to Bustamante.

In addition to founding a convent in celebration of his marriage, Terreros established a mission to the Apaches. Others inspired both these projects; the convent perhaps by Bustamante, and the mission by Alonso Giraldo Terreros, Pedro's first cousin, who was also born in Cortegana, the son of Terreros's mother's sister and a leading Franciscan administrator and missionary.

MISSIONS AND MISSIONARIES

Pedro Terreros played a small part in the history of the United States through one exceptional charity: the mission of San Sabá in Texas. Since the beginning of the eighteenth century, the Spanish government, the Franciscan Colegio de Propaganda Fide, and the Jesuits had been engaged in expanding the frontiers of New Spain to the north. They had established chains of missions for the conversion and settlement of the Indians and frontier forts or presidios to protect both Jesuit and Franciscan friars and to establish "the Spanish presence" among the Indian nations. When Friar Alonso Terreros founded the mission in 1757–58, he located it at the northernmost reach of Spanish presence in central Texas, 300 kilometers north of San Antonio. (See Map 7.)

Friar Alonso Giraldo Terreros, a former guardian of the Colegio de Propaganda Fide in Querétaro and a leading missionary on the Texas-Coahuila frontier, had a fierce desire to convert the Apaches, a group feared and hated by Spaniards and other indigenous peoples. His aims coincided with the plans of the new viceregal administration in Mexico, headed by the marqués of Amarillas, and with Spanish policy that centered on attempting to move the line of effective Spanish settlement to the north, both to subdue the Indians and to forestall occupation by other European powers. Local and peninsular authorities knew that the French and English governments and colonists had begun the French and Indian War, a conflict over who would control northern North America and that would later become entangled with the Seven Years' War. The French had already established a trading port on the Trinity River and had made other efforts to penetrate Texas and New Mexico from Louisiana.

Viceroy Amarillas, after whom the Presidio San Luis Amarillas would be named, planned the project under the direction of the crown and inspired by Fr. Alonso. The government planned to protect the mission of San Sabá from both hostile Indians and the French. Amarillas would in the future help Pedro Terreros in obtaining forced labor from Indian villages and in fighting his lawsuit against the marqués of Valleameno. His cousin, Friar Alonso, convinced Terreros to supply the money for the expenses of the mission, between 1,500 and 4,000 pesos for the expenses of each of twenty friars, up to a maximum of 100,000 pesos, including the costs of furnishing the chapel. It was one of two projects (the other was the convent) that Pedro selected to commemorate his marriage to María Antonia. The authorities agreed to appoint his cousin, Friar Alonso, as the director of the mission of San Sabá. The only project for the conversion of the Indians for which a private individual paid and never received financial recompense, the effort possibly won Terreros favors from Viceroy Amarillas.[19] The decision to move the missions to the Apaches from Coahuila, then to San Xavier in Texas, began as a military plan.[20] Pedro Terreros's intervention came as a result of familial loyalty, in honor of the celebration of his marriage, his patriotism, the desire to spread the faith, and with the expectation of rewards from the crown.

Friar Alonso, a man of strong will with a desire for martyrdom, but with a dedicated sense of mission, may have tried earlier to convince his cousin, Pedro Terreros, and his partner, José Alejandro Bustamante, that they were individuals chosen by God to convert the Indians on the northern frontier. In one earlier letter, he referred to them almost lyrically over and over again as Don Pedro Terreros and Don José Alejandro.[21]

Plans for financing the San Sabá mission, and perhaps two other missions, must have begun sometime in the early years of the 1750s. By October 10, 1755, Pedro Terreros had written a letter promising to provide all that was needed for the new mission sites. In April 1756 when Friar Alonso attended a meeting in Mexico

City with his cousin and the viceroy they planned to send up to twenty missionaries, half from the San Fernando College in Mexico City and half from the Santa Cruz College in Querétaro, to various sites to be established on the San Sabá River. The Apache Indians would be invited to settle around the missions and hopefully would be converted to Christianity and to the benefits of life as peaceful farmers. A contingent of one hundred soldiers would protect them from their enemies, and these military expenses would be borne by the government. All the mission expenses were to be paid by Pedro Terreros: he agreed to build and furnish the chapel and to contribute 4,000 pesos the first year, 2,000 pesos the second year, and 1,500 pesos the third year to pay the expenses of each friar. After three years, he assumed that the missions would be able to support themselves. He also agreed to pay compensation for the property of the older missions that were to be abandoned, the property turned over to Friar Alonso. One of Terreros's conditions was that his cousin be the director of the expedition, although he promised to continue his support of the missions if his cousin should die or be unable to serve.[22]

Friar Alonso and five other missionaries spent the spring and summer of 1756 collecting provisions and arranging their journeys. They arrived in San Antonio, Texas, in December 1756. They surveyed the region and decided on a site containing excellent agricultural land and abundant water. It was not until the spring of 1757 that the friars were able to proceed to the San Sabá River and to begin the construction of the new mission. Between April 1757 and March 1758, Friar Alonso and a slowly diminishing group of missionaries waited for the still-to-be-converted Apaches to settle. Quarrels broke out between the military at the presidio and the friars at the mission, and disputes occurred among the missionaries themselves—between the representatives of the Querétaro and Mexico City colleges, and between the fathers, who had worked on the previous missions of San Xavier and who wanted funds for their converts, and Friar Alonso, who refused to spend his cousin's money on Indians who had already been converted. Another difficulty arose from Friar Alonso's insistence that the presidio of San Luis Amarillas be located some distance from the mission, so that the soldiers could not easily molest Indian women. Although this humanitarian deed is admirable, it placed the mission in a vulnerable position with the protection of only a few soldiers.

The government indicated its dissatisfaction with the lack of progress in settling Indians by appointing an inspector (*visitador*) to oversee all the missions, implying a critique of the leadership of Friar Alonso. In a discouraged letter, one of the last the friar would write, he observed, perhaps in a mocking tone, that the two cousins, Friar Alonso and Pedro Terreros, had been the object of persecution ever since their birth, and that he would remain at San Sabá because it was better for him to die than to surrender.[23]

World events further complicated the difficulties of the mission. In 1756, the Seven Years' War began, and the French intended to use this opportunity to claim a share of territory in Texas that Spain claimed as its own. Indian nations, especially the Comanche and their allies, planned an attack against the Apache and insisted on their rights to this territory. The Apache had no claim to it and chose not to inform the Spaniards of their error in establishing a mission to them on land claimed by their enemies. Friar Alonso had placed his mission in a dangerous zone.[24]

Shifting alliances and the unwillingness of any group to submit themselves to the tutelage or restraints imposed by missionaries also hindered the project. The Apaches had promised to enter the mission, but really sought to enlist the military assistance of the Spaniards in their struggles with their enemies, as well as to secure gifts of food and tobacco. Groups of Apaches—men, women, and children—appeared several times and promised to return to live in the mission, but they had little incentive to do so.

On March 16, 1758, a group of about 2,000 Comanche Indians with their allies appeared. They had been equipped with guns and ammunition possibly by the French, or possibly purchased from Spanish sources. There had been news about the possibility of a hostile attack, but Friar Alonso refused to take refuge at the presidio, perhaps because he wished to protect the cattle and the mission or because martyrdom appeared an honorable solution in light of the failure of his plan to convert the Apaches. The Comanches and their allies killed Friar Alonso, another friar, and wounded a third. They also killed a number of other people. The Indians burned the mission so thoroughly that even its site was lost to view until 1997, when an architectural historian using aerial photographs identified the location. The vision of Friar Alonso and the Spanish authorities in the 1750s in Mexico City to extend Spanish control to the north proved difficult because Spain lacked the resources, the soldiers, and the colonists to occupy this section of the northern frontier. The Spanish military occupied the presidio only until 1769.

Thus the efforts of the two Terreros cousins to establish a new set of frontier missions failed. Beyond the loss of his cousin, Terreros suffered a severe disappointment: this was his second loss of the two institutions that he had supported as part of the celebration of his marriage. His anger at the authorities justified his decision to discontinue support for the project. He disbursed only small sums to clear the debts; his total contribution was 43,269 pesos, about 37 percent of the total he had pledged.[25]

Despite the spectacular failure of this venture, for several years Pedro Terreros referred to his involvement in the Texas missions as a justification for his request for a noble title and for favorable solution to the lawsuit against the heirs of Valleameno. Even as late as 1775, when writing his will, he referred to this contribution in explaining that the "*arras*," or jointure, of 50,000 pesos that he had granted to his wife in 1756 at the time of their marriage had been consumed in their joint sponsorship of the missions and implied that her family could have no claim on it from his estate.[26]

Included in Pedro Terreros's pledge to sponsor Texas missions was a promise to pay the expenses of twenty peninsular Franciscans on the frontier. This promise involved a parochial effort, which may have been closer to his heart, to recruit Franciscans in Spain and bring them to Mexico. This latter undertaking may have originated as part of a plan to establish a mining company in 1749, when the government suggested that a ship dedicated to transporting mining supplies could also bring missionaries.[27] Pedro Terreros agreed to pay for financing, equipping, and transporting friars. It appears that his friend, Friar Gaspar Gómez, went to Spain to collect the missionaries and by April 1758 found the twenty volunteers that he had been authorized to assemble in Puerto de Santa María to await transportation to the Indies. López de Carvajal, Pedro Terreros's chief representative in Spain, had purchased mattresses and pillows for their residence in Cádiz where they lingered for months until a ship departed for Mexico. López de Carvajal also invited them for dinner at his house, two at a time. Only in August 1759, after nearly a year of waiting did they finally depart under the leadership of Friar Gaspar Gómez, who had recruited them by inspiring them to leave their urban parishes to come to the Western Hemisphere to convert Indians.[28]

Whether Pedro Terreros's friends within the peninsular faction of the order encouraged him to seek recruits in Spain, or whether he simply preferred the idea of Spanish missionaries is uncertain. The words of López de Carvajal offer some insight about Terreros's goals. López de Carvajal believed that sending the missionaries would add splendor to the church and much merit to Pedro Terreros for his salvation.[29]

Perhaps in recognition of his cousin's martyrdom, at an unknown date, but probably before 1762, Terreros commissioned a large history painting of the massacre at San Sabá, one of the few history paintings about the frontier produced in colonial Mexico (see Figure 11). Friar Alonso and the other friar who died in the attack stand at either end of the painting, and in between is a detailed presentation of the mission, the people living there, and the procession of armed Indians approaching the mission. The painting, although it may have been intended as a gift to Charles III, resided until late in the twentieth century in the home of Manuel Romero de Terreros on Durango Street, Mexico City, and was then inherited by a family member who sold it to a purchaser in the United States. A group in Austin, Texas, tried to raise the money to buy it, so that it could be exhibited in the State Capital along with the paintings of the Alamo and of other events related to Texas history. Their aim, to commemorate for Texans an aspect of their Hispanic and Indian past, failed, like the San Sabá mission itself. The painting went back to Mexico to be displayed in the National Museum of Art.[30] One wonders whether Spain, in the middle decades of the eighteenth century, would have undertaken this particular expansion to the north if the viceroy had not been assured of financial support from a silver miner, if the silver miner had not been pressured into this donation, and, finally, if it had not been the dream of his cousin, Friar Alonso, to carry out a mission to the Apaches. Friar Alonso Giraldo de Terreros stands as one of the few Spanish individuals with good intentions and kindly feelings toward the Apaches.

MONTE DE PIEDAD

The Monte de Piedad, the most famous charity of the count of Regla, opened its doors to the public in 1775. It was a government-controlled pawnshop that lent cash in exchange for material goods such as jewelry, clothing, and furniture. In return for lending money up to an approximation of the value of the object, Pedro Terreros requested that the borrowers donate money for Masses for the repose of his soul and that of his family members. Thus the Monte combined the goals of a traditional chantry foundation with the more practical purpose of a lending institution to help the temporarily needy, but not the destitute who had nothing to pawn.

In the ten years between 1758 and 1768, however, Terreros did not establish a charitable institution. These were years of intense activity in the mines, as well as in his personal life. Thus charities received less attention and followed the conventional course of alms to the poor, donations to building funds, dowries to nuns, and assistance to family members, sons of colleagues and employees in Spain and in Mexico. Direct contributions to the church were made through Masses to be said for the repose of the soul of the deceased. Pedro Terreros excelled in the exercise of this kind of piety. When his wife died in 1766, he requested that thousands of Masses be said; five hundred of these Masses were to cost 1 peso, and the others, briefer Masses, would cost 2 reales each. In my examination of more than six hundred wills from Mexico City and Puebla in the eighteenth century, no other single testament comes close to this number. As a practical accompaniment to these Masses, Terreros also fulfilled the wishes of his wife by paying more than 9,000 pesos in aid to the poor.[31]

It is difficult to know when Pedro Terreros first conceived the idea of a Monte de Piedad. According to a somewhat suspect copy of a 1743 partnership agreement written in nineteenth-century script, José Alejandro Bustamante and Pedro Romero de Terreros pledged themselves to establish three institutions—convents for women, Montes de Piedad, and orphanages and shelters (*hospicios*)— in three different cities.[32] Each of them was to be established first in Mexico City, then in Querétaro, and finally in Pachuca, making a total of nine institutions or foundations. None of these institutions was founded during Bustamante's lifetime, and it was sometime between 1767 and 1770 that Pedro Terreros again considered the establishment of the Monte de Piedad. These were the years after the death of his wife and the strike in the mines of Real del Monte in 1766. One might speculate that the loss of his wife and the temporary closing of the mines released energy for other projects.

Fig. 11. History painting of the destruction of Mission San Sabá, c. 1762.
Courtesy of MUNAL, Museum of Mexican National Art.

It was from the Monte de Piedad established in Madrid between 1702 and
1713 that Pedro Terreros drew his inspiration. Francisco Piquier, a priest living in
Madrid at the turn of the eighteenth century, began collecting money to establish a capital fund for a Monte de Piedad, for "prayers for the souls in purgatory,
and for the aid of the needy." Ideally, the system would allow the needy to pawn
their possessions for cash; after a specified time, they could return the money
they had borrowed and redeem their pledges. Any unredeemed pawned items
could be sold at auction after a specified period of time. The donors would give
alms voluntarily for "prayers for the souls in purgatory." By 1713, Piquier had
accumulated enough money to open a Monte de Piedad in Madrid and to have
the statutes approved by the king. The Madrid Monte de Piedad, unlike those in
Italy, did not charge interest for loans, but existed through subsidies paid by the
crown. Each year, 70,000 pesos of income from the sale of tobacco paid employees'
salaries. The idea of such a lending institution spread, and additional Montes
were established in Granada, Salamanca, Barcelona, and Seville.[33]

Since Regla modeled his idea for a Mexico City Monte de Piedad after the
Madrid institution, he hoped that the king or the viceroy would act as a sponsor
to assure its continuity as well as to assume the financial responsibility for the
new institution. As envisioned by Regla, borrowers would pay no interest for
their loan, but when they redeemed their pledged items, they would be asked to

contribute to the celebration of Masses. The count of Regla would be the patron; he or his descendants would always sit on the governing board of the Monte and would have the right to propose the names of employees.[34]

More than five years elapsed between Regla's initial offer of 300,000 pesos in 1770 and the opening of the Monte de Piedad in 1775. The Council of the Indies ignored the request because it was mixed up with the additional titles and other privileges that the count requested for his children. As Regla's title had been delayed for many years because of his excessive demands, so the Monte de Piedad might have been stalled by a profusion of favors requested by the ambitious subject.

It was the pressure of a reforming and active viceroy, Antonio María Bucareli (1771–79), anxious to raise money for the crown and to establish social welfare institutions, that made possible the Monte de Piedad in Mexico City. As a recent historian observed, "At the Monte de Piedad, the state took on the role of pawn-broker as colonial paternalism married pious charity to social welfare policy."[35] It was Bucareli and his request for a loan from the Mexico City merchants of 2,800,000 pesos that gave the count of Regla his opportunity to meet the viceroy's demand. He offered 400,000 bars of silver, earmarking 300,000 pesos for the Monte de Piedad and thus displaying his ability to turn the disadvantages of a forced loan into a positive benefit for his proposed charity.[36]

Regla received preliminary approval for his institutions in a royal decree (*real cédula*) on September 26, 1772.[37] Between the final acceptance of the Monte de Piedad in June 1774, and the grand public opening in September 1775, a building had to be found to house it, the operating rules and statutes had to be formulated, and the employees had to be selected. Both Viceroy Bucareli and the count of Regla had requested that an expert from Madrid be sent to write the statutes, and the crown assigned Miguel Páez de Cadena, scheduled to become director of the Mexico City Customs, to gather information about the Monte in Madrid.

Finding an appropriate building in Mexico City proved difficult. The count of Regla had settled on a section of the former Jesuit College of San Pedro and San Pablo. This had been a center for the education of the creole elite until 1767 when the Jesuits were expelled from New Spain and the school was closed. The changed purpose of this building from an institution dedicated to the education of the creole elite to a large pawn shop dedicated to helping the needy symbolizes one of the changes in social priorities that occurred in the years before and during the reforming Bucareli administration.

From the time of its foundation in 1775 until the death of the count of Regla in November 1781, the purposes, functions, and procedures of the Monte de Piedad caused controversy among administrators, viceroys, treasury officials, and the count. Regla insisted that the Monte stay open on minor holidays when many employees wanted it to close. The count wanted the alms given for Masses for the Regla family, although not mandatory, to be accepted when the borrowers redeemed their pawn, but employees suggested that they should be required or accepted when the loan was given. To the end of his life, the count of Regla insisted on the optional nature of these alms. In these issues, he demonstrated a generosity that had not always been present in his relationships with workers and colleagues. Whether the Monte collected interest or not, however, affected neither his profits, nor his ability to meet his payrolls.

In a copy of a letter written on March 9, 1779, to Bucareli, he asserted that he would not agree to oblige the needy to leave their pawns at the Monte for a minimum of six months, nor would he request that alms be given at the time of the loan. He insisted that the rules of the Madrid Monte be followed, which did not require the payment of interest because it had the support of the tobacco monopoly, though the Mexico City institution did not receive these funds from the official sale of tobacco. We do not know if Regla tried to receive funds for the Monte from the recently established government monopoly of the sales of tobacco, but the Mexican Monte de Piedad did not receive official financial support.

Regla urged the employees of the Monte to treat the poor kindly when they came to pawn their property. The count was indeed, as a later historian of the Monte de Piedad wrote, a truly charitable giver, since the "Christian faith which animated him [had encouraged him to found] a truly pious work."[38]

Like many Mexican "pious works" of the eighteenth century, the Monte de Piedad was a family enterprise. Vicente Trebuesto, a brother of María Antonia, served as director of the Monte de Piedad from 1775 to 1795, and in any policy debates Trebuesto supported his brother-in-law (see Figure 12). The statutes now provided that a member of the count of Regla's family should always be a board member or president of the board. In this fashion, patronage of the Monte de Piedad provided dynastic continuity to the family of Romero de Terreros. At the beginning of the third millennium, the engineer-architect Luis Romero de Terreros, representing the seventh generation of the family, still presided over the historic offices of the Monte de Piedad.

Other debated aspects of the founding statutes proved more difficult to resolve and threatened the very existence of the institution. The provision for voluntary contributions for Masses for the soul of members of the Romero de Terreros family produced only 1,029 pesos in four years and eight months. Maintenance of the pawned goods and employee salaries consumed capital funds, and the government still refused to assign revenue from the tobacco monopoly to pay expenses. Many employees received only half of their stipulated salary. Moreover, some of the poor proved themselves less than deserving by exhibiting disorderly behavior in the patio of the Monte while waiting to pawn or redeem their belongings. Only a few years after the opening of the Monte, a jail and stocks were constructed in the patio to punish misdemeanors and to exact swift justice on those who pawned stolen articles.[39]

The debate over interest payments versus voluntary contributions pitted the count of Regla and his brother-in-law against the subdirector of the Monte de Piedad and other officials. The subdirector, arguing for the imposition of interest payments, insisted that the purpose of the Monte de Piedad was being traduced as wealthy people, with expensive jewelry, benefited from the Monte, and that these loans did not assist the poor. Another official retorted that the institution must be considered charitable, "because as the waters run down the mountains to fertilize the valley, the wealth of the Monte runs down to the Indians and the pious poor."[40] This statement reflected the conception of the Monte de Piedad as a "sum of money with pious and charitable ends."[41] This is an eighteenth-century version of the modern economic view of the "trickle-down" effect of assistance to the wealthy so they can better the lives of the poor but not destitute. It reflected the reality of giving access to loans to the deserving poor so that they could get through hard times or begin small businesses. It also demonstrated a Catholic vision of these institutions that helped those in need directly and that included the recital of prayers and the observance of the Mass.

It was only the death of Regla in 1781 that saved the Monte de Piedad from bankruptcy. Shortly after his death the Monte began to charge interest, a procedure followed to this day. The observance of the Mass continued to be practiced, but now it included not just the members of the family, but all souls. A chapel, with some of the original objects selected by Regla for the celebration of the liturgy still lies adjacent to the offices provided for the descendants of the count of Regla. Since it is a government institution, and the government is anticlerical, the Monte chapel has not had a Mass recited there for more than a century. The portraits of each of the family members who inherited this post, as well as all the directors, decorate the main office.

The Monte moved to the central square in Mexico City sometime between 1820 and 1830. Separated from the Cathedral by only a narrow street, and almost opposite the government palace where viceroys and later presidents of Mexico ruled during the nineteenth and most of the twentieth century, the location remained far more central to the life of the capital than its previous site. Along with the Catholic Church and the university, it endures as one of the only institutions to survive from the colonial period into the present.

OTHER CONTRIBUTIONS

Beginning with his Spanish connections, letters from his colleague Domingo López de Carvajal in Puerto de Santa María reveal pressures on Pedro Terreros to employ needy Spaniards, or to respond to pleas from Franciscan relatives to give money to young women (*pobres doncellas*), or to act as a conduit for people in Mexico to send money to their relatives in Spain. In the later years of his life, Regla also responded to requests for funds from institutions, often giving anonymously,

Fig. 12. Portrait of Vicente Trebuesto, first director of the Monte de Piedad and brother-in-law of Regla. Photograph by Juan Romero de Terreros.

so that only he and the abbess of the convent or the guardian of the college knew about it. These ranged from weekly contributions and building funds for the chapel at Guadalupe to donations to nuns. At his funeral, the orator announced that most establishments in Mexico had received proof of his generosity.[42]

Another series of donations, more patriotic than religious, is documented in a list of his "merits and services," prepared by his grandson, which included his response to governmental requests for assistance and his personal view of the contributions that he had made.[43] Aside from his donation to the Texas missions in the 1750s, these gifts occurred mainly during the decade of the 1770s and the administration of Viceroys Croix and Bucareli. These included lending the government the money to start the National Lottery. The government considered the lottery a charitable organization because it regulated gambling, provided income for the treasury, and gave alms to the poor. Regla gave money to establish the tobacco monopoly and considered this a contribution to the government, which hoped to profit from control of the product. He lent at no interest 20,000 pesos to the city of Querétaro so it could purchase grain during a famine. On a number of other occasions, he lent money to the king, as did other merchants and miners in Mexico City. These loans were only partially voluntary, because most of the wealthy were expected to contribute. They often expected to, and did, in fact, receive favors in return.[44]

Another particularly flamboyant and original contribution of the count to the king of Spain was the donation of 200,000 pesos to construct a battleship with three bridges and eighty cannon to sail in the Spanish navy. This original ship, constructed in the town of Regla near Havana, participated in many battles.[45] The count stipulated that the Spanish navy should always possess a ship called La Regla. The existence of a battleship bearing the family name would be yet another way in which Regla hoped to publicize and preserve the family name, an expectation lamentably doomed to disappointment.[46] When the Spanish navy retired the battleship La Regla sometime in the 1820s, they decided not to replace it with another ship of the same name, doubtless under pressure to honor living subjects and special events.

Regla and his son believed their mining activities to be a contribution to the towns of Pachuca and Real del Monte because their investment provided employment and brought wealth to the town. But neither Pachuca nor Real del Monte, which the count of Regla dominated from 1755 until his death, bear outstanding architectural evidence of that enormous mining boom. Regla did not neglect the area, for he contributed to the Caja Real (provincial treasury) built in 1774 and gave 80,000 pesos to the former Friary of San Francisco, succeeding in raising it from a simple friary to a Colegio de Propaganda Fide. Money that he spent on the Franciscans in Pachuca was used to construct living quarters, kitchen, stables, gardens, and infirmary, rather than a flamboyant church.[47]

If we were to compare the nature of the first count's philanthropies with those of his contemporaries, we should note that the other two most successful mining leaders, José de la Borda and Ignacio Obregón, the count of Valenciana, who rivaled the count of Regla in wealth, left resplendent architectural monuments. Both the town of Guanajuato, in which the count of Valenciana operated, and the town of Taxco, where Borda made one of his fortunes, still contain the elaborate baroque decorations of buildings and churches built by eighteenth-century mining wealth. Regla's relative failure to leave his architectural mark on Pachuca, Real del Monte, and the mining area around it can be explained in part by the separation between his mines and his refining haciendas. Much of the building undertaken by Regla occurred in the vicinity of the small village of Huasca some 18 miles from Real del Monte, where Pedro Terreros constructed and embellished three refining mills, the most impressive of which still stands in an isolated ravine several miles from the town of Huasca. If the count of Regla failed to leave an impressive public artistic monument in Mexico, his leading contribution, the Monte de Piedad, has enjoyed longevity and the capacity to adapt to changing conditions.

Regla's charities reflected his efforts to reform the habits of workers that he had deplored in the past. He instructed the three missionary colleges to which he had been so generous, Santa Cruz of Querétaro, San Fernando of Mexico, and San Francisco of Pachuca to conduct missions to his haciendas and mines so that the workers would fulfill their annual obligation of confession and communion. At the end of the sermon preached by the friars, the whole group was to recite the Lord's Prayer and one Hail Mary. The purpose of this recital was "to improve their habits and to serve God," another example of Reglas's efforts to improve the religious life and, by implication, the behavior of those who worked for him.[48]

Pedro Terreros's charitable projects were carried out alone, without the participation of other important individuals in the community. The man who "made a mansion in the wilderness" was solitary in his choice of charities: he did not contribute to general dowry funds, nor did he seek to administer them, or participate in most community ceremonies, with the exception of the ones he himself organized around the entry of nuns into convents, or the celebration in Pachuca of the coronation of Charles III.

His contributions to the missionary activities along the northern frontier of New Spain make him a participant in one of the great colonizing movements of the eighteenth century—the strengthening of Spanish power in northern Mexico and the southwestern United States. In his founding of the Monte de Piedad, he was certainly adding to one of the important charitable movements of his era. The Monte became another occasion to establish an institution in which his family would have the patronage and where their names would be remembered in prayers. A marked emphasis on funds for the remembrance of the souls of the dead continued to flourish as the most popular bequest in wills even among those most closely connected to educational institutions.[49]

But behind many of Regla's charities was the traditional notion that these were family contributions and that the recipients ought to recognize his charity, given out of a sense of Christian obligation, by saying Masses for the repose of his soul. Reciprocal relationships between giver and recipient supported a hierarchical view of society. His contributions to Mexico and to Spain, from lending money without interest, to resuscitation of the mines, to purchases of many former Jesuit haciendas for money in order to relieve the financial exigencies of the crown, were all, in his view, charitable donations. Even if they made his family wealthy and aggrandized his name and reputation, their charitable aspect was equally important. His family also needed the wealth that he was convinced could only come from the mines. This mingling of private interests and public benefits also characterized Regla's charities in the last years of his life.

CHAPTER 8

The Final Years: 1766–1781

Elongavi fugiens et mansi in solitudine.
—Ruiz y Villafranca y Cárdenas, *Sermón*

I fled far off and made a mansion in solitude.
—Psalm 55, Modesto Suárez, "Mansión en la soledad"

Pedro Terreros's flight from Real del Monte at midnight on August 15, 1766, when he escaped from crowds of angry, violent mine workers, followed closely on the death of his wife the previous June. These two events were the milestones that caused him grief and fury. His flight, commemorated fifteen years later in the Latin words "Elongavi fugiens et mansi in solitudine," characterized the way in which he lived between 1766 and 1774. The words surrounding his portrait were included as a frontispiece in the published version of the eulogy read at his funeral (see Figure 13). One source indicates that he himself might have used this refrain, writing in Spanish that he fled and made a mansion in the wilderness, surely a more accurate statement of the way he lived in these years.[1] These words, taken from the fifty-fifth Psalm and surrounded by several Psalms expressing anger and betrayal, reflect Regla's feelings toward workers of Real del Monte and the government that, in his opinion, had refused to punish those responsible for the riots, rebellions, and attempts on his life. These thoughts also defined Regla's actions in the years between 1766 and approximately 1774, when he refused to leave the refining hacienda of San Miguel. Taking refuge at this hacienda, Regla lived adjacent to the town of Huasca, surrounded by agricultural land, but close to his other refining haciendas. During this eight-year period, he seldom appeared in Mexico City, and then only to consult, perhaps in disguise, with Viceroy Antonio Bucareli.[2]

Regla chose to avoid the tumult of the towns of Pachuca and Real del Monte as well as the spirited social life of Mexico City. Surrounded only by servants and the men and women engaged in processing ore, his visitors were mainly the men who worked for him, his trusted aides, such as the Catalan Luis Marrugat, and the hacienda administrator Pedro Villaverde and his numerous sons.

Had Terreros been killed by his workers in 1766, he would be known as one of the many, if not the most contentious, of the successful eighteenth-century silver miners. But the activities he undertook during the last decade and a half of his life elevated his reputation beyond that of his contemporaries. These deeds included his charitable foundations, his applications for noble titles and entails, and the procedures leading to his emergence as the largest landowner in colonial Mexico.

Thanks to all these activities from 1766 to 1781, the public records abound. These include Regla's correspondence to obtain titles, land, and honors, as well as to benefit the organizations which he had taken under his protection or desired to establish such as the Monte de Piedad, which he first suggested to the Council of the Indies in 1767.[3] However, we are impoverished by a lack of personal correspondence. For the most part, letters from colleagues, partners, employees, and government officials preserved in the family archive run only until 1769.

Despite his absence from the scene of political power, Regla's influence, experience, and counsel continued to be heard by the viceroy and the personal representative of the King Charles III, José Gálvez, in Mexico City. Riots and rebellions like those that began in the Pachuca region in August 1766 later occurred in other places, such as Pátzcuaro, San Luis de la Paz, and Guanajuato. These outbursts stemmed from local discontents resulting from the effects of the Seven Years' War and the expulsion of the Jesuits. The government retaliated with lengthy sentences of imprisonment, exile, and public execution of those believed guilty, a policy facilitated by an increase in the number of troops.[4] The experiences from the riots and disturbances months before at Real del Monte, Pachuca, and Santa María Regla may have strengthened Gálvez's resolve to impose harsher penalties. Regla's own experiences and his claim that the rioters and strikers had not been sufficiently punished might have convinced Gálvez that only stern measures would suffice to stop what the authorities considered a movement threatening Spanish rule. Regla, who observed the unfolding of these rebellions, felt aggrieved as he recalled that the men who had almost killed him had only been exiled for five years and had returned by 1771.

In these years of what Terreros referred to as his "melancholy retreat at San Miguel," his relationship to the government improved at least superficially. Although he lent the viceroy, the marqués de Croix, the man who had been so critical of him in August 1766, 400,000 pesos without interest in 1771, he still continued to nurse complaints. Terreros, who had become the count of Regla by this time, took advantage of the arrival of the new viceroy, Antonio Bucareli, an Andalucían, to write a letter, accompanied by massive documentation, to the king via the viceroy. Written in the third person, and referring to himself not as I but as the count of Regla, he explained the suspension of work in his mines in the following way:

> The Count has often heard about the cruel censure of his conduct and his most noble intentions; and perhaps the influence of these vague unfounded rumors unsupported by the truth has prevented the government from undertaking the assistance and measures needed for this great

work of the Veta Vizcaína; for the Count has not wished for anything more than the most scrupulous perseverance.[5]

These lines indicate that Regla was still concerned about the fate of his mines and by what he saw as a misinterpretation of his actions. Here, he also expresses his belief that some of the leaders of the work stoppages, returning from their exile from Real del Monte, still menaced his physical safety. More than that, at a later date, he threatened the authorities with the ruin of the Veta Vizcaína if these rioting men, who wanted "violently to take the life of the Count of Regla," were permitted to return to the mining region.[6]

Another motivation for this flood of documentation sent to the crown might have been the denuncio, the request of another miner for a license to work one of his mines, which had been registered with the mining judge on August 9, 1771. Regla needed to explain why he had ceased working many of his mines after 1766–67. He asserted that he kept at full production only those mines that could be staffed by slaves and forced levies of Indians, but he kept token crews of administrators and workers in his other mines. He also wrote that he had spent 800 pesos each week to drain the San Cayetano, since it was the key to keeping water out of his other mines. Regla's arguments led both the viceroy and the Council of the Indies, representing the crown, to conclude that the mines could produce more silver if Regla would consent to open his mines and employ free workers, as he had done in the past, helped by the use of press-gangs.

Regla's stance of "abiding in the wilderness" and his assertion of partial retirement as a miner appears to have been undermined in 1768 when he purchased mines in the mining center of Zimapán, about two days' journey northeast of Real del Monte. He explained to the authorities that he intended to mine magistral (used in refining silver with mercury) and tin, but it is probable that he also intended to mine silver there. He did receive permission to employ press-gangs who rounded up laborers and forced them to work in the mines. One of these men met his end as a victim of workers' anger.[7]

There is more evidence to suggest that Regla's assertion—that he had closed all his mines in Real del Monte except those that he could work with slaves—was not trustworthy. Documents from the archives of the Real del Monte Company indicate that Regla continued to employ free labor, despite his protestations to the contrary. For example, two new administrators of the mines had been appointed, and in 1770 they disciplined workers for robberies, complaining that when the men went to jail, they were punished with only twenty-five lashes, instead of a sentence of exile to a presidio, which Regla advocated.[8] These workers must have been free miners, as forced Indian laborers and slaves, who were unable to leave the mines and refining haciendas, had little opportunity to steal.

Whether Regla's explanations for his decreased mining activity were accurate,

Fig. 13. Portrait of the count of Regla published in his funeral oration. Courtesy of the Bancroft Library, University of California at Berkeley.

in the interest of increasing revenue, royal authorities pressed Regla to work all his mines. But before Regla would agree to work his allegedly closed mines, he sought to guarantee his personal safety by having severe punishments inflicted on the men he presumed were responsible for the work stoppages and riots of 1766 and 1767. He also wanted the authorities to permit him to cease paying partido.[9]

Regla, assisted by the alcalde mayor of Tulancingo, Pedro Leoz, and by the chief prosecutor (*procurador mayor*) in Mexico City, José Antonio Areche, who would become famous for his ruthless efforts to reform the governments of both Mexico and Chile, determined to exile the parish priest, José Rodríguez Díaz, from Real del Monte. Doris Ladd, a historian of the Real del Monte strikes, argues that these men initiated judicial proceedings against Díaz, perhaps because it was one way to mollify Regla, or perhaps because in 1766 Regla implicated him as a supporter of the workers with their complaints over partido and press-gangs. This priest may have saved the count of Regla's life by placing his own cloak over him and later convincing the striking men to keep the mines drained, paying them out of his own pocket for this service. Witnesses differed about whether the priest alone saved the Real del Monte mines from the workers' rage, or whether it was the Franciscans with their processions and prayers who actually calmed the men that were bent on destruction.[10] Leoz testified that the priest "Díaz is or was the root and origin of the former revolts and harassments of this Real." The administrator of the mine of La Palma testified that "the Count of Regla has his sword unsheathed, and has told the viceroy that if the investigation was not conducted correctly, he, in spite of his age, would go to Spain."[11] He went on to say that Regla's anger at the strike and his near escape from death at the hands of the workers, could be appeased by punishing the priest. Placating Regla by removing the priest from his parish in Real del Monte succeeded and it did not provoke riots, as might have occurred if the authorities had tried to punish workers after so many years. Regla insisted that the priest leave Real del Monte, perhaps because of an ancient feud over parish funds for the slaves of the mine La Palma, or because Díaz had more sympathy for workers than Regla.[12] Regla alleged that the priest had disrupted his view of the proper hierarchical relationship between owners and workers.

During his years of theoretical exile, Regla began a series of complex financial transactions with the crown. Years later, these resulted in the crown bringing a major lawsuit against his family for the payment of money allegedly still owed the crown for the purchase of the Jesuit estates. That permeable boundary between debtor and creditor was crossed by Regla many times. In January 1771, acting on a request of the viceroy, the marqués de Croix, Regla lent the crown 400,000 pesos with no interest. (Lending money to the crown was always risky but necessary if one hoped to attain honors and privileges.) The next viceroy, Bucareli, could not repay the loan, although two years later Regla did receive the money from the Casa de Moneda; the following day Regla allegedly lent it once again to the crown, in a separate transaction. Regla explained that he had the silver bars and that he was always ready to serve the king, and in his second loan, of August 1773, he lent the crown more than 400,000 pesos. This money was sent by the viceroy to the Council of the Indies with the request that the king personally acknowledge this gift. Although we have a record of the return of the first 400,000 pesos, so far no record (if it was returned) of the repayment of the next loan has been located.[13] Later, Regla asserted that he had lent the crown 800,000 pesos.[14] To these loans might be added money given to the crown for the battleship or for the Monte de Piedad, as well as for the purchase of the Jesuit haciendas.[15] (The figures never explain the complex relations between the royal treasury, the Casa de Moneda, and the wealthy subject, the count of Regla, and his sons and daughters.) It is obvious only that Regla contributed substantial amounts of money to the royal coffers and received substantial privileges in return.

TURNING OF FORTUNE'S WHEEL: THE SILVER MINES BETWEEN 1763 AND 1781

Regla's highest production from the silver mines occurred in both 1763 and 1764 when Terreros's share of silver from the Pachuca region reached 69 percent of the total. In 1768, the year after the riots and work stoppages, Terreros's percentage of silver marcos dropped to 25 percent.[16]

A severe political crisis occurred in the Pachuca region after the stoning death of the alcalde mayor, Miguel Ramón de Coca, on August 15, 1766, when Regla almost lost his life. The government, not wanting to appoint a creole, hurriedly named a peninsular soldier and never checked his credentials. They sent him to Pachuca where he proceeded to act like a conquering soldier, raping and violently seducing the wives and daughters of the important families in Pachuca. Residents took refuge in their houses because of the depredations of the new alcalde mayor. After many protests, he was removed from office, but these events, combined with fears of more riots and rebellions, affected the production of silver bars from the treasury.[17]

Treasury figures indicate that Terreros sent a lot of his ore to be made into silver bars between June and September 1767, some months after the last disturbances in February 1767. In April 1767, the Veta Vizcaína had suffered a 70 percent reduction in its workforce.[18] Remissions from the Pachuca treasury fell to the lowest amount registered since 1743, the year when Bustamante had called on Terreros for assistance in his mines. Table 3 indicates the total amount of silver sent from the Pachuca Treasury by all the miners in the region.

Table 3 Silver Sent to Mexico City from the Pachuca Treasury, 1769–1775

Year	Marcos (for an approximate value in pesos multiply each figure by eight)
1769	117,042
1770	150,801
1771	118,827
1772	68,513
1773	112,392
1774	82,212
1775	82,901

Source: AGI, Contaduria, leg. 937; Canterla, *Vida y obra*, 40–41.

It is difficult to reconcile these figures with the statements made by the investigator, Pedro Leoz, in which he reported that Regla had only three mines in Real del Monte producing ore and had drainage works in two other mines.[19] There were few other mine owners working in Real del Monte and Pachuca. It is also around this time that Regla had 400,000 pesos to lend to the crown. The possible profitability of the newly opened mines in Zimapán might explain these figures. Or more likely, Regla had preserved silver bars from previous years.

In the family archives, there is a manuscript called *Book of Accounts* (Libro de cuentas), probably collated at the settlement of Regla's estate; in it, figures (Table 4) differ from those figures (Table 5) used by Francisco Canterla and by Bernd Hausberger.[20]

Table 4 Amount of Silver Marcos Produced by Regla, 1768–1781

Year	Amount (for an approximate value in pesos multiply each figure by eight)
1768	82,550
1769	105,884
1770	132,587
1771	79,534
1772	44,547
1773	64,611
1774	Missing
1775	48,142
1776	64,968
1777	32,358
1778	56,786
1779	25,664
1780	34,583
1781	27,502

Source: AMRT, Libro de Cuentas, uncertain date.

Table 5 Regla's Percentage of Silver from
Pachuca Treasury Accounts, 1776–1781 (in Marcos)

Year	Pachuca	Regla	Percentage Contributed by Regla
1776	106,396	55,199	51.88
1777	136,316	87,230	64.00
1778	100,669	40,190	30.00
1779	103,865	35,931	34.59
1780	85,603	32,663	38.15
1781	49,875	22,410	44.93

Source: Figures compiled by Canterla, *Vida y obra,* 41; AGI, México, legs. 2133, 2134, 2135, 2136; AGI, Contaduría, 937. Hausberger's *La Nueva España* has a graph indicating Regla's relative remissions of silver to the Pachuca treasury, 102.

Fig. 14. Pachuca treasury building, constructed c. 1776.
Photograph by Marco Hernández.

In his various statements to the crown and to viceroys in the last period of his life, Regla emphasized the wealth that he had extracted from the mines, mentioning only once the flood that he suffered in 1757, and describing over and over again the "rich and inexhaustible treasure" of the Veta Vizcaína. These statements continued through 1775 and even occur in his testament. But based on the figures in Tables 4 and 5, in the latter part of the decade of the 1770s, the downturns that had plagued his predecessors in Real del Monte, as well as every other miner in the region, also afflicted Regla. He only once acknowledged that his mines began to decline in productivity sometime in the mid-1770s. Humboldt reported that Regla's profits began diminishing in 1774: both official and family figures confirm this statement.[21]

Despite differences in methods of calculating the number of bars of silver registered in the mines and the percentages produced by Regla, figures tell us that total production for the years 1776 to 1781, both from the Pachuca mines and Regla's share in them, rose to their highest amount in 1770, exactly when Regla said that his mines were partially closed, and when his administrators were concerned about the level of thievery and tried to convince officials to administer more severe punishments. According to Doris Ladd's research and the government's investigations (*veedurías*) 1770 was also the year in which Regla had closed many mines. The most severe decline in production occurred in 1779 and rose slightly the next year, only to decline again in 1781, the year of Regla's death. The official figures reflect the decline in Regla's share. Regla, at least once, indicated that he was aware of the severe decline in production.

During the thirty years that Regla controlled the Veta Vizcaína, he suffered few of the calamities that befell other miners. Only once did his mines flood seriously (in 1757–58). He complained about a lack of cheap labor and implied that this was his greatest difficulty. The closing of the Real del Monte mines in 1766–70 may have been compensated by new mines in Zimapán and by the ability of administrators and workers to find rich veins of ore there. In his long period of success from 1747 to around 1774, he kept the mines producing enough to sustain his expensive aspirations, an achievement none of his predecessors could rival. Hence, when the inevitable decline of silver production occurred around 1774, he was probably unprepared, but it may have encouraged him to invest what profits he had in land and other sectors.

KNIGHT OF CALATRAVA AND COUNT OF REGLA:
THE PURSUIT OF NOBLE TITLES

Pedro Terreros, like many of his contemporaries, craved recognition and noble titles. Aspirations were not enough, however, because one needed money to purchase such titles. Spending money to be accepted into a military order, or if the fortune was large, in a title of nobility, seemed a good use of family resources in colonial Mexico.[22] During the course of the eighteenth century, the financial bonanza to be garnered attracted the crown, which collected heavy fees when awarding a new title and again taxed the successor when the title passed to the next generation. Recognition by the crown for services could be essential to the future of a family. The hundreds of documents called "Relations of Merits and Services" attest to the significance of royal service in furthering one's family and fortune. On a more spiritual plane, as the Jesuit Navarrete wrote, "Nobility is the glue of all the most excellent virtues: Religion, Charity, Justice, and Clemency."[23]

Regla had always coveted renown. His pursuit of honors began early but accelerated in the last years of his life. For a man who differed from his colleagues in so many ways—who stayed away from Mexico City, who worked only in one mining region, and who was neither Vizcayan nor Montañes (the two dominant wealthy ethnic groups of eighteenth-century Mexico) —he nonetheless shared the common desire to possess noble titles. Within less than a decade, he accumulated three titles for his sons, all accompanied by entails. He did not personally need to be in an important seat at official events, or ride at the head of a procession, or administer a dowry fund, but he strove to achieve abstract recognition—titles, membership in a military order, and all the personal

honors that the king or his agents could assign to him—perhaps because he
sought to overcome the memory of a life begun in poverty, but more likely because he wished to have his name and fortune preserved into the future.

Terreros originated his pursuit of noble titles when he began to receive profits
from the mines. In about 1748 he applied for the title of knight of the military
order of Calatrava, an honor he received in 1753.[24] For years, he referred to himself and others called him Pedro Terreros or Pedro Romero de Terreros of
Calatrava. Six years later, in 1759, flushed with even more success in the mines,
he applied for the title of Conde de Regla en El Salto. When he submitted his
petition for the title, he explained his principal contribution: "Aside from the
countless hours of toil, hardships, vigilance, that this work [mining] has brought
with it, I have distributed huge quantities of pesos especially in the arduous
but useful enterprise of the draining of the Veta Vizcaína." His other benefactions included sponsorship of the missions on the Texas frontier, in which his
cousin became a martyr, bringing twenty peninsular friars to Mexico, as well
as providing dowries for nuns.[25]

The king refused to grant the title and persisted in denying it to him for the
next nine years. This delay was astounding, as the crown awarded these titles for
a price, and the sale of titles to colonials became a source of revenue. One reason
for this refusal might be that in Terreros's original application in 1759, he had
requested additional favors. He wanted the crown to give him the ownership of
the San Vicente mine. He also requested two memberships in military orders for
the sons of his friend, Domingo López de Carvajal, and the right to cast silver
bars in his own refining hacienda. When the crown demurred at granting all
these requests at once, especially the favors to López de Carvajal, Terreros explained that his friend had provided him with more than 600,000 pesos to invest in the mines. He might have added that López de Carvajal had not only
supplied him with cash but also arranged for the import of mercury and other
materials for the mines, purchased European goods for his retail stores in
Querétaro and Pachuca, and organized the transportation of Spanish friars to
Mexico. In addition, he oversaw assistance to his family in Cortegana, contributed to peninsular charities, and legally represented Terreros in Spain.[26]

These requests based on Terreros's success in the mines had a peremptory
quality and came to the attention of the king, Charles III, who ascended the
throne just at the time that Pedro Terreros's applications appeared in Spain. In
one of the first cases heard under the rule of Charles III, an official wrote that
these petty quarrels about property, assignment of judges, and crown attorneys
(*fiscales*) wasted endless time, even though in later years the authorities went to
considerable trouble over appointments to these jobs.[27] In conclusion, the crown
denied Pedro Terreros all his requests. Believing that it would be unwise not to
award him some sign of gratitude for his services, he was offered the title of King's

Gentleman with voice and the right to enter the king's chambers (*gentilhombre de voca con entrada*) and a promise of more careful consideration of his other requests in the future. This title was prestigious, and his older son would be grateful for the same title years later, but it did not please Terreros. According to a note of Carvajal's on June 17, 1760, the king had personally opposed granting him his desired title of the count of Regla.[28]

López de Carvajal, acting as an agent in Spain, continued to write to Pedro Terreros of his efforts with the "negocio de Regla," that is, his title. When Terreros asked that the matter be dropped and that the 20,000 pesos he had given to his agent to pay the appropriate people be returned, Carvajal replied that the money could not be retrieved, and that he had been given the right to plead for this favor and to represent Terreros at the court to a hundred different people—surely hyperbole. He also urged Terreros to persist because he knew how important a title would be to him.[29] While awaiting the title, Terreros also shortened the name for it. He dropped the Mexican portion of the title, El Salto, which referred to the name of his principal refining hacienda formerly named after the waterfall that provided the water used to refine silver, and left only the Spanish part that referred to the Virgin of Regla.

After the strikes and riots of 1766–67, officials in Mexico City remonstrated with the Council of the Indies about the crown's failure to reward Pedro Terreros with the title. He began his "melancholy retirement," or self-imposed exile, at San Miguel, and informed officials in Mexico City that he had withdrawn from active management of many of his mines. Officials in Mexico City persuaded the Council of the Indies that Pedro Terreros should receive his long-delayed title so that he would more actively resume the supervision of his mines. They convinced the king that he must grant the title of the count of Regla that Terreros had requested so long before. Delays continued while the king waited for an appropriate occasion, such as a royal wedding, but on September 20, 1768, the king approved the title. Terreros had to send another 12,000 pesos, despite the fact that the king had granted him exemptions from the most common taxes on titles.

THREE ENTAILS AND TWO ADDITIONAL TITLES: MARQUÉS OF SAN FRANCISCO AND MARQUÉS OF SAN CRISTÓBAL

"Those properties that heirs are free to sell . . .easily pass to other owners, families run through their fortunes, and are often reduced to a wretched state, as experience has demonstrated." So wrote Regla in explaining his reasons for wanting to put much of his property into entails, which would protect his children from dissipating their large inheritance. Regla's desire to establish three entails for each of his sons began even before he had received his first title of count of Regla in 1768. He began to fear that his sons would squander the family fortune, and entailing part of their inheritance would make it difficult for them to sell the property included in the entail. The expenses of maintaining a noble lifestyle placed strains on even the most abundant fortunes, and no form of productive investment provided an income secure enough to underwrite these expenses. He included a copy of the entail, attached to the title of the count of Regla, in his testament written in 1775.[30]

The first entail, to be given to his oldest son, Pedro Ramón, was issued in Spain in August 1766 and then later added to his title.[31] After lending money to the crown in 1770, he felt confident that his application would be granted for two additional entails for his two younger sons, Francisco and José María. Using his excellent relationship with Viceroy Bucareli, he began to request these titles to accompany the entails. To the objections of royal officials that his four daughters were being deprived of their patrimony, he promised to provide 300,000 pesos in cash and in properties for each of them.[32]

Regla planned the title and entail of the marqués de San Francisco for his second son, Francisco, and a third entail, San Cristóbal, for his son, José María. The reason for the choice of the second entail and title reflected again Regla's devotion to Franciscan causes, although his son had been named for the Jesuit saint, Francisco Javier. Perhaps Saint Christopher was chosen as the third title because of his charitable deeds, although they involved physical prowess rather than the distribution of wealth. Christopher was rewarded by God with wealth, and perhaps the count of Regla believed that he too succeeded through his strength and had been rewarded by God with money and a charitable nature. Approval of both titles came in December 1776, free of the customary charges because they were given in thanks for the 200,000 pesos for the battleship to be named *Count of Regla.*[33]

But around 1775, perhaps a bit earlier, Regla conceived of the idea of adding his mining property to the entail that was to be inherited by his oldest son, Pedro Ramón, in order to assure that his son would continue to work the mining veins of the Veta Vizcaína, Santa Brígida, and in Zimapán. Because silver mines as well as all products of the subsoil belonged to the crown, entailing his mines posed possible problems. If the son stopped working the mines, nobody else would be able to undertake this task, and the crown would lose a potentially rich source of revenue, as well as opportunities to offer the mines to other miners. Regla, aware of these objections, emphasized in his petition to the crown that he wished to continue the bond between his own name and the silver mines. He also promised to assure that his son would spend 100,000 pesos each year for the purchase of the elements necessary in silver production such as mercury, salt, pyrites, and leather for buckets, and that he himself would undertake the preparation of the *obras muertas*, the maintenance of the tunnels, air shafts, and drainage works. As he summed up his goals, he hoped that God would help him to leave very little mining maintenance for his son to do for many years because of his past practices and future intentions. He also vowed to provide property worth 500,000 pesos, which would presumably permit his son to invest this amount of money in mining. Although he seems to have thought of everything, he failed to mention how he expected his son to meet the extensive payrolls. Apparently the authorities did not consider this expense either and gave him permission to include the mines in the entail attached to the title of the count of Regla.

A special example of Regla's grandiosity and confidence in his own ability to do anything and in the rightness of his projects shines forth from his statements. "When I die, it will not be easy [for Pedro Ramón] to serve with the vigor, will, and spirit that animate me," he wrote on October 14, 1774. While this indicated that he did not believe that his son had his energy and dedication, it did not prevent him from increasing his efforts to control his son's activities. Despite the decline in his fortune that was so palpable in the late 1770s, the prospect that the mines might fail to provide for his son could not be acknowledged, perhaps because it meant an admission that his own family name and wealth might not continue for long.

One example of Regla's overwhelming insistence on the preservation of the family name concerns his actions after the death of his second son, Francisco, in Madrid in 1778, three years before the count's own death. The question of who would inherit the second entail came to the attention of the crown, and officials suggested that Regla decide which of his heirs would inherit the entail of San Francisco. Regla died without resolving the issue. The obvious heir was his oldest daughter, María Micaela, but he pointedly did not name her as the heir. Possibly he lacked confidence in her, or possibly he did not wish a woman to inherit the property because should she marry, it could then pass out of the hands of a male bearing the Terreros family name. In fact, his fears were realized in the nineteenth century when properties in one entail did pass from the family, as the male offspring of his youngest daughter chose to leave the property to somebody not in the family. Regla's resistance to naming María Micaela the heir to the *marquesado* resulted in additional expense to his heirs in legal fees and taxes from which his daughter might have been relieved if he had named her the heir.

PURCHASES OF THE FORMER JESUIT HACIENDAS

Like most miners and merchants, Regla purchased agricultural land. In part this was an effort to diversify his investments, focused initially on commerce and mines, both far less secure than agricultural land. Although farming could be risky with the failure of crops in bad years and the lowering of the price of agricultural products after too many good years, land still possessed a dependability not shared by mines and commerce. Also miners needed agricultural lands to pasture livestock, including the mules that operated their winches and processed ore and to produce feed for livestock, rations for workers, and leather for buckets and ladders.

Regla purchased haciendas before he received his titles and entails. Several times he acquired them through his money-lending activities. When borrowers could not repay their loans, Regla sometimes purchased their property at auction. The full story of his acquisition of haciendas is difficult to determine, in part because he used many different notaries in Mexico City. The result has been the dispersal of records. Terreros purchased property in Huichipán, especially a large hacienda called Ajuchititlán, in the area between the Querétaro region and the extended Pachuca mining area, now part of the state of Hidalgo. In about 1763, he purchased the hacienda of Las Vaquerías with its abundant flocks of sheep whose valuable wool enabled him to get the cash he needed to buy the urban house on the street of San Felipe Neri in Mexico City.[34] (See Map 5.)

But Regla did not become the major landowner in Mexico until 1776–78, when he purchased most of the properties belonging to two former Jesuit institutions, the Colegio de San Pedro y San Pablo and the novitiate of Tepozotlán. Charles Gibson, the historian of Aztec and colonial Mexico, judged this acquisition to be "the largest transaction of the colonial period."[35] The land became available when the crown expelled the Jesuits from Mexico in 1767, an act asserting the supremacy of the state over the church, and it expropriated their properties. The Jesuits had supported their extensive educational and missionary activities from the proceeds of their landed estates, and they became the largest single landowner in Mexico.

The Jesuit Colegio de San Pedro y San Pablo owned the largest group of haciendas surrounding Regla's mines. This complex of estates, known collectively as Santa Lucía, included lands in thirty-three areas of the Valley of Mexico and Actopán, and additional haciendas in Colima and Guadalajara.[36] By the early seventeenth century, Santa Lucía supplied the mining region with most of the basic necessities—mules, oxen, maize, leather, barley, wheat, straw, tallow, and other agricultural products.[37] An important section of the property lay along the road between Mexico City and Pachuca. By 1739, Santa Lucía and its annexed haciendas covered at least 200,000 acres on the Pachuca plain and in the northwestern region.

Regla had close ties with the functioning of the hacienda of Santa Lucía as early as 1750, when the compadre and chief servant of José Alejandro Bustamante, Pedro Villaverde, first rented the *pulque* operations and then administered all the estates from 1751 to 1764. This was the only time a non-Jesuit served in this capacity.[38] It was suggested that Terreros had some influence in securing this post for Villaverde. One might speculate that Pedro Terreros could promise the Jesuits exclusive rights to his business if the Jesuits appointed his friend and most intimate employee as administrator of the hacienda complex. Herman Konrad suggested that the Jesuits appointed Pedro Villaverde while in the process of secularizing their operations and responding to public apprehensions about their wealth, power, and influence. Thirteen years later, in 1764, the Jesuits discharged Villaverde as the administrator of the Santa Lucía haciendas, alleging significant financial losses. His removal could also be explained by the fact that his patron and compadre, Ignacio Gradilla, the business manager of the Colegio de San Pedro y San Pablo, went to another position in the Jesuit order. In the end Villaverde's departure from his post as administrator remains as enigmatic as his entrance.[39] But while Villaverde ran the hacienda complex, Regla enjoyed connections to the operation of Santa Lucía.

In early 1767, after the expulsion of the Jesuits, the crown took over the administration of their haciendas in every region of Mexico and sought to sell the order's property to laymen. In a society in which cash, in the form of silver coin, was the accepted currency, there were few who could buy the haciendas at their appraised value. The crown wished to have cash as quickly as possible and declined to underwrite mortgage payments. Only Regla, and another miner, José Borda, had the money to buy a significant number of haciendas. Whether Regla had been pressured by the crown to buy a large number of haciendas, as a lawyer for the family later alleged, cannot be known.

In June 1776, nearly a decade after the estates had been expropriated, Regla offered to buy the properties of two of the Jesuit institutions, one the college of San Pedro and San Pablo, of which the most valuable property was the hacienda of Santa Lucía. The Temporalidades, the crown-appointed agency in charge of the Jesuit properties, had evaluated all the properties of the two institutions at 1,956,681 pesos. Regla initially offered 1 million pesos, but after some adjustments about what would be included, he increased his offer by 200,000 pesos. He also agreed to demonstrate that he had 700,000 pesos before the transfer process began. As usual, he drove a hard bargain by setting five conditions. One was that if any of the property in the original inventory was missing, he would subtract its value from the purchase price. Temporalidades would pay the costs of measuring the lands that composed the estates, as well as the formalities of turning over ownership to Regla. Furthermore, Regla stipulated that he had to be free of disputes about boundaries. The only other serious bidder offered to show 100,000 pesos, so Temporalidades accepted Regla's offer. The amount of money that Regla agreed to pay for his purchase was an astoundingly large sum.

The costs of turning over the properties to a new and very demanding owner proved enormous. Regla's representatives, principally Pedro Villaverde and four of his five sons, traveled to each of the haciendas and rode hundreds of miles around them placing markers made of mortar and stone (*cal y canto*) with the initials of S.C.de R. (Señor Conde de Regla) surrounding the borders of all the haciendas. As the Villaverdes and their witnesses marked boundaries, representatives of Otomi, Nahuatl, and mestizo villages and individual owners presented opposing views. The disputes about the boundaries were based on continuing lawsuits, personal memories, and documentation of prior ownership before the Jesuits had purchased or received the land in gift. The papers relating to these disputes, preserved in the National Archives in Mexico City, amount to at least ten volumes of six hundred double-sided folio volumes. Protests arose from disputes over boundaries, water rights, and the right of groups of peasants living within hacienda lands to a minimum area (*fundo legal*) around their houses. Whether these new measurements provided villagers, peasants, and small landowners with additional information for future protests, or whether Regla's purchases silenced future protests can only be determined by new research. For the moment, Regla's representatives and the government ignored the protests, and the boundary markers were placed as the officials and the Villaverdes determined. As late as 1798, legal claims continued over the payment for paper, scribes, and witnesses. Pedro Villaverde asserted that neither he nor his sons had been paid for their enormous labor.[40] Villaverde believed that Regla owed him the money, but perhaps Regla expected him to collect the money from the government.

On January 27, 1778, Regla presented 420,000 pesos of the money he had promised and four years later, on March 4, 1780, he paid another 220,000 pesos, a total of 640,000 pesos for the cost of the haciendas belonging to the two former Jesuit institutions. Later, both he and the government agreed that he had paid 700,000 pesos (although when the extra 60,000 pesos was paid is uncertain). He refused to pay more because so many of the objects included in the inventories could not be found when he took possession; furthermore, the aqueduct on the hacienda of Jalpa had never been finished and thus had no value to him. Expensive objects used for the celebration of the Mass were worthless to him and he would not pay for them. The judges of the Temporalidades in 1778 still refused to turn over the land. As late as 1780, disputes over the properties continued and the officials of Temporalidades still retained some of the documentation necessary to clear title.[41] Regla's continual attention to detail and unfailing concentration on receiving the most land at the lowest possible cost is evidenced in these documents.

Despite the guarantees from Temporalidades that Regla had demanded and perhaps even received, debates continued about the wisdom of accepting slightly more than half of the value of the Jesuit haciendas formerly belonging to the two colleges. For example, one of the tax people noted that the hacienda of Santa Lucía had been sold for 200,000 pesos, but that it had an actual value of 600,000 pesos, as admitted by one of the Villaverde sons. These contradictions would return to haunt Regla's heirs many years after his death.[42]

Nevertheless, these haciendas, coupled with those that Regla had purchased earlier, helped to support the family for the next three and possibly four generations. Before the Jesuit expulsion, the income from these haciendas had supported the Colegio de San Pedro y San Pablo, the chief educational institution in Mexico City for the education of young creole men, and the novitiate of Tepozotlán where all the creole Jesuits had been educated for more than a century. It is a tribute to Reglas's financial astuteness that he was able to transfer the income that supported two valuable educational institutions to his own family's personal use. It might be argued that perhaps some of the money he had paid for the purchase of the haciendas was dedicated by the crown to charitable activities such as the foundation of a work house (*hospicio*) for the poor.

CONCLUDING ARRANGEMENTS AND FAMILY AFFAIRS

Sometime after 1774, Regla partially ended his self-imposed exile in San Miguel and began to spend his time in Mexico City. He now referred to himself as a resident, or vecino, of Mexico, rather than either Querétaro or Pachuca. Changes in the house at San Felipe Neri Street provide evidence of his presence. In his testament signed in 1775, he instructed his executors to bury him in any of the three Franciscan Colegios de Propaganda Fide that he was closest to at the time of his death.

Despite the assertion that he had taken refuge in the wilderness, affirmed in the publication of the eulogy read at his funeral, he kept informed about economic and political activities in Mexico City. If Regla felt concerned about his own financial position and the declining revenues from his mines, it is rarely mentioned in his public statements. However, the old magic that had turned the silver mines into what he had characterized as an inexhaustible source of wealth had begun to diminish. The silver production resulting from his mines proved disappointing, although he still said that the amount of wealth that his mines produced was too great to count.

His absence from the mines (although not from the refining haciendas) between 1766 and 1774 gave him the opportunity to devote more energy to his other interests such as charities, land purchases, and the pursuit of honors. Even after he emerged from San Miguel he dedicated less attention to his mines. Regla, aware that the last period of his life was approaching, worked harder on ventures that would assure that his name and deeds would last into perpetuity; almost frantic activity filled the last period of his life as he tried to guarantee that his heirs would inherit a sizeable and well-balanced estate. Having already viewed the activities of Pedro Ramón, his oldest son, with dismay, he tried harder to ensure that the 5 million pesos that he estimated he would leave in his estate in the value of mines and property would cushion future blows. One of his deeds in these last years backfired. Around 1780 he sent agents to the north of Mexico to purchase Jesuit haciendas belonging to Jesuit Colegio de Zacatecas. His heirs amassed debt to pay for them, which the count of Regla had usually avoided, and which would begin to debilitate the family.

The establishment of the Monte de Piedad with the provision that a member of the family had to be the head of the governing board was more successful.

This provision has been honored by the government from 1781 to the present, giving his family a continuity that no other family in Mexico would enjoy. Other arrangements made during these last years for his children proved more evanescent, but represented the best that any father seeking to govern his family from beyond the grave could manage. Regla did make some investments that enriched his heirs' future estate. For example, he purchased and established the rights for four *pulquerías*, places where the extremely profitable beverage, pulque, made from the cactus plant was sold. This secured for his family another business based on a profitable crop—from the production of the cactus plants on the former Jesuit haciendas to its sale in Mexico City.[43]

The pace of Regla's activities to assure the continuity of his family sped up in the last six years of his life. During these years of semi-exile in San Miguel he did not remain completely solitary; instead, his life took another path. Perhaps during these years he even remembered some aspects of the book called *David Perseguido* found in his uncle's house in those far-off days when he was a young merchant in Querétaro in the 1730s. Decades later, Regla may have believed himself to be in a position similar to David, persecuted by his enemies and many leagues from the center of power. Like David, but in different ways, he managed to overcome this isolation. His request to sponsor the Monte de Piedad began a few months after the beginning of his self-imposed exile. It appears that his aim was not to retreat in the wilderness in silence and despair, but to construct a mansion and to collect around him symbols of his wealth and services and to insist on the continuation of that name and fame into the future. No longer the persecuted David, Regla had become a powerful and successful man whose name and fame have survived for generations.

The elements that Regla chose for his coat of arms demonstrated symbols of wealth and tradition. As part of his coat of arms he chose two wolves, symbols often used on Basque coats of arms, thus distancing himself from his Andalucian-Extremaduran past and aligning himself with a more powerful group of peninsulares in Mexico. He included symbols of the names of Romero and Terreros, crosses, the logo for membership in the order of Calatrava, and other elements such as honeycombs, bee hives, and deer. (See Figure 15.)

Perhaps remembering his uncle's will with its elaborate instructions for everything from the number of candles, the dress of the mourners, to the participation of the members of his confraternities, he asked only that his funeral be a simple one and that all the members of the unnamed confraternities to which he belonged should pray for him. He requested that he be buried in the Franciscan habit, a common practice in eighteenth-century Mexico, and in one of the three Franciscan Colegios de Propaganda Fide that he had endowed.

As a man who had lent money to a great many people, and sometimes very large sums, he forgave no debts. To collect the debts, he told his heirs to proceed first with prudence and Christian piety; if that brought no results, then they were to use force and finally a court of law.[44] He instructed his heirs to continue the procedures that had permeated his business dealings. This may have been the first of his instructions to be broken, possibly because his heirs had not been prepared for this kind of strict business operation.

Regla had indeed been concerned about the kind of education his sons would receive. About a year after the death of his wife and after surviving the threats to his life by the workers of Real del Monte, he wrote to his friend, Domingo López y Carvajal in Puerto de Santa María, Spain, asking that he and his wife bring up his three sons. In this letter, Regla explained that he asked this favor in order not to have his sons grow up with the customs or manners (*modalidades*) of Mexico. Risking the loss of a friendship and an important business relationship with Regla, Domingo López refused to undertake this task, partially because of the difficulties of raising three boys in a household with his daughter, but above all, because no matter what education and training Regla's sons received, they would still be creoles. In the view of Domingo López, race and birthplace determined much, while nurture and education would count for little.[45] Regla apparently had written that he did not wish his sons to grow up like other wealthy creoles who were reputed to be lazy and pleasure loving.

Regla delayed sending his sons to Spain until 1775 when they had reached the ages of nine, thirteen, and fourteen, and by then had obviously been influenced by the culture of the country where they had spent their early years. By this time, Regla had no intention of training them to be merchants, but sent them to Madrid to be educated as gentlemen. So in 1775, the same year that Regla wrote his will, Pedro Ramón, Francisco, and José María departed for Spain with abundant Masses to be said for their safe journey. Pedro Ramón and his brothers were presented at the Spanish court by the secretary of state, Floridablanca, "as the sons of the richest vassal of the Spanish monarchy." The boys attended the Semanario de Nobles in Madrid, which had been a Jesuit institution closed on their expulsion in 1767 and recently reopened. Nothing in the curriculum of the Semanario prepared Pedro Ramón to administer agricultural haciendas or to run the silver mines. Instead, he studied moral philosophy, moral and natural law, Latin, dancing, and apparently some military subjects. His school companions appear to have been middle class, often the sons of bureaucrats, and overwhelmingly creole, as the Spanish nobility tended to educate their sons at home. The character of this student body frustrated efforts of Regla to educate his sons as peninsulares.[46] When the oldest son, Pedro Ramón, left the Semanario at the age of eighteen, about a year before his father's death, he received a commission in the army. The combination of an inadequate education and continual reminders of his wealth sent Pedro Ramón down a path filled with contradictions, stumbling blocks, and temptations.

Fran.^{co} Sylverio.   ex .   ā. 1759.

Fig. 15. Regla's coat of arms. Courtesy of the Bancroft Library,
University of California at Berkeley.

His affluence entitled him to make the acquaintance of the future king of
Spain, Charles IV, a friendship that had an unfortunate outcome. At an unknown
date, Pedro Ramón lent the Prince 4 million reales, which were not repaid until
1791, three years after Charles had become king.[47] He also came to know one of his
father's business partners, the count of Repárez, who inducted him into the world
of commerce, selling him enough Spanish brandy (*aguardiente*) and other commodities to fill one of Repárez's ships and send it to Mexico. Regla refused to accept
the goods and returned them to Spain. The debt of half a million pesos remained
unpaid during the lifetime of the first count of Regla and continued to grow after
his death, compounded not just by interest, but by sums of cash added by Repárez
for unstated reasons.[48] Before his death, when becoming aware of his son's fiscal
incompetence and irresponsibility, the old count apparently decided to arrange
matters so that Repárez could not easily collect the debts.

Confronted, apparently, with the knowledge of his oldest son's dubious
activities, Regla may have decided that he needed to tie up more of his cash in
landed estates, perhaps to be added to the entails, which would hinder his offspring
from profligate spending, and he instructed his envoys to buy additional ex-Jesuit
haciendas in the north.

As for the daughters, many men in his position would have married them to capable peninsular merchants; the kind of young man he had once been himself. Regla refused to take that path, perhaps because he feared that in the future the names of his sons-in-law would take precedence over his own, leaving the name of Romero de Terreros in official oblivion, to be remembered only in family stories told by women about their illustrious ancestors. Even the family position on the Monte de Piedad could be given to a relative through marriage, which indeed did happen briefly during the nineteenth century. Thus he sought to avoid this eventuality by keeping his daughters unmarried. None of them entered a convent.

Regla's doubts about how to proceed with arrangements after his death is exemplified by the fifty blank pages he left in his will and by his failure to appoint a capable executor. Although he must have known that the appointment of an able executor of his estate was crucial, he found himself unable to decide how to proceed. The two men whom he had appointed in his outdated 1766 will had died, and he apparently had little confidence in his current business associates, a judgment that posterity would partly confirm. His 1775 will remained deficient because he had appointed only his two oldest sons and two oldest daughters as executors, none of whom had any relevant experience or knowledge. Two of them had already predeceased him: Francisco, who died in 1778, and Juana María, who had died in 1762, at the age of four. Whether this oversight stemmed from his unwillingness to decide among a series of bad choices or whether he simply neglected the matter cannot be known. It is possible that he did not distinguish among his daughters, or perhaps he refused to name the next oldest daughter, María Antonia, as she already displayed signs of the ineptitude that would later consume most of the cash in her share of the estate. We can only conclude that for all his care in these last years, there were many details and actions, some of the greatest importance, that he failed to resolve. Perhaps he felt that his closest friends and assistants might betray him and feast on the estate. Executors enjoyed 10 percent of the value of the estate, and he may have resented having any of his friends possessing that amount of his money. He informally appointed a Franciscan friar, a specialist in the settlement of testaments, to work on arranging his estate.[49]

The activities of these last years—the establishment of entails, purchases of Jesuit estates, his attempts to make his sons into peninsulares and members of the Spanish nobility, his vastly expanded charities, and judicious investments—all made possible the continuation of his family, fame, and fortune well into the latter part of the nineteenth century.

CHAPTER 9

Death and its Aftermath: 1781–1878

I am surprised that writers on society ... have not accorded rules on inheritance a greater influence on the story of mankind. ... They confer a godlike power over the fate of one's fellow human beings.
—De Tocqueville, *De la démocratie en Amérique*, quoted in Casey,
The History of the Family

In the name of God, our Lord, all powerful, Amen.
—Beginning of all eighteenth-century wills and testaments

At 8:30 on the evening of November 27, 1781, in his refining hacienda of San Miguel, at the age of seventy-one, the count of Regla died after an illness lasting only three days. His four daughters wrote to the viceroy, explaining that his death from pneumonia came on him so suddenly that he hardly had time to speak with his confessor before he became delirious. They were so astounded by his death that they could scarcely breathe.[1] The chronicler of Mexico City reported a different cause of death when he announced that "the most powerful miner that this century has known had died of herpes."[2] There is no way to confirm either of these causes of death.

For more than thirty years, Regla had enjoyed bonanza after bonanza, which may have produced more than 20,000,000 pesos worth of silver. His estate, valued at between 4,500,000 and 5,000,000 pesos at his death, may have been the largest estate of any noble in the colony. At the time of his death, he had in his possession 200,000 pesos in the form of silver coins and bars, twice the quantity in the royal treasury ten years earlier.[3]

Despite Regla's great wealth, six months after his death his family faced a fiscal crisis caused by his purchase of northern landed estates. Regla had utilized all the available institutional arrangements to assure the perpetuation of his family and assumed that the continuation of his mining enterprises ranked high among the priorities of the king, the minister of the Indies, José de Gálvez, and the viceroy, Martín de Mayorga. He was proved right in this assumption: these officials combined to prevent the full severity of the crisis from totally decimating his family fortune and debilitating his heirs.

The conflicts, contentions, and challenges began only a few hours after Regla's death when the alcalde mayor of Pachuca, José Muzquiz, acting as an official of the secular power, tried to take the count's body from the house. He also claimed Regla's keys and goods.[4] His actions illustrate the conflicts around Regla's death and the numbers of people anxious to make claims on this fortune.

Contrary movements to preserve the family fortune (and also to make it available to higher ranking government men) took only a short period of time to materialize. Regla's nephew, the son of his older brother, the priest Antonio Romero de Terreros, protested the actions of the alcalde mayor. The viceroy intervened by sending troops, which were placed under the command of the oldest daughter, María Micaela Romero de Terreros. Other nongovernment individuals, such as the family retainers José Marrugat and Pedro Villaverde, sought to maintain the family intact, but they too exacted a price. Each of them received 30,000 pesos from the estate, claiming that Regla had not sufficiently paid them for their services, and Micaela herself took 30,000 pesos in addition to her inheritance for her work as executor of the will.[5]

THE FIRST SIX MONTHS: THE FUNERAL

Immediately after Regla's death, a group of friars from the Franciscan colegio in Pachuca, who must have been present in the refining hacienda of San Miguel from the onset of the illness, ignored the protests of the alcalde mayor and carried the body of their benefactor on their shoulders to the city of Pachuca about 20 miles away. Family legend recalled that "workers of the mines of Real del Monte and their families, . . .dependent on the Count of Regla, cried at his death as though he were their father and exclusive benefactor."[6] A modern historian of his funeral mused "that it would be interesting to know the opinion of the workers who, on this rainy night, saw the count of Regla on his last journey [*recorrido*] between San Miguel and Pachuca, passing through the mining region that had given him so much wealth."[7] He was temporarily buried the next day, on November 28, in a space normally reserved only for friars in the church of San Francisco. He was entitled to this honor as a patron. (See Figure 16.)

He had requested, as he had done for the funeral of his wife, a large number of Masses said for his soul by members of confraternities to which he belonged and that money be given to the poor. Unlike his uncle, Juan Vázquez, he did not spell out where the Masses should be held, nor did he provide specific bequests for either the Masses or for the poor.[8]

In the future, the friars had intended to construct a burial chapel that would include Regla's coat of arms and statues of him and his wife. But the money that Regla had put aside for the construction of the chapel, he instead gave to celebrate the installation of a bishop.[9] It is remarkable that during the final period of his life, Regla elected to donate money to another person and for an ephemeral purpose that would not celebrate him and his wife. Because of this act of generosity (if true), it was his own burial chapel that was without support, making it easy for his body to be mislaid; in fact, the location of his body was lost for more than one hundred years, only to be discovered in 1999.[10]

The funeral, separated by six months after his burial, was elaborate, despite orders in his 1775 will that these services be "without ostentation and mundane pomp."[11] But the friars declined to honor this request, contradicted in spirit as it had been by Regla's intention to construct a chapel. Centuries earlier, the Jesuits had buried their patron, Alonso de Villaseca, with great pomp despite his ascetic lifestyle.[12] Clearly, both orders felt it incumbent on them to honor their patron with "funeral rites and praises" that included elaborate ceremonies.

The Franciscans waited six months to hold an extensive funeral so that they could complete preparations, including the production of a vast monument, or pyre, which would be consumed by flames after the funeral. The funerals of kings commonly boasted such constructions.[13] Planned with unusual care, the funeral pyre consisted of series of candelabra containing four candles each and an elaborate monument of wood. At the base of the monument, there were canvasses with painted inscriptions in Latin, sonnets in Spanish, and lyric poems. The four columns sustaining the monument contained written words demonstrating the virtues of the deceased: his devotion to the Virgin Mary, his avoidance of praise, his fleeing from applause and persecutors, and the sober and abstemious nature manifested in the midst of his riches. Above these columns hung paintings on each of the four sides. One depicted his work on the conversion of the Indians (referring to San Sabá); another his contributions to the reedification and improvement of the three apostolic colegios of Pachuca, Querétaro, and Mexico; a third referred to the Monte de Piedad, picturing a statue of Piety giving money to the poor; and the last had a painting of a ship that alluded to his contribution of money to build a Spanish warship. The fourth section of this gigantic monument portrayed other virtues of Regla, most importantly indicating that his path was directed toward the heavens and demonstrating his considerable generosity. Finally a representation of a man with a sword and shield of snakes threatened another one who remained silent. It symbolized Regla's "tranquility of spirit" in the face of the violence of others. Also depicted was the insignia of the Order of Calatrava, the military order the count had belonged to since 1752. The topmost horizontal section supported a statue of Religion.

The title of the publication describing the funeral services was "Call to Religion." It contained no mention of Regla's silver mining, mercantile career, or of his accumulation of property. This pyre and the sermon that accompanied it declared the importance of accumulating wealth, not boasting of it, and then distributing it to religious, charitable, and patriotic causes.[14]

Although it was not yet the season for heavy rains, when the appointed day

Fig. 16. Church of San Francisco in Pachuca, where Regla was buried.
Regla was its patron and benefactor. Photograph by Marco Hernández.

of the funeral in Pachuca arrived in May 1782, many guests failed to attend because three days of torrential downpours preceded the services. The sparse attendance at the ceremony did include neighbors from Pachuca and the surrounding areas, a choir from the village of Zumpango, the clergy who led parts of the Mass, and Regla's four daughters. His two sons were still studying in Spain. The musketeers from Real del Monte, who may have been stationed there since 1766, stood in the atrium and cemetery of the colegio and fired their muskets at appropriate times during the service. Dragoons guarded the funeral pyre, just as they may have guarded the count's property for many years.

FINANCIAL DIFFICULTIES

The problems that complicated the life of Regla's family for the years after his death began in the count's lifetime. His mines began to produce less silver. He realized that his sons might not be prepared for the responsibilities of supervising and caring for the extensive properties they would inherit. Fearing that already established entails might not protect his heirs from the consequences of their inexperience and the habit of indulging in the luxury in which they had been raised, the old count sent his representatives to buy still more former Jesuit properties. There is also the possibility that the government pressured him into this act. One representative went to Colima and another negotiated for haciendas belonging to the former Jesuit Colegio de Zacatecas. In both cases, his representatives overpaid for the haciendas. In Colima, they paid more than 150,000 pesos for a hacienda that Regla had wanted to purchase for 70,000 pesos. In Zacatecas and in Aguascalientes, they offered more than 700,000 pesos for haciendas that had been valued at around 300,000 pesos, already an inflated figure. These extravagant transactions not only terminated the count's cash reserves but also required that 200,000 pesos would have to be borrowed to complete the purchases. It is uncertain if Regla knew about these prices or had agreed to them before death overtook him, but these additional properties added to the fiscal crisis faced by the family in the year and a half after Regla's death.

Confusion over who should be the executor of the estate also complicated matters. The oldest child, María Micaela, had not yet reached the age of twenty-five, which would legally permit her to act as executor. After the customary ten days of mourning had passed, she journeyed to Mexico City to assure her appointment. Viceroy Mayorga placed himself in overall charge of the estate and selected Fernando José Mangino, one of the most important officials in Mexico City, as the individual in charge of the settlement. The crown had a special interest in Regla's estate and hoped to gain some of the cash; it also expected little resistance from the inexperienced daughter whose education had been devoted to "sewing, weaving, [and] embroidering to perfection . . .which were [her and her sisters'] constant activities when not reading devout books."[15] In the weeks following the count's death the government concentrated on keeping the House of Regla in good working order.[16]

Luis Marrugat, a Catalan merchant whose close relationship with Regla began around 1761, to whom the count had lent money, and who was the agent for the purchase and decoration of the house on San Felipe Neri Street, became María Micaela's chief advisor. One of their principal actions was to borrow 200,000 pesos from various ecclesiastical chaplaincies and pious funds to pay for the haciendas in the north of Mexico, chiefly one of the former Jesuit haciendas called Tetillas.[17] Marrugat himself had negotiated and been the guarantor for the purchase of those haciendas in 1780 and had paid double the evaluated price for them. An additional 250,000 pesos was taken from other family funds to complete the payment. To objections raised by Lucas de Lasaga, guardian of the three younger sisters, that Luis Marrugat and Micaela Romero de Terreros had agreed to excessive prices, they responded that the honor of the count of Regla required them to carry through on these purchases, because the money had been promised by Regla's representatives.[18] The question of honor seems like a far-fetched excuse to pay the extra money.

Micaela also had an interest in gaining control of the San Francisco entail, which had originally been created for her now-deceased brother Francisco. Micaela took money that was accumulating in the cash reserves of the estate and purchased for herself the hacienda of Tiripitio in Tuzantla, Michoacán, for 192,075 pesos. Since this property had been sold for 40,000 pesos four years earlier, and the money had not been paid, in repossessing the hacienda, the crown thus received an additional 150,000 pesos for it. Whether Micaela paid this money out of ignorance of the previous sale, or from a desire to convince the government to let her assume the ownership of the San Francisco entail is unknown.

Overpaying for former Jesuit haciendas constituted one form of indirect contribution to the crown. Another more direct form was a donation of 3,000 *cargas* (48,000 bushels) of wheat for Havana, Cuba, from the haciendas under the general administration of María Micaela. The total cash value of the gift may have been as high as 24,000 pesos. Much of the money paid out in these months came from cash belonging to the three younger sisters who had been promised an inheritance of 300,000 pesos each. While it appears that the crown profited from these transactions, these payments helped to compensate the government for the low prices (as they perceived it) that Regla had negotiated in 1775–78 for the haciendas that had belonged to the Colegio de San Pedro y San Pablo and the Novitiate of Tepozotlán.[19]

Some of this "generosity" may be explained not as innocence, stupidity, or even corruption, but fear. María Micaela and her sisters perceived that they were threatened by men who were trying to force marriage on them. The Regla daughters had lived in virtual isolation in San Miguel Regla, and their father had not arranged marriages for them. Now they may have resisted any matrimony because the motive for such a union could only have been to strip further the Regla estate. Given that their father had decided to keep the wealth in the masculine line by avoiding either a wastrel or a capable son-in-law, and that they lived in a society in which filial obedience enjoyed a high premium, the threats of forcible marriage must have been viewed with horror by the women.[20] Only the favor of the government could help them resist forced marriages. Preventing such marriages was advantageous for the viceroy, because an astute husband for one of the daughters might have hindered some of the hemorrhaging of cash from the estate to the crown. These fears of a forced marriage also drove Micaela further into the confidence of Marrugat. However, he seemed to have been more interested in serving the government by paying double the evaluated price for properties than in serving the family of his deceased employer. Marrugat and María Micaela had encumbered the estate with more than 29,000 pesos a year in interest. Still worse, they borrowed this money to buy haciendas that would not appreciate in value for more than a century, long after the family had sold them.

Immediately after Regla's sons returned from Madrid in 1783, the family tried to sell the haciendas of Tetillas. Lacking potential buyers, they retaliated against Marrugat and refused for several years to pay the interest, forcing Marrugat, the guarantor, to pay it. Although one of the Regla sisters had previously mortgaged one of her haciendas to assist him, the government, despite his complicity in transferring excessive sums from the estate to the crown, enjoined her from lending him any more money.[21] Not until four years after Marrugat's death did the Reglas finally find a buyer for the Tetillas haciendas—the conde de Rul, to whom they sold the haciendas for an estimated loss of nearly 200,000 pesos. Even at 500,000 pesos, Rul probably overpaid for the haciendas in order to add lands to his entail.[22]

Despite these unfortunate transactions, the Regla fortune in lands and silver mines was still immense. However, much property could not be sold or converted into cash for at least fifty years because it was tied up in entails. The crown had exacted 900,000 pesos from the family; or to put it another way, the crown had appropriated 20 percent of Regla's fortune in the course of settling his estate. The continuation of the Regla businesses made it possible for the Spanish count of Repárez to continue to collect money on Pedro Ramón Terreros's debts to him, which he had contracted while still living in Spain. That gave Repárez funds to pay the crown as well as his other creditors. Also, the government itself could sue the functioning family business for an additional million pesos for the haciendas that Regla had purchased in earlier years.[23]

A GLIMPSE AT THE LIVES OF THE SUCCEEDING GENERATIONS

Two members of the elite did succeed in sharing the Regla wealth by marrying into the family. The second count of Jala scored a dramatic success, breaking his daughter's engagement to Teodoro de Croix, viceroy of Peru, and marrying her to Pedro Ramón Terreros, second count of Regla, in 1785. The count of Jala added between one-third to one-half of the value in all the objects that he gave his daughter as a dowry and included no productive property.[24] Vicente Herrera, at one time regent of the audiencia and one of the most powerful officials in Mexico, married the youngest Regla daughter, María Dolores, with the connivance of her brother. Pedro Ramón doubtless hoped that Herrera's age and ill health might diminish his capacity to produce heirs, who would have a more valid claim on María Dolores's property than Pedro's own children. It was also possible that Herrera would be able to represent the Regla family interests with influential officials in Spain. María Dolores and Vicente Herrera had no offspring, and we are so far unaware of any help that the latter gave to the family in legal cases in Spain.

Although the Reglas entered the second generation of their existence with a reduced cash reserve, they still had substantial properties in silver mines, at least five urban houses, and the bulk of the property of three former Jesuit colleges. A good deal of their property was entailed and could not be sold or legally be used to pay off either the government or the count of Repárez. Given a certain competence in estate management and luck in the silver mines, the Reglas might have retained their leading position as the wealthiest family in New Spain.

The economic status of these early years is revealed in an early will of the second count, written about five months after the birth of his only son and heir, born in 1788. In a simple will, he requested that at the time of his death, Masses with a value of 1 peso each be said in all the more than one thousand churches in the archbishopric of Mexico. Twenty years later, after he had suffered bankruptcy, the second count of Regla dictated his final testament and demanded that he be given a pauper's burial in the fields of Santa María Redonda, ordering his executors not to provide an ornate funeral.[25] Certainly his family did not follow through on this request: the eulogy read at the funeral was published, and he did not have a pauper's burial.

The outlines of some of the family's economic difficulties appear in notarial documents. New business dealings are rarely mentioned, but there are many long-term rental agreements, appointments of general managers for various kinds of businesses, and powers of attorney for people to act in place of the second count in his business dealings. These may be indicators of neglect toward his properties. Despite the fact that in 1789 he inherited the property of one of his sisters, this additional infusion of land, while it certainly improved his economic condition, failed to shelter his family from severe economic difficulties ending in bankruptcy proceedings against Pedro Ramón. On the contrary, since this newly acquired property was not entailed, it could be mortgaged and these additional lands became the vehicle by which new funds could be raised, old debts paid off, and new debts created. Some of these mortgages helped to pay off the Repárez obligations, others were used to found chaplaincies for family members as directed by the sister whose land he had inherited and to maintain an aristocratic lifestyle.[26]

In 1804, when the government required that Mexicans repay their long-term loans from various convents, confraternities, and other religious organizations, the house of Regla owed enormous debts. Although we do not know the extent of their obligations, they owed at least 165,000 pesos to church endowments and probably paid no more than 50,000 pesos through requesting and receiving permission to consolidate and reduce their indebtedness (*composiciones*), which permitted them to pay less. Raising even 50,000 pesos must have been difficult. The fact that they paid less than one-third of their total debt might have been facilitated by their close personal friendship and ritual kinship with Viceroy Iturrigaray. An insistence on payment of the full amount owed the government agency of Consolidación might have eliminated the Regla family, and in the final analysis, the government had as little desire to exclude them from the upper ranks of the elite in 1808 as it had in the 1780s. Other elite families enjoyed the same privileges and were able to reduce the amount of money that they had to pay the crown.[27]

The second count of Regla died in 1809 shortly before the beginning of the Wars of Independence. Although he had passed from his days as a playboy-soldier in Madrid to a pious and often hard-working middle age, it was his wife who displayed the necessary energy to keep the family functioning in the difficult years of the Wars of Independence (1810–21).[28]

In fact, the second countess of Regla managed the family estates from 1809 to 1819, while her son, the third count of Regla, Pedro José María, was in his twenties. Despite the time that had been granted to the third count to mature, when he assumed full charge of his estates at the age of thirty-one, the notary records and the diminution of the family wealth under his charge indicate an ineptitude for business, a possible addiction to gambling, and a willfulness and an inability to follow through on his projects that created new difficulties.[29]

In the period following the death of the second count of Regla in 1809, the attitude of other members of the elite proved decisive in preserving the family. The business associations derived from the old count, such as the Villaverde and the Marrugat families, continued to serve the Reglas as they had done since 1781. For example, they acted as aides in various Regla affairs, as guarantors for loans, and even cared for the natural children of José María Romero de Terreros, the marqués of San Cristóbal, the younger brother of the second count. Leading lawyers, such as Juan Francisco Ascárete, arranged the Regla estates and lent their talents to help the family preserve its status. Their peers, such as the mining financiers like the Fagoaga family, and institutions, such as the Tribunal de Minería and the Inquisition, lent them money and pressured them only slightly for repayment.[30] When the marqués of San Cristóbal died in Paris in 1815, the crown awarded the marquesado land to the third count of Regla, even though the marqués of San Cristóbal had willed the entail properties to another individual. The government refused to honor claims of two offspring of the marqués of San Cristóbal's two children, who had been conceived and born out of wedlock.[31]

By 1819, two years before Mexico's independence from Spain, the third count of Regla not only enjoyed his own estates but also those of his deceased uncle and two of his aunts. He had also received two additional titles from the maternal side of his family. The only other entail, that of the marquesado of San Francisco, still remained in the hands of another aunt and her heirs.

During the quarter-century between 1819 and 1845 when the third count of Regla acted as family patriarch, the monarchical institutions that had created and sustained the Reglas's privileges were abolished. The entails and titles of nobility were eliminated in the early 1820s, although custom prevailed to the extent that holders of titles were referred to as ex-condes and ex-marqueses in official documents.[32] As late the 1850s the family and properties and businesses of the Romero de Terreros were referred to as the House of Regla.

The abolition of entails, favored by the nobility as a way of achieving liquidity and borrowing money, since these arrangements had made it difficult to sell or mortgage property, removed the last brake on the irresponsibility of the third count of Regla. He could now mortgage and lose almost all his property. Unfavorable economic conditions for the old colonial nobility added to the estate's downturn. In the first half of the nineteenth century, mining and agricultural properties, even if well-managed, often lost money. Moreover, Regla's most important estates lay on one of the invasion routes of local and international forces into Mexico, and his lands served as a free commissary for competing armies seeking national power.

Around 1835, at least ten years before the third count's death, two of his sons enlisted the assistance of other members of the elite and succeeded in wresting some part of their estates and inheritance from their father. The government was no longer in a position to control the Reglas, either to give assistance or to exact money from their estates as Charles III, the minister of the Indies, José de Gálvez, and Viceroy Mayorga had done in the early 1780s. Nor was there any longer a compelling reason for the government to intervene, because the silver mines of Real del Monte had passed into the administration of an English mining company who paid rent to Regla. They then came to belong to a group of Mexican investors, leaving the descendants of the Reglas as shareholders who soon sold their stock.

Other members of the elite, acting as guardians, judges, and lawyers, did succeed in saving some aspects of the Regla businesses and maintaining the family's high status. With the death of the third count in 1845, his second son, Manuel Romero de Terreros, assumed family leadership, and with the assistance of such friends as Mariano Riva Palacios, succeeded in removing his stepmother and half-brother from the ancestral home at San Felipe Neri Street, so that the house could be sold. A third son of the third count of Regla, Juan Romero de Terreros, took his share of the estate and traveled to Spain and procured the newly created title of Duke of Regla. He also collected and published documents about the deeds of the first count of Regla.[33] The oldest son of the third count, Pedro, the heir to the remnants of the most valuable entail, was mentally handicapped and placed in the care of a guardian who assisted him in husbanding his resources. The less capable younger sons of the third count of Regla fared badly.

The recovery of the Romero de Terreros family from its low point at the death of the third count in 1845 belongs to another epoch in the history of both Mexico and the family. The story of the first three generations of the family indicates the vulnerability of even the wealthiest family to wasteful sons who had been shaped by an education that seemed appropriate only for maintaining their noble status.

During the eighteenth century, the wealthy tried to preserve their families, their names, and their enterprises by joining an aristocracy and gathering entails, thus establishing a close connection between monarchy and nobility. Failure to train heirs to manage family businesses and assets, combined with structural weaknesses in the economy, vitiated both the powerful families and the government that supported them. Beginning most dramatically with the confiscation of the pious funds (Consolidación) in 1804, when the crown expropriated about 1 million pesos from the money that had been used to support clergy through chantries, and ending with the Wars of Independence, civil conflict threatened the state and a part of the bureaucracy and weakened the aristocracy and other elite families. The end of entails and titles weakened the fragile supports that had preserved the colonial aristocracy. The fabric of monarchical institutions was destroyed. Only the patriarchal family, elite solidarity, and the extraordinary wealth of the Jesuit haciendas sustained the remnants of the Regla family.

The weakening of this noble family provided avenues to some prosperity for other, less exalted families and permitted the rise of smaller property owners and opportunities for the middle class in both town and country. But new powerful families arose in the nineteenth century, some of them with eighteenth-century roots. The tradition of strong patriarchs formed during the colonial period continued into the twentieth century. While the Reglas had dynastic continuity, their economic fortunes suffered.

During the lifetime of the third count, some political events that might have been disasters ended by advantaging the family. The government moved the Monte de Piedad to its location in the central square in Mexico. What might have been a difficulty ended by providing them with an even more advantageous site. The family's decision to rent their mines to a British company provided 16,000 pesos a year in rent. In fact, the independence of Mexico and the legends of her enormous mineral wealth attracted the attention of Europeans and North Americans, and diplomats and potential investors began to visit Mexico. Several travelers wrote extensively about the silver mines of the grandfather, the first count of Regla. The suppression of the entails meant that the third count could divest himself of land as the demands of an upper-class lifestyle and the education of his sons necessitated more cash. This could be obtained only by the sale of land— at times voluntarily, at other times forced. These sales provided Pedro José María, the third count of Regla, with cash, but ended by lowering his income when he lost his agricultural lands. Shortly after his death, the mines were sold to a group of Mexican investors.[34]

Manuel Romero de Terreros (1818–78), the third son of Pedro José María, struggled to preserve the family property through judicious marriages of his daughters, striving to make astute political decisions when the violence of post-independence Mexico rendered such calculations uncertain. Although the factional wars often benefited smaller landowners (as well as the military, those with cash, politicians, and some foreigners), men like Manuel Romero de Terreros, heirs to declining and mishandled fortunes to be shared among sons, ended their lives as insecure and perhaps even impoverished members of the upper class.

CONCLUSION

Ambiguous Legacy

*Regla always viewed laziness with mortal aversion and found
the bread made from his own hands to be sweet and tasty, and [he]
enjoyed the fruit of his own work.*
—Ruiz y Villafranca y Cárdenas, *Sermón*

Regla lived out a dream that young immigrants from Spain cherished and treasured. Born into poverty, like many eighteenth-century immigrants, he was one of the few who became wealthy. He succeeded in becoming the richest man in his new country and close to the richest in Spain; perhaps if we were to count the silver that passed through his hands, he might have been the wealthiest man in the Atlantic world.

If we were to imagine Regla's evaluation of his own legacy, he would probably have considered himself a successful man, a good subject of the king, a faithful member of the church, a good husband, father, and a friend of his friends. He would probably have considered himself a just employer—fair to his employees without indulging in any emotional weakness that would endanger the proper relationship between master and worker.

He may not have been so pleased about the future of his descendants. Although the silver mines had periods of both prosperity and depression in the centuries after his death, they could not produce enough ore to sustain a large elite family forever and eventually drained family resources. But however much the family's wealth declined, Regla's name lived on, marking the region in multiple ways. The Regla name became a defining appellation to all sorts of businesses and haciendas: the refining hacienda of San Miguel Archangel became San Miguel Regla, El Salto became Santa María Regla, and even the former hacienda of San Antonio, which was flooded by the electric power company around 1940, is known in local memory as San Antonio Regla. Regla's portrait still decorates the halls of the Hotel San Miguel Regla, and commercial establishments in the town of Huasca bear his name.

Although it might not have pleased him that the family's control lasted only a little more than a century, compared with other mining or agricultural families of the colonial period, such as the Fagoagas, the Adalids, the Bordas, and the Obregóns, the Terreros family still exists in Mexico and also in Spain as notable presences because of the work of the first count of Regla. Heirs continue to validate all the titles that Regla had established with the crown. Perhaps the only comparable mining figure in colonial Hispanic America is Antonio López de Quiroga, the most successful, innovative, and daring silver-mining entrepreneur of the mines of Potosí in South America.[1]

Regla's charities constituted the aspect of his legacy of which he would have been most proud. But here also, the legacy dwindled. He dedicated many of his charities to the recital of Masses for the repose of his soul and that of his family, an exercise of devotion that had the practical consequence of supporting the church and his own relatives who came to enjoy the chaplaincies dedicated to reciting Masses. In addition, instead of building a flamboyant church, Regla used his charitable expenditures to provide dowries for nuns, to give alms to religious organizations, and to expand the size of existing friaries. These contributions left far less impressive physical monuments than those of other eighteenth-century wealthy miners, but they expressed values of concern for the needy required by members of the lay or Third Order of the Franciscans. At his funeral services, the friar spoke of his many anonymous gifts to nuns and convents.

Did Regla continue to consider himself a peninsular, even though he had married into an old aristocratic creole family and fathered creole sons and daughters? As a peninsular, he enjoyed an elevated social position. He and his principal mining partners, Bustamante and Valleameno, married younger creole women who produced children almost annually. He sent his sons to be educated in Spain and did not arrange the marriage of any of his four daughters.

Regla employed both creoles and peninsulares in his enterprises, and both his Spanish contacts and Mexican family and friends often wrote recommending one or another person to him. He depended on both groups. At one point, he went to a great deal of trouble to bring peninsular Franciscan friars from Spain to Mexico. By contrast, in the biography of Regla written by his great-great-great grandson, Manuel Romero de Terreros, there is an undocumented anecdote recounting that the administrator of the Convent of Carmen had refused to accept a candidate that Regla had sponsored because he was creole and had been born in Mexico. Regla customarily donated a bag of 1,000 pesos on January 1 of each year to the Carmelites. When the administrator came to collect his annual contribution on the first of January in one year, Regla asked him to select from his warehouse one of the bags of 1,000 peso coins that did not contain Mexico pesos. Because that proved impossible, Regla told him that the coins were Mexican pesos and that, being Mexican, they could not be received in the convent.[2]

His own definition of where he belonged is ambiguous. He was not a creole. He did not want his sons to grow up with the customs of Mexico, but he failed to make other arrangements soon enough. He did not arrange the marriage of his daughters, thus preventing them from creating a new creole family. Nevertheless, he was not anticreole; in fact, he employed creoles in his businesses, formed partnerships with them, and even supported the Franciscan creoles.

Regla asserted his identity as one of the most important servants of the king of Spain, a faithful and active church member who provided in his will for Franciscan friars to visit his haciendas each year at Easter and to administer the sacraments and hear confessions for all those who lived there. He also considered himself a good and generous husband, sending expensive jewelry to his wife and celebrating her after her death in the house he had purchased in Mexico City. We know that Regla was keenly interested in the material prosperity of his children, but of his affectionate relationship to them we know very little.

Regla fell into a pattern that existed before his ascent. He tried to eliminate the middle class or small mine owners when he could, but that was an inevitable result of the new cost of technologies needed to dig deeper into the earth to get minerals. Given the nature of technological progress, with the concentration of capital transferred into fixed works of mining and improved methods for refining silver, the triumph of men like Regla seems fated. The policies of the crown and its constant need for money also facilitated the rise of men like Regla, making possible their control over the mines and over land. During most of his and his son's lifetimes, governments favored larger enterprises and monopolies in the hands of wealthy Spanish merchants.

The eighteenth-century wars also affected him favorably. The first war, that of the Spanish Succession (1700–14), ended by making possible an era of peace in his birth community of Cortegana. The second war, that of the Austrian Succession (1740–48), favored provincial merchants over the large Mexico City merchant guild and facilitated much of Regla's initial success. During the Seven Years' War (1756–63) Regla became a wealthy silver miner, finishing his gigantic adit that made possible increased production of silver. He suffered from one incident in that war when his cousin was killed by Comanche Indians who also destroyed the mission that Regla had supported. In the war of the American Revolution (1776–83), which began just when his mining crisis started and which ended after his death, he contributed the money for a battleship that bore his name. After his death, the battleship was useful in Spain's continuing participation in European conflicts.

The count of Regla had many faces and different ways of appearing. How should one evaluate a man who, when he was sued over the seizure of a mine belonging to somebody else and was ordered to turn back the mine to its owner, invited the officials who issued the order into his house for dinner? This was also a man who negotiated in the mines with a group representing the workers with only a few assistants around him and with a large gathering of antagonistic mine workers surrounding them. Should we evaluate as brave or foolhardy a man who oversaw workers and attended Mass in one of his mines on the day of the major festival of the region when he knew that dangerous discontent prevailed among hundreds of men working all around him? Taking such risks confirmed his capacity to act like a man who could control any situation with his mere presence.

That calculation proved to be incorrect. After narrowly escaping death by stoning, Regla retreated into his refining hacienda and proceeded to acquire additional mining property, later buying more agricultural land in Mexico than any individual in his time. Although angered by rebellious workers, he proved undaunted in carrying out his entrepreneurial dreams and projects.

A person of great contradictions, he was sometimes known as a stubborn man with an insistent temper, but the friar who preached his funeral sermon emphasized his soft voice and gentle manner of speaking. Despite his spending on luxurious furnishings and clothing, a high-ranking Spanish official noted his humble black suit, typical of a man of moderate possibilities. Although he was parsimonious with workers and partners, as was a man like Henry Ford, he also had a reputation for generosity. He chose to have himself depicted in his portrait as a man with an outstretched hand; in the icons of eighteenth-century portraits, that gesture suggested a charitable man. After his death, in the publication of the description of the funeral services, his face was copied from the original portrait, with an image of his coat of arms at the top and laurel leaves, the symbol of praise and honor, at the bottom. The eulogy included a phrase from Psalms about fleeing from his enemies and taking refuge in the wilderness, which has also been translated as making a mansion in solitude, as Terreros did in his final years. These years were marked, in part, by his residence far from his active mines, a testament to his anger at the workers in the mines and at the government's failure to punish them adequately. A third rendition of the portrait made after his death and still displayed in the Monte de Piedad depicts him wearing a well-made black suit and a shirt with a lace collar, standing at a table with a few papers and books—rather like a mild-mannered man of affairs. All these portraits and visions contrast with those of other portraits of noblemen in Mexico who chose to be depicted in elaborate, highly decorated clothing with many symbols of nobility and national origin.[3]

With regard to the most controversial aspect of his life, his relationship with labor, can we evaluate Regla as a man who treated his workers ruthlessly, or as an individual who acted like other employers of the eighteenth century? There is some indication that he might have been a harsher taskmaster than other mine owners, but not necessarily an exceptionally cruel boss. He owned slaves and used them in the mines when other Mexican mine owners did not; he made as much use as he could of forced labor from Indian villages; he used press-gangs as often as he could obtain permission from the government and expected these men to capture many workers. When responding to accusations of bad treatment, he answered by indicating his concerns for the upper levels of the workforce, bosses, and captains of work gangs. He resented the workers' practice of buying expensive clothing and then gambling all night. Such behavior offended his austere nature. Yet there was also an unconfirmed report that mine workers mourned his death.

Regla seems to have fomented and advocated the repression of labor rather than mediation, a practice that had sometimes prevailed earlier. In the 1757 rebellion at Actopán, the authorities hardly punished anybody. After 1768, Regla paid for troops in Real del Monte; he also had obtained the right to appoint judges, who were not likely to be impartial in cases of disputes over labor. The exile of a priest, whom he apparently accused of helping the workers, created an example that warned the population that powerful mine owners had influential advocates and extraordinary powers.

Regla did, in fact, provoke rebellions from both forced laborers and free workers, but suffered some of this because of a tradition of worker militancy and independence in the mining region. Perhaps the geography of Real del Monte, which separated mine workers from the upper levels of administration, increased solidarity among workers. One of his contemporaries and colleagues, but also his enemy, the marqués del Valleameno, found him to be an unjust boss when he tried to deprive his workers of between one-quarter and one-third of their former pay. He might have replied, and did imply, that he paid wages when others did not, and that, in the language of early-twentieth-century American business, he had to meet a payroll and could have had problems with cash flow. Regla's aversion toward the workers might have encouraged them to be more militant. But would he have been so successful as a miner if he had been less intransigent as an employer? We cannot answer this question, of course, but to pose it suggests the existence of a vast gulf between workers' rights and employers' needs.

As to the issue of slavery, Regla had a commitment to resurrect the mines and could afford to purchase slaves in a period in which slavery in the Hispanic world bore no moral stigma. But some slave owners did not wish their slaves to be put to work in the mines, perhaps because of their close personal connection with them. Slavery was dying out in late-colonial Mexico, and slave owners tended to possess few slaves, who were largely used in households rather than in fields and mines. Regla's use of slaves in the mines indicates that he had the money to purchase slaves while other mine owners depended on a growing population to supply paid labor.

Regla's life raises the troubling issue of how to interpret a man who often did good in his charities, according to the customs of his time, but departed from our ideal concepts of the qualities that define a moral or virtuous life. Looking to times before his own, beyond his own time, and at the history of businessmen in the European tradition, we find similarities, for example with the thirteenth-century merchant of Prato whose life has been so elegantly described by Iris Origo and whose relations with his employees, servants, and slaves seemed also to lack charity and kindness. In fact, Regla was a unique combination of past practices combined with the forward-looking efforts of a merchant who combined "ambition, shrewdness, anxiety, tenacity, and greed."[4] He coupled risk taking and extravagant spending with parsimonious actions toward workers, employees, and colleagues. He could be generous toward the upper levels of his colleagues and their offspring, but through acts of charity, not by paying them earned money. His interest in his family and in the enterprise he ran differentiate him from a prototype of a certain kind of twentieth-century businessman whose aim is to make money and provide well for his family, but not necessarily to assure the continued success of the enterprise he heads. Regla did indeed care about the mines, although he ceased to work some of them at times because of his mistrust of the men on whose labor he depended. The mines were not simply an investment for him, but a kind of hallowed trust for the creation of wealth to be used to sustain his family, to provide for his charities, and to enhance the power of Spain.

In a larger vision of the historical role of silver in the world economy, Regla's and the crown's economic and industrial innovations take on a more moderate role, as the gold standard, industrial capitalism, financial markets, and globalization have reduced the role of silver and impoverished silver-producing communities. As William Schell, Jr., the recent historian of "Silver Symbiosis," states, "In the U.S. as well as in ancien regimes, silver was the standard of traditional, populist regimes while gold was seen as the money of international finance and of the elite."[5] Perhaps seeing Regla's role as a greedy merchant and exploiter of labor will recede in the twenty-first century, to be replaced by an understanding of him as a benevolent charitable man who represented the religious aspect as well as goals of economic progress of eighteenth-century life. We may also gain greater insight into the degree to which Regla was driven by the aspirations of his time: for personal fortune, honor as a nobleman, and the almost universal Western desire to leave a rich legacy for one's descendants. Perhaps one indication of this change has already been evidenced in the city of Pachuca: the fact that the museum and cultural center that had been named after Bustamante, whose reputation as a kindly employer has been emphasized by recent historians, now no longer bears his name. Pachuca is a place where the labor movement has considerable strength, and the museum could not be named after Regla, although his presence is palpable in the region that he controlled. But the importance of silver production to the whole area is marked by the memorial presence of old mining machinery placed at appropriate intervals along the highway entering Pachuca on the road from Mexico City.

Regla lived in the period of great prosperity of this region, so close to Mexico City, but still a backwater to the major tourist and industrial routes in all direc-

Fig. 17. Real del Monte in 1999. Photograph by Marco Hernández.

tions from Mexico City. Now Pachuca is a bedroom community for Mexico City, and Real del Monte has been painted in glowing pastel colors, known as a monument to the past (see Figure 17). A house that Regla purchased there a year before his death has a plaque on its facade memorializing him. In a period when the silver industry in Mexico is in one of its worst depressions, the memory of the days when Regla and his descendants tried to maintain its prosperity seems like a vision of an ideal past.

Appendix

List of the Children of Pedro Romero de Terreros, first Count of Regla (1710–1781) and María Antonia Josefa Micaela Trebuesto Alvarado Dávalos Orosco y Bracamontes y Dávalos, first Countess of Regla (1733–1766)

1. María Micaela Gregoria, b. May 9, 1757–d. 1817
2. Juana María Ignacia Josefa, b. May 16, 1758–d. 1762
3. María Antonia Manuela Silveria, b. June 20, 1759–d. 1788
4. María Ignacia Josefa Seferina, b. August 6, 1760–d. [?]
5. Pedro Ramón Mariano José, b. August 30, 1761–d. 1809
6. Francsico Javier María Ciriaco, b. August 8, 1762–d. 1778
7. María Dolores Josefa Gertrudis, b. February 18, 1775–d. 184[?]
8. José Maria Antonio, b. May 10, 1766–d. 1815

Abbreviations

AAFTNC: Antiquo Archivo de Fomento, Terrenos Nacionales y Colonización, Departamento Agrario, Mexico City, Mexico
ACLDS: Archive of the Church of Latter Day Saints, Salt Lake City, Utah
AGI: Archivo General de Indias, Seville, Spain
AGN: Archivo General de la Nación, Mexico City, Mexico
AGS: Archivo General de Simancas, Valladolid, Spain
AHCRMP: Archivo Histórico Compañía Real del Monte y Pachuca, Pachuca, Mexico
AHEQ: Archivo Histórico de Estado de Querétaro, Querétaro, Mexico
AHN: Archivo Histórico Nacional, Madrid, Spain
AHPJEH: Archivo Histórico Poder Judicial Estado de Hidalgo, Pachuca, Mexico
AHPM: Archivo Histórico Palacio de Minería, Mexico City, Mexico
AMRT: Archivo Manuel Romero de Terreros, Mexico City, Mexico
ANA: Archivo de Notarias, Aracena, Spain
ANC: Archivo de Notarias, Cádiz, Spain
ANM: Archivo de Notarias, Mexico City, Mexico
AXA: Archivo ex-ayuntamiento, Mexico City, Mexico
BLAC: Benson Latin American Collection, University of Texas, Austin, Texas
BNMA: Biblioteca Nacional, Madrid, Spain
BNME: Biblioteca Nacional, Mexico City, Mexico
CHLA: *Cambridge History of Latin America*
corr.: correspondencia
ELAHC: *Encyclopedia of Latin American History and Culture*
exp.: expediente
INAH: Instituto Nacional de Antropología y Historia, Mexico City, Mexico
leg.: legajo
LAMM: Latin American Ms. Mexico, Lilly Library, Indiana University
MNH: Museo Nacional de Historia, Mexico City, Mexico
PCR: Papeles del Conde de Regla, Washington State University, Pullman, Washington
Probert Coll.: Lilly and Alan Probert Collection, Benson Latin American Collection, University of Texas, Austin, Texas
UNAM: Universidad Nacional Autónoma de México, Mexico City, Mexico

Notes

PROLOGUE

1. Castro Santa Anna, *Diario*, 5:243 (May 5, 1754).
2. Leonard, *Baroque Times*, 118–19; Curcio-Nagy, "Spectacle in Colonial Mexico," 3, 52, passim.
3. Ramírez Montes and Iturrate, *Un ilustre ayalés*, 20–30.
4. Navarrete, *Relación peregrina*, 48.
5. Ibid., 82. Poem translated by Ruth Morales.
6. Calderón de la Barca, *Life in Mexico*, 261–66, for a description of such elaborate ceremonies.

INTRODUCTION

1. Contemporaries referred to him as Pedro Terreros until he received the title "Count of Regla," and I have followed that usage.
2. AGN, Civil, 2242; AHCRMP, Cartas de Monjas, ca. 1757.
3. Ruiz y Villafranca y Cárdenas, *Sermón*, 15, 18, passim.
4. J. Romero de Terreros, *Apuntes biográficos*, 17–18.
5. Marroquí, *Ciudad de México*, 2:449.
6. M. Romero de Terreros, *El conde de Regla*, 170–71.
7. Probert, "Pedro Romero de Terreros."
8. Chávez Orozco, *Conflicto de trabajo*, 12, 13, 18.
9. Ladd, *Strike*, 26, 98.
10. Ramos, *Tu eres Pedro*. Ramos's book, though interesting and well written, was published without following the scholarly practice of documenting sources.
11. Brading, *Miners and Merchants*, 254. AGI, México, leg. 2251, Informe fiscal, May 30, 1764.
12. Randall, *Real del Monte*, 10–16.
13. Ladd, *Mexican Nobility*, 41.
14. Torales, *La compañía de comercio*; Torales, "La familia Ireata"; Torales, "Del nacimiento a la muerte."
15. Pazos, "Un español ilustre."
16. Garner, *Economic Growth*; Jacobsen and Puhle, *Economies of Mexico and Peru*; Morín, *Michoacán*.

CHAPTER 1

1. Casey, *Early Modern Spain*, 25.
2. Archive of Church of San Salvador, Cortegana, Libro de Bautismos, fol. 215r.
3. Rubio Mañé, "Gente de España," A29, no. 16; see Chapter 2, below, for Pedro Ochoa.
4. Romero de Terreros Castilla, *San Sabá*, 1–2; Ortega y Pérez Gallardo, *Historia genealógica*, vol. 1, "Duque de Regla," sec. 1, and vol. 3, "Condes de Regla," sec. 15.
5. AGS, Dirección General de Rentas, 1633, exp. 4; Candau Chacón, "Presencia y jurisdicción," 2:410; Pescador, "New World inside a Basque Village," 214.
6. AMRT, Testimonio . . .de Juan Vázquez de Terreros, 1735.
7. ANA, González Maestre, Dec. 29, 1736, 80–83.
8. AHN, Ordenes Militares, Calatrava 2258.

9. AGS, Dirección General de Rentas, 1633, exp. 4.

10. AHN, Ordenes Militares, Calatrava, 2258.

11. AHCRMP, Domingo López de Carvajal, Apr. 1765.

12. Ibid., Aug. 20 and 28, 1763.

13. I have used the word "entail" to refer to the Spanish *mayorazgo* throughout, even though the conditions for their establishment and continuation were different.

14. *Población general de España, con sus trofeos, blasones, conquistas heroycas* (1645), fol. 184v, quoted in Cortés, *Huelva;* Cortés, *Fuentes,* 19.

15. Dalyrumple, "Viaje," 3:712; Núñez Roldán, *En los confines del reino,* 34–35.

16. ANA, Cortegana, González Maestre.

17. Stein, "Concepts and Realities," 107; "Cortegana" in Madoz, *Diccionario,* vol. 9; Cortés, *Huelva,* 7–11; Cortés, *Fuentes,* 11–15.

18. Ponsot, "En Andalousie occidentale," 1203–4; Ringrose, *Transportation and Economic Stagnation,* 43–45.

19. Canterla and Martín de Tovar, "Hombres de Huelva," 1:307–27.

20. Madoz, *Diccionario,* 9:74–75.

21. Cortés, *Fuentes,* 13.

22. Domínguez Ortiz, "La crisis de Castilla," 437–42.

23. Lynch, *Bourbon Spain,* 8–10.

24. Moreno Alonso, "Los hombres," 13–14.

25. AGI, México, leg. 2789. It is also possible that Domingo López and Pedro Terreros met on the voyage or in the Spanish mercantile community in Mexico.

26. Pazos, "Un español ilustre," 10.

27. Cortés, *Fuentes;* Cortés, *Huelva.*

28. Heredia Moreno, *La orfebrería.*

29. ANA, Cortegana, González Maestre.

30. Cortés, *Huelva;* Heredia Moreno, *La orfebrería,* 1:291–301, 2:93–101; ANA, Cortegana, González Maestre, Dec. 29, 1736, 80–83; Maddox, *El castillo,* 71–72, 76–80.

31. González Rodríguez, "Armadores y navegantes"; Ramos, *Tu eres Pedro,* 31.

32. Pazos, "Un español ilustre," 105–9.

33. AMRT, Segundos Condes de Regla, Mar. 12, 1785.

34. Information from Juan Romero de Terreros, the present owner of the family home in Cortegana, Mar. 1999.

CHAPTER 2

1. Gemelli Carreri, *Viaje,* 2:246–48.

2. BLAC, Manuscritos, Ulloa, "Descripción."

3. Calderón de la Barca, *Life in Mexico,* 54, 56.

4. Wolf, "Mexican Bajío," 177–200; Moreno Toscano, "Economía regional," 114–23.

5. Moreno Toscano, "Economía regional," 115; Chevalier, *La formation,* 29.

6. Villaseñor y Sánchez, *Teatro americano,* 1:90-94.

7. Reyes, *Los caminos;* Super, *La vida en Queretaro,* 17; AGN, Civil, 2085, exp. 4, July 31, 1790.

8. LAMM, "Título del mesón."

9. Wolf, "Mexican Bajío."

10. Bazant, "Evolución," 489; Moreno Toscano, "Economía regional," 117–18; Super, "Querétaro Obrajes," 200–2, 211–14.

11. Humboldt, *Ensayo político,* quoted in Ramírez Montes and Iturrate, *Un ilustre ayalés,* 142.

12. Guillermo Prieto, quoted in E. Cervantes, *Santiago de Querétaro*, n.p.
13. Gómez Canedo, *Sierra gorda*, 15–29, 46–50; Zorilla, *El poder colonial.*
14. Wright, *Querétaro*, 29–31.
15. Wright, "Vida cotidiana," 13–43.
16. Ramírez Montes and Iturrate, *Un ilustre ayalés*, 105–7.
17. Zelaa y Hidalgo, *Glorias de Querétaro.*
18. INAH, Fondo Franciscano, 4th series, leg. 197, 1728.
19. AGI, México, leg. 546.
20. AGI, Indiferente General, leg. 107. Published version of this report written by Gómez de Acosta, *Querétaro en 1743.*
21. Super, *La vida en Querétaro*, 115–24.
22. ANM, Antonio de la Torre, Aug. 3, 1764, 213ff. Even as late as 1764, Pedro Terreros still invested in businesses as this contract with Buenaventura Taxonera indicates.
23. Serrera Contreras, "Ciudad de Santiago de Querétaro," 536.
24. AHEQ, Francisco Vitarica, June 23, 1723, 191r–v.
25. Ibid., Aug. 20, 1728; Heredia Moreno, *La orfebería,* 1:292; 2:95, 99; Heredia Moreno, "Valoración de la platería," 300, 302, figures 9, 11, 12, 13.
26. AHEQ, Francisco Vitarica, Aug. 25–26, 1728, 368v–69v.
27. Ramos, *Tu eres Pedro*, 14–21; Knaut, "Yellow Fever," 621.
28. Probert, "Pedro Romero de Terreros," 54–55; Ruiz y Villafranca y Cárdenas, *Sermón*, 9–10.
29. AHEQ, Francisco Vitarica, Mar. 3, 1733, 22.
30. Rubio Mañé, "Gente de España," 48.
31. MNH, Serie Micropelícula, Querétaro, Rollo no. 50, Salvador Perea, 1708, 69.
32. Gunnarsdóttir, "Religious Life and Urban Society," 54.
33. AMRT, "Testimonio," Querétaro, 1733–35.
34. AHEQ, Civil, 1732–33, no. 16, 1732.
35. AHEQ, Francisco Vitarica, Mar. 7, 1729.
36. Ibid.
37. Ibid., 104.
38. Alamán, *Historia de México*, I:19.
39. Brading, *Miners and Merchants,* 109–11.
40. AHEQ, Diego Antonio de la Parra, Oct. 10, 1734.
41. AHEQ, Felipe Suasnabar y Sosa, Feb. 17, 1742, 11; Mar. 1742, 18v–19r; Mar. 13, 1744, 21. AHPJEH, Ambrosio Zevallos y Palacio, Oct. 22, 1764; AHCRMP, Corr. del primer Conde, Juan Manuel Vázquez Terreros, 1752–64.
42. *ELAHC*, Schwaller, "Cofradías."
43. AMRT, Testimonio . . .de Juan Vázquez de Terreros.
44. Ruiz y Villafranca y Cárdenas, *Sermón*, 13.
45. AMRT, Testimonio . . .de Juan Vázquez de Terreros.
46. Serrera Contreras, "La ciudad de Santiago de Querétaro."
47. AHCRMP, "Cartas de Monjas," letters written from Mexico City and Querétaro between 1752 and 1768.
48. Ruiz y Villafranca y Cárdenas, *Sermón,* 13.
49. AMRT, Testimonio . . .de Juan Vázquez de Terreros.
50. AHEQ, Felipe Suasnabar y Sosa, July 8, 1743.
51. Ibid., May 12 and 24, 1747, 46r–47v, 50v–51r.
52. Socolow, *Merchants*, 60, 212.

53. AHEQ, Felipe Suasnabar y Sosa, July 8, 1743, May 12 and 24, 1747.

54. AHCRMP, "Cartas de Monjas," Querétaro, letters from María Luisa de San Salvador, c. 1758–60.

55. AHCRMP, Juan Manuel Vázquez de Terreros, Querétaro, 1758[?] (date illegible).

56. Ruiz y Villafranca y Cárdenas, *Sermón*, 14.

57. AHCRMP, "Esclavos del Conde de Regla"; AHEQ, Felipe Suasnabar y Sosa, Mar. 3, 1744, recorded the purchase of nine slaves for a total of 1,130 pesos.

58. Gunnarsdóttir, "Religious Life and Urban Society," 137–39.

59. AHCRMP, letters of Domingo López de Carvajal.

60. ANM, Antonio de la Torre, Aug. 3, 1764, 213v–18v.

CHAPTER 3

1. Ober, *Travels in Mexico*, 447; Almárez, *Memoria de los trabajos*, 75–76.

2. Gemelli Carreri, *Viaje*, 1:89.

3. Ilarione da Bergamo, *Daily Life*, 154.

4. Calderón de la Barca, *Letters of Fanny Calderón*, 237; Robertson, *Visit to Mexico*, 2:163.

5. Bakewell and Brown, "Mining," 4; *ELAHC*, 59–61; Brading and Cross, "Colonial Silver Mining," 552–55; Probert, *En pos de la plata*, 97–142.

6. Villaseñor y Sánchez, *Teatro americano*, 1:145–47. Mining towns were called *Real* in the colonial period because of special royal ordinances. Beginning in the mid-nineteenth century, the politically neutral word *Mineral* came to replace the idea of royal rules. Hence, Real del Monte, where Pedro Terreros's principal mines were located, came to be called El Mineral or El Monte. In recent years, the old name of Real del Monte, used in this study, has been gaining popularity.

7. AGN, Reales Cédulas Originales, 84, 293–301; AGI, México, legs. 1123, 2251, Testimonio, 143; AGN, Minería, 148, 142–44; Probert, "Pedro Romero de Terreros," 56–57.

8. Bakewell, "Mining," 2:151.

9. Humboldt, *Political Essay*, 3:215–16; *Geology and mineral deposits*, 155.

10. See Prologue, above; AGI, México, leg. 2251.

11. Gemelli Carreri, *Viaje*, 1:129, quoted in Brading and Cross, "Colonial Silver Mining," 549–50.

12. Bakewell, *Silver and Entrepreneurship*, 46.

13. Brading, *Miners and Merchants*, 171; AXA, Nobilario Primero, no. 8, Oct. 14, 1708, 151–55; Vargas-Lobsinger, "Ascenso social," 601–19.

14. AGI, México, leg. 1919, fol. 61.

15. Ward, *Mexico*, 2:142. Ward reported that in one year alone, Rodríguez de Madrid received more than 4 million pesos. The *Gazeta de México*, in February 1728, stated that was the amount produced in six years, indicating the uncertainty of many of these figures. Some of this wealth belonged to other miners and to profit-sharing workers.

16. "Pachuca," *Enciclopedia de México*, 10:6111.

17. Gamboa, *Comentarios*, 478.

18. AGI, México, leg. 1123, mentions a 1754 document referring to the "desertion and abandonment of the mines by D. Isidro"; AGI, México, leg. 2251.

19. Probert, "Episodes of Mining History," 15–18; AGI, México, leg. 1929, 72.

20. AGI, México, leg. 1129; Sarabia Viejo, *Juego de gallos*, 38–39; Cuello Martinell, "Renta de naipes," 291–94.

21. AGI, México, leg. 1129. In 1728, he paid for a celebration.

22. TePaske and Klein, *Ingresos y egresos*, 2:13–16.

23. AGN, Civil, 1425, no. 10, fol. 49.

24. Ibid.

25. AGN, Minería, 149, record of a Veeduría of 1732.

26. Ibid., 149 and 29.

27. Velázquez, "José Alejandro Bustamante"; Ramos, "Herencia de los Bustamante."

28. AGN Minería, 29, 340–55; AGI, México, leg. 2251, Pliego de condiciones, 1737–39.

29. Ramos, "Herencia de los Bustamante," 6.

30. Pajarón Parody, *Gobierno en Filipinas*; Probert, "Pedro Romero de Terreros," 58–61; Ramos, *Tu eres Pedro*, 10–11; AGN, Filipinas, I, exp. 1.

31. Both Alexander Humboldt and Henry Ward, writing at the end of the eighteenth and the beginning of the nineteenth centuries, reported that Bustamante had practical mining knowledge.

32. ANM, Raymondo González de Ulloa, May 2, 1749.

33. ANM, Juan Antonio de Arroyo, Feb. 17, 1748, 148r–50v. On that date he borrowed 25,000 pesos from his mother-in-law, which was secured by his estates in Zumpango de la Laguna.

34. AGI, Contaduría, 937, Nov. 22 and Dec. 14, 1740.

35. Randall, *Real del Monte*, 12–13; Trabulse, "Orígenes de la tecnología," 69–78.

36. Brading and Cross, "Colonial Silver Mining," 549; Bakewell, "Mining," 2:420–22.

37. AGI, México, leg. 2251.

38. AHCRMP, caja l, no. 1, 1746; AGN, Minería, 48, 148. The notarial documents for 1746 in the archive of the state of Hidalgo seem to be missing.

39. Gamboa, *Comentarios*, 381–82.

40. ANM, Juan Antonio de Arroyo, Sept. 27, 1743, 630–32; original document signed on Mar. 17, 1743.

41. AMRT, contracto; M. Romero de Terreros, *El conde de Regla*, 13–15; ANM, Juan Antonio de Arroyo, 1743, 630v–32v, 636–37; AGI, México, leg. 1123.

42. AHCRMP, letters of the first count, San Sabá, Nov. 18, 1751.

43. AGI, México, leg. 1123, undated.

44. Velázquez, "José Alejandro Bustamante," 341–44.

45. AHPM, "Representación"; Velázquez, "José Alejandro Bustamante."

46. AHCRMP, Fondo Colonial, caja 2; AGN, Civil, 2243, June 6, 1749, 4v.

47. Klein, *American Finances*, 80.

48. Klein, "Economía," 566.

49. AGI, México, leg. 2251.

50. Probert, "Pedro Romero de Terreros," 59–62.

51. AHCRMP, Fondo Colonial, caja 4, exp. 2.

52. They called the store "Tienda del Puente de Santo Tomás."

53. AGI, México, leg. 546. He claims to have had no profits until 1752; AGI, México, leg. 2251.

54. AGN, Civil, 2243.

55. Sarrablo Aguareles, *Conde de Fuenclara*, 2:320–49.

56. Ibid., 300–5; AGI, Indiferente, leg. 28, doc. 8, Mar. 10, 1747; AGI, México, leg. 1339, doc. 6; Gamboa, *Comentarios*, 44–145, 159–71; Brading, *Miners and Merchants*, 162; Howe, *Mining Guild*, 46–59.

57. AGN, *Bandos*, vol. 4, exp. 5.

58. AHPM, "Representación"; Velázquez, "José Alejandro Bustamante."

59. AHCRMP, Fondo Colonial, caja 2, exp. 3.

60. Brading, *Miners and Merchants*, 120–24, 173–77, 184.

61. AHPJEH, Agustín Joaquín de Zúbira, Nov. 2, 1748 (files of 1782 and 1785).

62. Velázquez, "José Alejandro Bustamante," 361.

63. ANM, González de Ulloa, 1749; Antonio de la Torre, May 7, 1765, 131–44.

64. AMRT, Libro de Caja, fol. 29, Dec. 12, 175[?] (date illegible).

65. Velázquez, "José Alejandro Bustamante," 361.

66. ANM, Juan Antonio de Arroyo, 1743, 636–37; AGN, Minería, 144, 1751.

67. AMRT, Primeros Condes de Regla, Mar. 28, 1753; Chávez Orozco, *Conflicto,* 71; Brading, *Miners and Merchants*, 176; AHPJEH, Nov. 3, 1748, Aug. 29, 1777; AGI, México, leg. 2240 (June 22, 1753, sale of Santa Brígida), Mar. 7, 1761.

68. AMRT, Libro de Caja, fol. 40. For other materials about Tello, see AHPJEH, Ambrosio Zevallos y Palacio, Oct. 5, 1761, 65v–66r; Sept. 18, 1762, 31v–33r.

69. AAFTNC, exp. San Juan Hueyapán; Couturier, *Hacienda de Hueyapán,* 72–73.

70. AGN, Minería, 65; Ramos, "Herencia de los Bustamante," 12.

71. Solano, *Antonio de Ulloa.*

72. BLAC, Antonio de Ulloa (17 Divulgación); see also Solano, *Antonio de Ulloa.*

73. BLAC, García Granados Collection, Ms., vol. 15, Antonio de Ulloa, "Descripción de parte de Nueva España," piezas sueltas, vol. 2, no. 4, fol. 188; AMRT, Libro de Caja, 40.

74. AHCRMP, letters of the first count, Manuel Fernando Bustamante to Regla.

75. AGI, México, leg. 2251.

76. Probert, "Pedro Romero de Terreros," 63. The Rosenbach Collection has a copy of the appointment of Valleameno as governor of New Mexico; Gamboa, *Comentarios,* 320–25; AGN, Minería, 48, Vínculos 203, 204, 209, 210; AGI, México, leg. 1123.

77. Riva Palacio, *México através de los siglos,* 802.

78. AHPJEH, Ambrosio Zevallos y Palacio, Nov. 2, 1748.

79. Probert, "Pedro Romero de Terreros"; Pedro Terreros later claimed that he began to receive profits from his mines only in 1752. AGI, México, leg. 2251.

80. Probert, "Pedro Romero de Terreros," 63; Gamboa, *Comentarios,* 320–25; AGN, Minería, 48; AGN, Vínculos, 203, 204, 209; AGI, México, leg. 1123.

81. Gamboa, *Comentarios,* 477.

82. AHCRMP, Fondo Colonial, caja 3, no. 6; ANM, Molina, Apr. 28, 1756, 152r–62v (refers to meetings of the workers and their obligations to work for all owners).

83. Probert Coll., Box 2\4.

84. Probert, "Pedro Romero de Terreros," 78.

85. AMRT, Miravalles, Mar. 24, Apr. 28, Apr. 29, and May 9, 1757; AGN, Vínculos 209, "Cuaderno Secreto"; AGI, México, legs. 1123, 1259.

86. Riva Palacio, *México através de los siglos,* 2:810; AGN, Vínculos 210.

87. Gamboa, *Comentarios,* 321–25.

88. AMRT, Miravalles, Apr. 1757.

89. Gamboa, *Comentarios,* 327–28; AGI, México, leg. 1087.

90. AGN, Vínculos 210; AHCRMP, letters of the first count; Servicios de los Villaverde a la casa de Regla.

91. AMRT, Miravalles, Dec. 13, 1759, and Apr. 25, 1760.

92. AGN, Tierras 2272, exp. 3, Jan. 10, 1766.

93. AHCRMP, Cartas de Monjas, letter written in 1752 by an *indigena* Capuchin; AGN, Minería, 29, contains a reference to a letter by the archbishop to the viceroy giving him this title.

94. Langue, *Mines,* 185.

95. Canterla, *Vida y obra*, Fig. 7, opposite 40.
96. Hausberger, *Nueva España*, 100.
97. Mullen, *Architecture*, 138; Bakewell, "Mining," 2:117.
98. Probert, "Pedro Romero de Terreros," 62; AGI, México, leg. 2251; Canterla, *Vida y obra*, 38; Humboldt, *Ensayo político*, claimed that it cost more than 2 million pesos (416,700 pounds sterling) 3:217.
99. AGI, México, leg. 2251. The viceroy was probably Bucareli.
100. Calderon de la Barca, *Life in Mexico*, 240–41.
101. Hausberger, *Nueva España*, 103.
102. Mullen, *Architecture*, 138–39.
103. Probert Coll., Box 2\4, record of a Veeduría of 1762.
104. AMRT, Primeros Condes de Regla, Mar. 28, 1753; AHPJEH, Zevallos y Palacio, Apr. 25, 1761; Chávez Orozco, *Conflicto*, 71.
105. Brading, *Miners and Merchants*, 183–87.
106. AMRT, Primeros Condes de Regla, copy of a letter written by Domingo López de Carvajal in March 1770.
107. Probert Coll., Box 1\24; AHCRMP, Luis Marrugat, Apr. 25, 1765.
108. The phrase, "bellicose habits of the Spanish nation," comes from F. A. Navarrete, *Relación peregrina*, the chronicler of the fiestas in Querétaro in 1737.

CHAPTER 4

1. Ladd, *Strike*, 19–28; AHCRMP, Fondo Colonial, caja 1, exp. 14; AGN, Criminal, 303.
2. AGN, Minería, 148.
3. Gamboa, *Comentarios*, 337; possible statement by Terreros in AGN, Minería, 148.
4. Bakewell, *Silver Mining and Society*, 125.
5. Valdés, "Decline of Slavery," 170–74.
6. Velázquez, "José Alejandro Bustamante," 343.
7. Ibid., 342; Brading, *Miners and Merchants*, 147–48; Ladd, *Strike*, 42–44.
8. Danks, "Revolts of 1766 and 1767," 257; AGN, Minería, 148, 332–33.
9. AHCRMP, letters from Luis Marrugat and Domingo López de Carvajal.
10. AGI, México, leg. 747, Aug. 4, 1724.
11. Ibid., leg. 2252.
12. Palmer, *Slaves of the White God*.
13. BLAC, Ulloa, "Noticia de Nueva España," 188; AGN, General de Parte, Complaint of Pachuquilla, 1779.
14. AHEQ, Felipe Suasnabar y Sosa, Mar. 13, 1744, refers to earlier purchases; AGI, Testamentaria, leg. 1323.
15. AGI, México, leg. 543B.
16. AHCRMP, Fondo Colonial, Cuenta de 1743; ANM, Rivera Buitrón, Oct. 31, Nov. 5, 11, and 23, 1743.
17. AHCRMP, Miravalles, Jan. 26, 1757, Nov. 8 and Dec. 13, 1761, Apr. 19, 1762.
18. AMRT, Libro de Cuenta, papel suelto de gastos, 1768.
19. ANM, Antonio de la Torre, June 18, 1770, Aug. 17 and Nov. 25, 1771.
20. AGN, Civil, 2243.
21. AHPJEH, Jan. 7, 1761; Ladd, *Strike*, 15.
22. AHCRMP, Fondo Colonial, caja 3.
23. Zavala and Castelo, *Fuentes de trabajo*.
24. AGN, Minería, 29, 330; AHCRMP, Fondo Colonial, caja 1.

25. Zavala and Castelo, *Fuentes de trabajo*, 1–8; AGI, México, leg. 743.

26. AGN, Minería, 149, 190–95; Ladd, *Strike*, 30, 165; AMRT, Títulos de la Veta Vizcaína.

27. AGN, Minería., 148, 470v; AHCRMP, Miravalles, Jan. 9, 1757.

28. AGN, Minería, 148; Ladd, *Strike*, 36–39.

29. Ladd, *Strike*, 33–34.

30. Taylor, *Drinking, Homicide, and Rebellion*, 124–25; Ladd, *Strike*, 39–40; AGI, México, leg. 747.

31. AGN, Minería, 148; Ladd, *Strike*, 39–41.

32. AHCRMP, letters of Domingo Trespalacios, May 1, 23, and 29, 1757.

33. Ibid., May 1, 1757.

34. Ibid., undated letter; AGN, Minería, 48, 583.

35. AGI, México, leg. 2251; AGI, Real Cédula, Sept. 29, 1764.

36. Ladd, *Strike*, 40–42; AGN, Minería, 148, 590–91, 461–64, 602; AGN, Minería, 149, 153–153v; AHPJEH, Alcaldía Mayor; AGN, Tributos, 7,15,37.

37. Velasco, "Trabajadores mineros," 280.

38. AGN, Minería, 148, 494ff; also Probert Coll., Box 1.

39. AMRT, Miravalles, May, 1757.

40. AGN, General de Parte, 41, exp. 173, fol. 121v; AGN, Indios, 66, exp. 152, fols. 194–95.

41. Haskett, "Sufferings with the Tasco Tribute."

42. AGN, Minería, 148, 494ff.

43. Ladd, *Strike*, 42–44; Probert, "Pachuca Papers"; AHCRMP, letters of the first count, Zimapán, c. 1772.

44. Ladd, *Strike*, 14–16; Ilarione da Bergamo, *Daily Life*, 158.

45. Martin, *Governance and Society*, 50.

46. Ladd, *Strike*, 52; Chávez Orozco, *Conflicto*, 37.

47. Chávez Orozco, *Conflicto*; Probert, "Pachuca Papers"; Danks, "Revolts of 1766 and 1767"; Ladd, *Strike*, 45–97.

48. Rodríguez, "Spanish Riots of 1766," 117–46; Castro Gutiérrez, *Nueva ley y nuevo rey*, 83–93 and passim, contends that the Real del Monte work stoppages should be differentiated from disorders in other parts of Mexico, such as in San Luis Potosí, Guanajuato, and Michoacán.

49. Ladd, *Strike*, 128; Randall, *Real del Monte*, 23.

50. Langue, "Trabajadores," 484.

51. Danks, "Revolts of 1766 and 1767," 204.

52. Probert, "Pachuca Papers," 104; Ladd, *Strike*, 55, Chávez Orozco, *Conflicto*, 57.

53. Bobb, *Viceregency*, 177–78.

54. AGN, Minería, 148; Ilarione da Bergamo, *Daily Life*, 160–62; M. Romero de Terreros, *Conde de Regla*, 93–101; Canterla, *Vida y obra*, 45–61; Probert, "Pachuca Papers"; Danks, "Labor Revolt of 1766," 143–66, Ladd, *Strike*, 45–84.

55. Ladd, *Strike*, 58–59.

56. Letter of Viceroy Croix to Francisco Gamboa, Sept. 10, 1766, quoted in Chávez Orozco, *Conflicto*, 215–16.

57. Navarro García, "Virrey Marqúes de Croix," 1:250.

58. Ladd, *Strike*, 60–68; AGN, Criminal, 303.

59. Danks, "Revolts of 1766 and 1767," 202–53; Ladd, *Strike*, 45–84.

60. See Chapter 8, below.

61. AGI, México, legs. 2252, 1130.

62. Hausberger, *Nueva España*, 98–112; Canterla, *Vida y obra*, 35–42; TePaske and Klein, *Ingresos y egresos*.

63. Unworked mines could be denounced and a new entrepreneur could receive title.

64. Ladd, *Strike*, 85–86; AGI, México, leg. 2252; Velasco Ceballos, "Administración," cviii; AHCRMP, letters of the first count, Domingo López de Carvajal, undated letter, c. 1765.

65. AGI, México, corr. de virreyes, c. 1772, letter of Viceroy Antonio de Bucareli to Minister of Indies, Julián Arriaga, about repayment of 400,000 pesos borrowed during the time of Viceroy Croix's reign.

66. Gálvez, *Informe*, 71; Priestley, *José de Gálvez*; Brading, *Miners and Merchants*, 143, 162–63; AGN, Minería, 148.

67. Bobb, *Viceregency*; Ladd, *Strike*, 91–96; AGN, Minería, 148; AGN, Real Cédula, 21, 27 (1772).

68. AHCRMP, Fondo Colonial, caja 1, no. 14.

69. Velasco Ceballos, "Administración," 2:362; Bobb, *Viceregency*, 177–78; Danks, "Revolts of 1766 and 1767," 202.

70. Gálvez, *Informe*, 72; AGI, México, legs. 1130, 1273; AGN, Historia, 133; Ladd, *Strike*, 104–9.

71. Velasco Ceballos, "Administración," cvii, 369.

CHAPTER 5

1. Arrom, *Women*, 143–49; Pescador, *Bautizados*, 145–62.

2. Socolow, *Merchants*, 37.

3. Langue, *Mines, terres*, 184.

4. Chipman, "Isabel Moctezuma," 214–27.

5. Couturier, "Viuda aristócrata," 327–39.

6. Couturier, "Women," 133.

7. AMRT, Miravalles, María Antonia to Pedro Terreros, June 2, 1757.

8. Ibid., June 2, 1757, Sept. 13, 1757.

9. Ibid., Sept. 13, 1759.

10. AHCRMP, letters of the first count of Regla, Luis Marrugat, Pedro Villaverde, Domingo López de Carvajal, 1759–66.

11. Couturier, "Women," 134. We cannot be certain that he wrote this letter.

12. ANM, Ambrosio Zevallos y Palacio, June 26, 1756; PCR, folder 94.

13. Casey, *History of the Family*, 89.

14. Lavrin and Couturier, "Dowries and Wills," 284–85.

15. Lavrin, "Sexuality," 72–74; Casey, *Early Modern Spain*, 205.

16. ANM, Juan Antonio de Arroyo, 1744, 762r–63v.

17. Pescador, *Bautizados*, 224.

18. AGN, Vínculos, 93, exp. 3.

19. Their youngest son presented a different and simpler description of the wedding ceremony. See AHN, Ordenes Militares, Santiago, no. 14.

20. Calderón de la Barca, *Life in Mexico*, 248.

21. AMRT, Cuenta de Eliseo Vergara, July 1756.

22. ANM, Ambrosio Zevallos y Palacio, June 1756.

23. AHCRMP, letters of Ana Terreros y Sosa begin c. 1752.

24. AMRT, Miravalles, Sept. 27, 1759.

25. AHCRMP, Miravalles.

26. Ibid., Dec. 13, 1759, and Dec. 1761[?].

27. Ibid., Dec. 1756.

28. Ibid.

29. Ibid., Mar. 1757.

30. *Padrecito* was a term also used by a supplicant to Pedro Terreros. She wished him to supply a dowry for her sister. See Chapter 7, below. Some of his relatives who were nuns sometimes used the term.

31. AMRT, Miravalles, Apr. 1757.

32. Ibid., Apr. 28, 1757.

33. Castro Santa Anna, *Diario* (May 4, 1757), 129; also see Chapters 3 and 4, above; and 1757 letters from the countess of Miravalle.

34. Lavrin and Couturier, "Dowries and Wills," 284.

35. AHCRMP, Miravalles, Apr. 1757.

36. See Chapters 7 and 9, below.

37. ACLDS, 035186, Baptisms, Sagrario, 1756–59; Castro Santa Anna, *Diario* (May 6, 1757), 134–35.

38. AHCRMP, Miravalles, June 26, 1757.

39. Ibid., letter of July 24, 1757.

40. AMRT, Miravalles, June 16, 1757. The countess wrote that "she continues to go out of the house, and I fear that people will talk; it is necessary that you return, as somebody might insinuate something."

41. AHCRMP, Miravalles, July 4, 1757.

42. Ibid., Cartas de Monjas, Mar. 23, 1757; AMRT, Miravalles, Aug. 11, 1757.

43. ACLDS, Baptisms, Sagrario, 035186, 1756–59.

44. AMRT, Miravalles, June 14, 1759.

45. Ibid., undated letter of 1757.

46. Couturier, "Women," 135–40.

47. AHCRMP, Miravalles, Aug. 20, 1761.

48. ACLDS, Pachuca, 266509, 108v; M. Romero de Terreros, "Segundo conde."

49. Calderón de la Barca, *Life in Mexico*, 237.

50. AHCRMP, Miravalles, Sept. 3, 1760, Cuentas de 1768.

51. Ibid., Feb. 6, 1761.

52. Ibid., "Se fuere necesario que vaya Angela, me avise," Feb. 28, 1763.

53. Ibid., Dec. 6, 1761.

54. Ibid., May 1, 1760, and Aug. 7, 1761.

55. Ibid., July 22, July 29, and Aug. 8, 1762.

56. Ibid., Nov. 19, and Dec. 9 and 23, 1762.

57. Ibid., Feb. 28, 1763.

58. Ibid., Nov. 17, 1763.

59. Ibid., Feb. 8, 1759.

60. M. Romero de Terreros, "Los hijos menores," 191.

61. AHCRMP, Miravalles, Nov. 1, 1759.

62. AMRT, Miravalles, Sept. 27, 1759.

63. Ibid., Primeros Condes de Regla, statement made sometime in 1770s.

64. AHCRMP, letters of Pedro Villaverde, Jan. 29 and Mar. 5, 1758, and of Luis Marrugat. See Chapter 6, below.

65. Lavrin, "Sexuality," 73–74.

66. Ramos, "Herencia de los Bustamante"; ANM, Juan Francisco Triguera, Jan. 19, 1734, 10v–12r; ANM, Juan Antonio de Arroyo, 1744, 277r–80v.

67. Socolow, *Merchants.*
68. Lavrin, "Sexuality," 72–78.

CHAPTER 6

1. AMRT, Miravalles, Jan. 19, 1763.
2. AHCRMP, Marrugat, Jan. 5, 1764; Villaverde, Jan. 18, 1764.
3. Tovar de Teresa, *Ciudad de palacios,* vol. 2.
4. Felstiner, "Larrain Family," 48.
5. AHCRMP, Miravalles, Jan. 21, 1764.
6. Ibid., Marrugat, Mar. 15, 1764.
7. Jiménez Condinach, *México,* eighteen of the introductory essays.
8. AHCRMP, Marrugat, Apr. 1764.
9. Ibid., Apr. 7, 1764.
10. Ibid., Apr. 18, 1764.
11. Ibid., May 26, 1764.
12. Ibid., June 1, 1765.
13. Ibid., Nov. 13, 1764.
14. Ibid., Aug. 16, 1764.
15. The copper paintings had been purchased by Madre Azlor, founder of the convent for the education of girls, La Enseñanza; AHCRMP, Marrugat, Sept. 27 and Oct. 11, 1764.
16. M. Romero de Terreros, "Casa del conde de Regla," 426.
17. AHCRMP, Marrugat, Nov. 13, 1764.
18. Jiménez Condinach, *México,* 14.
19. M. Romero de Terreros, "Casa del conde de Regla," 427.
20. Ibid.
21. Ibid., 429.
22. Ibid.
23. Couturier, "Philanthropic Activities," 28.
24. AMRT, Libro de Cuenta, 1768 sheet.
25. Ibid.
26. AMRT, Segundos Condes de Regla; AMRT, Libro de Caja; Couturier, "Women," 146.
27. AHCRMP, "Servicios de los Villaverdes a la casa del conde de Regla," 1782.
28. Ruiz y Villafranca y Cárdenas, *Sermón,* last eight pages.
29. Archivo de Churubusco, *Ciudad de México.*
30. Origo, *Merchant of Prato,* observed this characteristic behavior of a fourteenth-century Florentine merchant.

CHAPTER 7

1. Couturier, "For the Greater Service," 119–20, 135–36.
2. Ruiz y Villafranca y Cárdenas, *Sermón,* 22; PCR, *Testamentaria.*
3. McCloskey, *Formative Years.*
4. AGI, Indiferente General, leg. 1609; Probert, "Name in Spain," 52.
5. AMRT, Primeros Condes de Regla, 1764.
6. AHCRMP, Juan Vázquez Terreros, Apr. 21, 1763.
7. Castro Santa Anna, *Documentos,* 4:123–24; Brading, *Miners and Merchants,* 201; Langue, *Mines, terres,* 137.
8. AMRT, Cartas del Conde de Jala, Nov. 1791; AGN, Vínculos, 59, exp. 6.
9. AHCRMP, Cartas del Pedro Villaverde, Aug. 28, 1763.

10. Ibid., Cartas de Monjas, June 15, 1752.

11. Lavrin, "Female Religious," 165–72; Couturier, "For the Greater Service of God," 125–26.

12. AHEQ, Felipe Suasnabar y Sosa, 1743, May 20, 1747, 49r–50v. The latter document gives Bustamante power to begin procedures for establishing a convent in Mexico City.

13. BNMA, Ms. 494, "Testamento otorgado por d. Fernando Bustamante y Bustillo, July 1, 1721." The will may have been written in 1717.

14. Costeloe, *Church Wealth*, 1–60; Knowlton, "Chaplaincies," 421–23; Lavrin, "Role of Nunneries, " 371–81.

15. BNME, Fondo Franciscano, Ms. 2\52 (14).

16. Couturier, "Philanthropic Activities," 17.

17. Lavrin, "Indian Brides of Christ"; Gallagher, "Indian Nuns," 151–53.

18. AGN, Civil, 1432.

19. White, *Painting*, Appendix D, E, 221–26.

20. Weddle, *San Sabá*, 23–24.

21. AHCRMP, San Sabá, Nov. 18, 1751.

22. BNME, Fondo Franciscano, Ms. 15, 1755–56.

23. Romero de Terreros Castilla, *San Sabá, Misión para los Apaches*, 51.

24. Weber, *Spanish Frontier*, 188–91; Weddle, *San Sabá*, 112–14, 131, 139–40. Information from Elizabeth John in an interview in Austin, Texas, in early April 1999. AHCRMP, San Sabá, letter Fr. Alonso, 1757–58.

25. AMRT, Libro de Caja, 164.

26. BLAC, Hackett Transcripts, Box 394; AGN, corr. de virreyes, vol. 321, Apr. 21, 1759; PCR, *Testamentaria*.

27. AGN, Bandos 4, exp. 5, 8.

28. AHCRMP, San Sabá, Pedro Terreros' draft, July 25, 1758; Domingo López de Carvajal, Nov. 10, 1759.

29. AHCRMP, Domingo López de Carvajal, Aug. 20, 1759.

30. White, "Painting," opines that José de Paez and his workshop executed the painting, 92–105, 149–55; Sloan, *Untitled Painting*.

31. Based on notarial records in ACLDS, Puebla, and ANM, 1715–75.

32. AMRT, the document is dated 1743, but the handwriting appears to be from the nineteenth century.

33. Rumeu de Armas, *Historia de la previsión social*, 418–19.

34. Villamil, *Monte de Piedad*.

35. François, "When Pawnshops Talk," 123.

36. Alamán, "Disertaciones," vol. 3 (or vol. 8 of the complete works), 382; Pajarón Parody, "Bucareli," 2:582–86.

37. AGN, corr. de virreyes, first series, vol. 14

38. Villamil, *Monte de Piedad*, 44.

39. Rubio, *Nacional Monte de Piedad*, 23–26.

40. Statement by Mariano Velasco, official of the Monte, AGN, Historia, 303, 334r.

41. François, "When Pawnshops Talk," 126.

42. M. Romero de Terreros, *Conde de Regla*, 37–42, 105–28; Ruiz y Villafranca y Cárdenas, *Sermón*; AMRT, Primeros Condes de Regla; AHCRMP, Cartas de Monjas.

43. PCR, 1803.

44. AMRT, Primeros Condes de Regla; the contribution to Querétaro is in AMRT, Libro de Caja, 111v; M. Romero de Terreros, *Conde de Regla*, 119–20.

45. Pérez Galdós, *Trafalgar*, 19.

46. J. Romero de Terreros, *Apuntes biográficos;* Ortega y Pérez Gallardo, *Historia genealógica*, 219. AMRT, Cartas de Marqués del San Cristóbal, 1786; M. Romero de Terreros, *Conde de Regla*, 136–38.

47. Fernández, *Catálogo de construcciones*, 2:26; Vergara y Vergara, *Convento y colegio*, 19–20; Couturier, "For the Greater Service," 28.

48. ANM, Rivera de Buitrón, 1775, Testamento del Conde de Regla.

49. Couturier, "For the Greater Service," 131–32.

CHAPTER 8

1. Jiménez Condinach, 3, *Episodios mexicanos*, no pagination.

2. AGN, Minería, 48; AGN, Criminal, 297.

3. M. Romero de Terreros, *Conde de Regla*, 121.

4. Gálvez, *Informe*, 78–79, 85–86; Archer, *Army in Bourbon Mexico*, 16–17.

5. AGI, México, leg. 2252; Canterla, *Vida y obra*, 90–97.

6. Canterla, *Vida y obra*, 92.

7. AGN, Minería, 148; AHCRMP, letter from mine administrator.

8. AHCRMP, Fondo Colonial, caja 4, 1770.

9. Ladd, *Strike*, 91–94.

10. Ladd, *Strike*, 102; Ilarione da Bergamo, *Daily Life*, 161–65; AGN, Minería, 48; AGN, Historia, 133.

11. Ladd, *Strike*, 102.

12. Ibid., 98–110.

13. AGI, México, leg. 1241, letter of Bucareli, Aug. 27, 1773; AGN, Casa de Moneda; M. Romero de Terreros, *Conde de Regla*, 119; J. Romero de Terreros, *Apuntes biográficos*, 44–46.

14. J. Romero de Terreros, *Apuntes biográficos*, 17, 45; PCR, "Certificaciones relativas de la lexitimidad, . . .de Don Pedro José María Romero de Terreros . . .Rodríguez de Pedroso, 1803."

15. J. Romero de Terreros, *Apuntes biográficos*, 17, 45. He includes 200,000 pesos for the battleship.

16. Hausberger, *Nueva España*, 103; Canterla, *Vida y obra*, 41.

17. AHN, Escribanía de Cámara, Consejos, 20687.

18. Ladd, *Strike*, 83–84.

19. Ibid., 84.

20. Canterla, *Vida y obra*, 40–42. Hausberger, *Nueva España*, 81–103. Hausberger has marginally higher figures and percentages because he found more sources for the registration of silver than did Canterla.

21. Humboldt, *Political Essay*, 3:218.

22. Ladd, *Mexican Nobility*, 9.

23. Navarrete, *Relación peregrina*.

24. AHN, Ordenes Militares, Calatrava, 1752.

25. AGI, México, legs. 1123, 1265.

26. AGN, corr. de virreyes, second series, 1759; AGI, México, leg. 1123; AHCRMP, Domingo López de Carvajal, Sept. 26, 1768; AGI, Indiferente, leg. 1633, Bucareli to Armona, Nov. 26, 1771; AGI, México, leg. 2789.

27. AGI, México, legs. 1259, 1759; Burkholder and Chandler, *From Impotence to Authority*.

28. AHCRMP, Domingo López de Carvajal, June 17, 1760.

29. Ibid., probably around 1762.

30. PCR, folder 60.

31. AGN, corr. de virreyes, first series, vol. 14; Real Cédula, Aug. 31, 1766.

32. AMRT, Testamentaria and Albaceazgo de María Micaela Romero de Terreros; Couturier, "Women," 137, 147.

33. AGI, México, leg. 1814. Money arrived in Sept. 1777.

34. Couturier, "Women," 138–39; AMRT, Segundos Condes de Regla; AHCRMP, corr. de Marrugat, Nov. 25, 1763, and Jan. 5, 1764.

35. Gibson, *Aztecs,* 290; Velasco Ceballos, "Administración," 1:433; M. Romero de Terreros, *Conde de Regla,* 131; AGN, Tierras, 2033.

36. Konrad, *Jesuit Hacienda,* 68–69, Appendix A; Riley, *Hacendados jesuitas.*

37. Blood, "Historical Geography," 32, 54, 57, 66, 106, 108.

38. AHCRMP, Luis Marrugat, c. 1751.

39. Konrad, *Jesuit Hacienda.*

40. AGN, Vínculos, 178; Temporalidades, 205, about Villaverde's continuing dispute with the Jesuits over his pay; Tierras, 1556–57; haciendas of the novitiate of Tepozotlán; 2033–35, haciendas of San Pedro and San Pablo; AHCRMP, Servicios de los Villaverde.

41. AGN, Vínculos y Mayorazgos, 142, 45.

42. Domínguez, *Manifiesto;* Rico González, *Documentos;* AHCRMP, Francisco Villaverde, 1783.

43. Couturier, "Women," 135–39; Kicza, *Colonial Entrepreneurs,* 121–22; AMRT, Testamentaria.

44. PCR, Testamento; ANM, Rivera de Buitrón, 1775.

45. AHCRMP, corr. del primer conde, Domingo López de Carvajal, Apr. 1768.

46. M. Romero de Terreros, "Segundo conde de Regla," 349; Alvarez de Morales, *Ilustración,* 205–6; Simón Díaz, *Historia del Colegio Imperial;* Kagan, *Students and Society,* 40; AHN, Universidades, 673, 1314ff.

47. Ortega y Pérez Gallardo, *Historia genealógica,* 2:29–31, Real Orden of Nov. 6, 1791.

48. M. Romero de Terreros, "Segundo conde de Regla," notes that there was interest owed to Repárez from debts in Spain; AGI, México, leg. 1133; AGI, Indiferente General, legs. 1609, 2486. AMRT, Libro de Caja, fol. 126v.

49. AMRT, Testamentaria.

CHAPTER 9

1. AGN, Vínculos, 145, exp. 1, 1781.

2. Zúñiga y Ontiveros, *Diario y calendario,* Nov. 1781.

3. Ladd, *Mexican Nobility,* 184–86; ANM, Diego Jacinto de León, May 17, 1782; Rivera Cambas, *Governantes de México,* 1:423.

4. AGN, Vínculos, 145; Zarate, "Muerte," 192.

5. Couturier, "Women," 135; AMRT, Testamentaria; AHCRMP, Servicios de Pedro Villaverde, 1782.

6. J. Romero de Terreros, *Apuntes biográficos,* 29.

7. Zarate, "Muerte," 189–90, 192.

8. PCR, Testimonio del testamento, 1781 copy, folder 94.

9. Canterla, *Vida y obra,* 127; AGI, leg. 2252.

10. Information from José Vergara y Vergara and the friar of the church of San Francisco in Pachuca, Nov. 1999.

11. PCR, 194.

12. Konrad, *Jesuit Hacienda,* 380.

13. Maza, "Piras funerarias"; Zarate, "Muerte," 193–96.

14. Zarate "Muerte," 193–96; Ruiz y Villafranca y Cárdenas, *Sermón,* 11–38.

15. Couturier, "Women," 134, quoting the *Sermón* of Ruiz y Villafranca y Cárdenas.

16. AGN, Vínculos, 145; Couturier, "Women," 136; AGI, México, leg. 1161.

17. University of Chicago archives, box 2, folder 8, Confraternity Documents; ANM, Jacinto de León, May 14, 17, 1782.

18. ANM, Jacinto de León, May 14, 1782; ANM, Manuel de Ochoa, May 26, 1783, fols. 49v–57r.

19. AGI, México, legs. 1867, 1868; AGN, Tierras, 1153, exp. 3.

20. AGI, México, leg. 1511, in which officials discuss the possibility of their marriage to one of the daughters.

21. ANM, Manuel Puertas, Apr. 8, 1789, fols. 197–98; ANM, José Antonio Burillo, Apr. 26, 1787, fols. 206–8, and June 24, 1794, fols. 194–96.

22. AGI, México, leg. 1795; Brading, *Miners and Merchants,* 279–98.

23. Domínguez, *Manifiesto.*

24. AMRT, Cartas del Conde de Jala, Segundos Condes de Regla; Couturier, "Women" 141; M. Romero de Terreros, "Casa"; PCR, Carta Dotal de la Señora Condesa de Regla, 1785, no. 253 in Guido and Stark, *Regla Papers,* 23.

25. ANM, Manuel Puertas, 1788, fols. 133–36; ANM, Antonio Ramírez de Arellano, May 9, 1808.

26. PCR, folder 120; ANM, Francisco Calapiz, Oct. 11, 1788, Nov. 12, 1792; ANM, Antonio Ramírez de Arellano, May 28, 1800, Apr. 22, 1801.

27. Lavrin, "Execution of the Laws of *Consolidación,*" 47.

28. Couturier, "Women," 141–43; D. Navarrete, "Crisis y superviviencia"; Rojas y Andrade, *Elogio funebre,* 22, 23, 24; M. Romero de Terreros "Condesa escribe."

29. ANM. The second and third counts of Regla used two notaries active from the turn of the eighteenth century through at least the 1830s. They are Francisco Madariaga and Manuel García Romero; also, AHCRMP, corr. of Pedro Ramón and Pedro José María, the second and third counts of Regla.

30. AGN, Minería, 29; ANM, Antonio Ramírez de Arellano, June 4, 1794; AGN, Tierras, 2027.

31. AGN, Vínculos, 290.

32. Ladd, *Mexican Nobility,* 154–57, 160–61, 167; Calderón de la Barca, *Life in Mexico.*

33. J. Romero de Terreros, *Apuntes biográficos.*

34. Randall, *Real del Monte,* 27–31, 35–42, 49, 209–21, 221–26; Meyer, "Beisteguí," 126–29; Archivo Judicial (Mexico City), Testamento de Pedro José María de Terreros.

CONCLUSION

1. Bakewell, *Silver and Entrepreneurship.* López de Quiroga's fame continues locally, but not his family.

2. M. Romero de Terreros, *Conde de Regla,* 172–73.

3. Ruiz Gomar, "Pintura del retrato," 9.

4. Origo, *Merchant of Prato,* 18, 258–61.

5. Schell, "Silver Symbiosis," 131.

Works Cited

Ajofrín. fray Francisco de. *Diario del viaje que hizo a la América en el siglo XVIII el P. Fray Francisco de Ajofrín.* México: Instituto Cultural Hispano Mexicano, 1964.

Alamán, Lucas. "Disertaciones," 3 vols. In *Obras de D. Lucas Alamán,* 12 vols. Colección de Grandes Autores Mexicanos bajo la dirección de D. Carlos Pereyra. México: Editorial Jus, 1942.

————. *Historia de México.* 5 vols. 3d ed. México: Editorial Jus, 2000.

Almárez, Ramón. *Memoria de los trabajos ejecutados por la Comisión Ciéntifica de Pachuca.* México: Andrade y Escalante, 1865.

Alvarez de Morales, Antonio. *Ilustración y la reforma de la universidad en la España del siglo XVIII.* Madrid: Ediciones Pegaso, 1979.

Archer, Christon. *The Army in Bourbon Mexico, 1760–1810.* Albuquerque: University of New Mexico Press, 1977.

Archivo de Churubusco. *La ciudad de México y el patrimonio histórico: Proyecto del conjunto de San Felipe Neri. 52 República de el Salvador.* México: 1965, 1972.

Archivo General de la Nación. *La administración de D. Frey Antonio María de Bucareli y Ursua* II. México: Talleres Gráficos de la Nación, 1936.

Arrom, Silvia. *The Women of Mexico City, 1790–1857.* Stanford, Calif.: Stanford University Press, 1985.

Austen, Jane. *Pride and Prejuidice.* New York: Random House, 1950.

Azcue Mancera, Luis, et al. *Catálogo de construcciones religiosas del estado de Hidalgo.* 2 vols. México: Secretaría de Hacienda, 1940.

Bakewell, P. J. "Mining." In *The Cambridge History of Latin America,* 8 vols., ed. Leslie Bethel, 2:105–51. Cambridge: Cambridge University Press, 1984–91.

————. *Silver and Entrepreneurship in Seventeenth-Century Potosí: The Life and Times of Antonio López de Quiroga.* Albuquerque: University of New Mexico Press, 1988.

————. *Silver Mining and Society in Colonial Mexico, Zacatecas, 1546–1700.* Cambridge: Cambridge University Press, 1971.

Bakewell, P. J., and Kendall Brown. "Mining." In *Encyclopedia of Latin American History and Culture,* 5 vols., ed. Barbara Tenenbaum, 4:59–64. New York: Scribners, 1996.

Bazant, Jan. "Evolución de la industria textil poblana (1544–1845)." *Historia Mexicana* 13 (1962): 473–516.

Benedict, Bradley. *La administración de temporalidades y haciendas en Chihuahua colonial: 1767–1820.* México: Casa Londres, 1998.

Bethel, Leslie J., ed. *The Cambridge History of Latin America.* 11 vols. Cambridge: Cambridge University Press, 1984–91.

Blood, Richard. "A Historical Geography of the Economic Activities of the Jesuit Colegio Mayor of San Pedro and San Pablo in Colonial Mexico, 1572–1767." Ph.D. diss. University of Minnesota, 1972.

Bobb, Bernard. *The Viceregency of Antonio María Bucareli, 1771–79.* Austin: University of Texas Press, 1962.

Brading, D. A. *Miners and Merchants in Bourbon Mexico, 1763–1810.* Cambridge: Cambridge University Press, 1971.

Brading, D. A., and Harry E. Cross. "Colonial Silver Mining: Mexico and Peru." *Hispanic American Historical Review* 52 (1972): 545–79.

Burkholder, Mark, and D. S. Chandler. *From Impotence to Authority: The Spanish Crown and the American Audiencias, 1687-1808*. Columbia: University of Missouri Press, 1977.

Calderón de la Barca, Mme. *The Letters of Fanny Calderón de la Barca*. Ed. and annot. Howard T. and Marion Hall Fisher. New York: Doubleday, 1966.

———. *Life in Mexico during a Residence of Two Years in that Country*. Ed. Camille Destillieres Comas. México: Ediciones Tolteca, 1952.

Candau Chacón, María Luisa. "Presencia y jurisdicción eclesiásticas en la sierra de Aracena y sus aldeas a comienzos del siglo XVIII." In *Huelva en su historia*, 3 vols., ed. Javier Pérez Embid, 2:400–35. Huelva: Caja de Ahorros, Diputación, 1986–94.

Canterla, Francisco. *Vida y obra del primer conde de Regla*. Sevilla: Escuela de Estudios Hispano-Americanos, 1975.

Canterla, Francisco, and Francisco Martín de Tovar. "Hombres de Huelva en la América del siglo XVIII." In *Andalucía y América en el siglo XVIII en Actas de las IV jornadas de Andalucía y América*, 3 vols., 1:307–27. Sevilla: Publicación Conmemorativa del V Centenario, 1985.

Casey, James. *Early Modern Spain: A Social History*. London: Routledge, 1999.

———. *The History of the Family*. New York: Blackwell, 1989.

Castro Gutiérrez, Felipe. *Nueva ley y nuevo rey: Reformas borbónicas y rebelión popular en Nueva España*. Zamora: Instituto de Investigaciones Históricas, Colección Investigaciones, 1996.

Castro Santa Anna, José Manuel. *Diario de sucesos notables, escrito por D. José Manuel de Santa Anna y comprende los años de 1752–1754*. 6 vols. México: Juan de Navarro, 1856.

Cervantes, Enrique. *Santiago de Querétaro en el año de 1934*. México: 1934.

Chávez Orozco, Luis, ed. *Conflicto de trabajo con los mineros de Real del Monte, año de 1766*. México: Instituto Nacional de Estudios Históricos de la Revolución Mexicana, 1960.

Chevalier, François. *La formation des grands domaines au Mexique: Terre y société aux xvie xviie siècle*. Paris: Institut d'Ethnologie, 1952.

Chipman, Donald. "Isabel Moctezuma, Precursor of Mestizaje." In *Struggle and Survival in Colonial America*, ed. David Sweet and Gary B. Nash, 214–27. Berkeley and Los Angeles: University of California Press, 1981.

Chowning, Margaret. *Wealth and Power in Provincial Mexico: Michoacán from the Late Colony to the Revolution*. Stanford, Calif.: Stanford University Press, 1999.

Cortés Alonso, Vicenta. *Fuentes documentales para la historia de Huelva*. Huelva: Instituto de Estudios Onubenses, 1975.

———. *Huelva, población y estructura*. Huelva: Instituto de Estudios Onubenses, 1976.

Costeloe, Michael P. *Church Wealth in Mexico: A Study of Juzgado de Capellanías in the Archbishopric of Mexico, 1800–1856*. Cambridge: Cambridge University Press, 1967.

Couturier Edith. "Family and Fortune: The Origins of an Entrepreneurial Career in Eighteenth Century Andalucía and Querétaro, the Case of Pedro Romero de Terreros: 1710–1740." *Latin American Essays* 2, Middle Atlantic Council of Latin American Studies ll (1989): 61–75.

———. "For the Greater Service of God: Women's Philanthropy in Colonial Mexico." In *Lady Bountiful Revisited: Women, Philanthropy, and Power in Colonial Mexico*. New Brunswick, N.J.: Rutgers University Press, 1990.

———. "The Philanthropic Activities of Pedro Romero de Terreros: First Count of Regla." *The Americas* 32 (1975): 13–30.

———. *La hacienda de Hueyapán, 1550–1936*. México: SepSetentas #103, 1976.

———. "Una viuda aristócrata en Nueva España en el siglo XVIII." *Historia Mexicana* 41 (1992): 327–63.

————. "Women in the Family of the Mexican Counts of Regla, 1750–1830." *Latin American Women: Historical Perspectives,* ed. Asunción Lavrin, 129–49. Westport, Conn.: Greenwood Press, 1978.

Curcio-Nagy, Linda A. "Introduction: Spectacle in Colonial Mexico." *The Americas* 52 (1996): 275–86.

Cuello Martinell, María Angeles. "La renta de naipes en Nueva España." *Anuario Escuela de Estudios Hispano-Americanos* 22 (1965): 231–335.

Dalyrumple, Sir Hugh Whiteford. "Viaje por España y Portugal en el año 1774." In *España vista por los extranjeros,* ed. García Mercadel, 3 vols. Madrid: Biblioteca Nueva, 1918.

Danks, Noblet Barry. "The Labor Revolt of 1766 in the Mining Community of Real del Monte." *The Americas* 44 (1987): 143–66.

————. "Revolts of 1766 and 1767 in Mining Communities in New Spain." Ph.D. diss., University of Colorado, 1979.

Díaz-Trechuelo Spínola, María Lourdes, et al. "Antonio María Bucareli y Ursúa, 1771–79." In *Virreyes de Nueva España en el reinado de Carlos III,* 2 vols., ed. José Antonio Calderón Quijano, 1:385-658. Sevilla: Escuela de Estudios Hispano-Americanos, 1967.

Domínguez, Miguel. *Manifiesto del derecho que asiste al Conde de Regla,al Marques de San Cristóbal . . .en la demanda de la Real Audiencia . . .suponiendo que el ramo de Temporalidades padeció lesión . . .en el remate que se hizo á dicho conde de varias haciendas pertenecientes a los colegios de San Pedro y San Pablo.* México: Zúñiga, 1795.

Domínguez Ortiz, Antonio. "La crisis de Castilla en 1677–87." *Revista Portuguesa de Historia* 10 (1962): 435–51.

Enciclopedia de México. Ed. José Rogelio Alvarez et al. 14 vols. México: Instituto de la Enciclopedia de México, 1966–77.

Espinosa, Isidro Félis. *El peregrino septentional . . .vida del venerable Padre F. Antonio Margil.* México: Hogal, 1737.

Felstiner, Mary. "The Larrain Family in the Independence of Chile." Ph.D. diss, Stanford University, 1970.

Fernández, Justino. *Catálogo de construcciones religiosas del estado de Hidalgo.* 2 vols. México: Secretaría de Hacienda, 1940.

François, Marie Eileen. "When Pawnshops Talk: Popular Credit and Material Culture in Mexico City, 1775–1916." Ph.D. diss., University of Arizona, 1998.

Frost, Elsa, et al. *El trabajo y los trabajadores en la historia de México.* México: El Colegio de México; Tucson: University of Arizona Press, 1979.

Gallagher, Ann Miriam. "The Indian Nuns of Mexico City's Monasterio of Corpus Christi." In *Latin American Women: Historical Perspectives,* ed. Asunción Lavrin, 150–72. Westport, Conn.: Greenwood Press, 1978.

Gálvez, José de. *Informe sobre las rebeliones populares de 1767.* Ed. Felipe Castro Gutiérrez. México: UNAM, 1990.

Gamboa, Francisco Xavier de. *Comentarios a las ordenanzas de minas 1761.* Facsimile. México: Porrua, 1987.

Garner, Richard. "Silver Production and Entrepreneurial Structure in Eighteenth-Century Mexico." *Jahrbuch für Geschichte* 17 (1980): 157–85.

Garner, Richard, with Spiro Stefanos. *Economic Growth and Change in Bourbon Mexico.* Gainesville: University Press of Florida, 1993.

Gemelli Carreri, Giovanni Francisco. *Viaje a la Nueva España.* Ed. Francisca Perujo. 2 vols. México: UNAM, 1976.

Geology and Mineral Deposits of Pachuca and Real del Monte District. México: Consejo de Recursos no Renovables, 1963.

Gerhard, Peter. *A Guide to the Historical Geography of New Spain.* Cambridge: Cambridge University Press, 1972.

Gibson, Charles. *The Aztecs under Spanish Rule.* Stanford, Calif.: Stanford University Press, 1964.

Gómez Canedo, Lino. *Sierra gorda, un típico enclave misional en el centro de México (Siglos XVII-XVIII).* Pachuca: Centro Hidalgüense de Investigaciones Históricas, 1976.

Gómez de Acosta, Esteban. *Querétaro en 1743: Informe presentado al rey por el corregidor Esteban Gómez de Acosta.* Ed. Mina Ramírez de Acosta. Querétaro: Gobierno del Estado, 1997.

Gonzalbo Aizpuru, Pilar. *Familia y orden colonial.* México: El Colegio de México, 1998.

González Rodríguez, Adolfo Luis. "Armadores y navegantes en la Carrera de Indias en Sevilla del siglo XVIII." In *Andalucía moderna: Siglo XVIII. Actas de primer congreso de historia de Andalucía,* 1:269–80. Córdoba: Publicaciones del Monte de Piedad y Caja de Ahorros de Córdoba, 1978.

Gould, Alicia R. *Nueva lista documentada de los tripulantes de Colón en 1492.* Madrid: Real Academia de la Historia, 1984.

Gunnarsdóttir, Ellen. "Religious Life and Urban Society in Colonial Mexico: The Nuns and Beatas of Querétaro." Ph.D. diss., Cambridge University, 1997.

Guido, John, and Lawrence R. Stark. *The Regla Papers: An Indexed Guide to the Papers of the Romero de Terreros and Other Colonial and Early National Mexican Families.* Pullman: Washington State University Press, 1994.

Haskett, Robert S. "Our Sufferings with the Tasco Tribute: Involuntary Mine Labor and Indigenous Society in Central New Spain." *Hispanic American Historical Review* 71 (1991): 447–75.

Hausberger, Bernd. *La Nueva España y sus metales preciosos: La industria minera colonial a través de los libros de cargo y data de la real hacienda, 1761–1767.* Frankfurt am Main: Vervuet Verlag; Madrid: Iberoamericana, 1997.

Heredia Moreno, María del Carmen. *La orfebería en la provincia de Huelva.* Vol. 2. Huelva: Diputación de Huelva, 1980.

———. "Valoración de la platería hispanoamericana de la época colonial en la provincia de Huelva." *Huelva y América: Actas de las XI jornadas de Andalucía y América.* 2 vols. Huelva: Diputación de Huelva, 1980.

Hill, Lawrence Francis. *José de Escandón and the Founding of Nuevo Santander: Study in Spanish Colonization.* Columbus: Ohio State University Press, 1927.

Howe, Walter. *The Mining Guild of New Spain and its Tribunal General (1790–1821).* Cambridge, Mass.: Harvard University Press, 1949.

Humboldt, Alexander von. *Ensayo político sobre el reino de Nueva España.* Ed. Juan A. Ortega y Medina. México: Porrua, 1984.

———. *Political Essay on the Kingdom of New Spain.* 5 vols. Trans. John Black. 1811; rpt., New York: AMS Press, 1966.

Ilarione da Bergamo, Friar. *Daily Life in Colonial Mexico: The Journey of Friar Ilarione da Bergamo, 1761–1768.* Ed. Robert Ryal Miller and William J. Orr. Trans. William J. Orr. Norman: University of Oklahoma Press, 2000.

Jacobsen, Nils, and Hans-Jurgen Puhle, eds. *The Economies of Mexico and Peru during the Late Colonial Period, 1760–1810.* Berlin: Verlag, 1986.

Jiménez Condinach, Guadalupe. *México: Su tiempo de nacer: 1750–1821.* México: Fomento Cultural Banamex, 1997.

———. *Episodios mexicanas.* México: Dirección General de Publicaciones y Bibliotecas, 1981.

Kagan, Richard. *Students and Society in Early Modern Spain.* Baltimore, Md.: Johns Hopkins University Press, 1974.

Kicza, John. *Colonial Entrepreneurs: Families and Business in Bourbon Mexico City.* Albuquerque: University of New Mexico Press, 1983.

Klein, Herbert S. *The American Finances of the Spanish Empire.* Albuquerque: University of New Mexico Press, 1998.

———. "La economía de la Nueva España, 1680–1809: Un análisis a partir de las cajas reales." *Historia Mexicana* 34 (1985): 561–609.

Knaut, Andrew L. "Yellow Fever and Late Colonial Public Health Response in the Port of Veracruz." *Hispanic American Historical Review* 77 (1997): 619–44.

Knowlton, Robert. "Chaplaincies in the Mexican Reform." *Hispanic American Historical Review* 48 (1968): 421–37.

Konrad, Herman W. *A Jesuit Hacienda in Colonial Mexico: Santa Lucía, 1576–1767.* Stanford, Calif.: Stanford University Press, 1980.

Ladd, Doris. *The Making of a Strike: Mexican Silver Workers' Struggles in Real del Monte, 1766–1775.* Lincoln: University of Nebraska Press, 1988.

———. *The Mexican Nobility at Independence, 1780–1826.* Austin: University of Texas Press, 1976.

Langue, Frédérique. "La convergencia de los intereses particulares y estates: El alboroto de 1767 en Nueva Galicia." *Temas Americanistas,* Universidad de Sevilla, no. 7 (1990): 14–17.

———. *Mines, terres et société a Zacatecas (Mexique) de la fin du xviie siècle a l'indépéndance.* Paris: Sorbonne, 1992.

———. "Trabajadores y formas de trabajo en las minas zacatecañas del siglo XVIII." *Historia Mexicana* 40 (1991): 463–506.

Lavrin, Asunción. "The Execution of the Laws of *Consolidación* in New Spain: Economic Aims and Results." *Hispanic American Historical Review* 53 (1973): 27–49.

———. "Female Religious." In *Cities and Society in Colonial Latin America,* ed. Louisa Hoberman and Susan Socolow, 165–95. Albuquerque: University of New Mexico, 1988.

———. "Indian Brides of Christ: Creating New Spaces for Indigenous Women in New Spain." *Mexican Studies* 15, no. 2 (summer 1999): 225–60.

——— "The Role of Nunneries in the Economy of New Spain in the Eighteenth Century." *Hispanic American Historical Review* 46 (1966): 371–93.

———. "Sexuality in Colonial Mexico: A Church Dilemma." In *Sexuality and Marriage in Colonial Latin America,* ed. Asunción Lavrin, 47–95. Lincoln: University of Nebraska Press, 1989.

Lavrin, Asunción, and Edith Couturier. "Dowries and Wills: A View of Women's Socioeconomic Role in Colonial Guadalajara and Puebla, 1640–1790." *Hispanic American Historical Review* 59 (1979): 280–304.

Leonard, Irving. *Baroque Times in Old Mexico.* Ann Arbor: University of Michigan Press, 1966.

Lynch, John. *Bourbon Spain.* Oxford: Blackwell, 1989.

Maddox, Richard. *El Castillo: Politics of Tradition in an Andalusian Town.* Stanford, Calif.: Stanford University Press, 1993.

Madoz, Pascual, ed. "Cortegana." In *Diccionario Geográfico, Estadístico, Historico de España y sus possessiones de ultramar.* Madrid: La Ilustración, 1847.

———. *Diccionario geográfica de España.* Vol. 9. Madrid: Ediciones del Movimiento, 1957.

Marroquí, José María. *La ciudad de México.* 3 vols. México: La Europea, 1900–1903.

Mahr, Aaron Paine. "José de Escandón." In *Encyclopedia of Latin American History and Culture,* 5 vols., vol. 2, ed. Barbara Tenenbaum. New York: Scribners, 1996.

María de San José. *A Wild Country out in the Garden: The Spiritual Journals of a Colonial Mexican Nun*. Ed. and trans. Kathleen A. Myers and Amanda Powel. 1656–1719; rpt., Bloomington: Indiana University Press, 1999.

Martin, Cheryl English. *Governance and Society in Colonial Mexico: Chihuahua in the Eighteenth Century*. Stanford, Calif.: Stanford University Press, 1996.

Maza, Francisco de la. *Las piras funerarias en la historia y el arte de México: Grabados, litografías y documentos del siglo xvi al xix*. México: UNAM, 1946.

McCloskey, Michael. *The Formative Years of the Missionary College of Santa Cruz of Querétaro, 1683–1733*. Washington, D.C.: Catholic University Press, 1955.

Meyer, Rosa María. "Los Beisteguí: Especuladores y mineros, 1830–1869." In *Formación y desarrollo de la burgesía en México*, 108–39. México: Siglo XIX, 1978.

Moerner, Magnus. "Spanish Migration to the New World prior to 1810: A Report on the State of Research." In *First Images of America: The Impact of the New World on the Old*, vol. 2, ed. Fridi Chiapelli et al., 727–803. Berkeley and Los Angeles: University of California Press, 1976.

Moreno, Roberto. "Régimen de trabajo en la minería del siglo XVIII." In *El trabajo y los trabajadores en la historia de México*, ed. Elsa Frost et al., 242–67. México: El Colegio de México; Tucson: University of Arizona Press, 1979.

Moreno Alonso, Manuel. "Los hombres de la sierra de Huelva en las Indias." In *Huelva y América: Actas de las XI jornadas de Andalucía y América*, 3 vols., 1:11–25. Huelva: Diputación de Huelva, 1992.

Moreno Toscano, Alejandra. "Economía regional y urbanización: Tres ejemplos de relación entre ciudades y regiones en Nueva España a finales del siglo xviii." In *Ensayos sobre el desarrollo urbano de México*, 95–130. México: SepSetentas, 1974.

Morín, Claude. *Michoacán en la Nueva España en el siglo XVIII: Crecimiento y desigualdad en una economía colonial*. México: Fondo de Cultura Económica, 1979.

Mullen, Robert J. *Architecture and its Sculpture in Viceregal Mexico*. Austin: University of Texas Press, 1997.

Navarrete, Francisco Antonio. *Relación peregrina de la agua corriente, . . .de Santiago de Querétaro . . .describense las . . .fiestas*. México: Hogal, 1739.

Navarrete G., David. "Crisis y supervivencia de una empresa minera a fines de la colonia: La Vizcaína (Real del Monte), 1781–1809." Paper presented at the Fifth Reunión de Historiadores de la Minería Latínoamericana, San Luis Potosí, 1997.

———. "Propietarios y trabajadores en el distrito de minas de Pachuca. 1750–1810." Tesís de Licenciado en el Colegio de Historia, México, UNAM, 1972.

Navarro García, Luis. "El Virrey Marqués de Croix, (1766–71)." In *Virreyes de Nueva España en el reinado de Carlos III*, ed. José Antonio Calderón Quijano, 2 vols., 1:161–381. Sevilla: Escuela de Estudios Hispano-Americanos, 1967.

Núñez Roldán, Francisco. *En los confines del reino: Huelva y su tierra en el siglo XVIII*. Serie Filosofía y Letras, vol. 87. Sevilla: Publicaciones de la Universidad de Sevilla, 1987.

Ober, Frederick A. *Travels in Mexico and Life among the Mexicans*. Boston: Estes and Lauriat, 1884.

Ordenanzas de la minería de la Nueva España formadas y propuestas por su real tribunal. Ed. María del Refugio González. México: UNAM, 1996.

Origo, Iris. *The Merchant of Prato: Daily Life in a Medieval Italian City: Francesco di Marco Datini*. 1957; rpt., London: Penguin, 1992.

Ortega y Pérez Gallardo, Ricardo. *Historia genealógica de las familias más antiguas de México*. 3 vols. 2d ed. México: A. Carranza, 1904–1906.

Osante, Patricia. *Orígenes del Nuevo Santander (1748–1772)*. México: UNAM and Universidad Autónoma de Tamaulipas, 1997.

Osborne, Wayne. " 'Comentario' on Roberto Moreno, 'Régimen de trabajo.' " In *El trabajo y los trabajadores en la historia de México*, ed. Elsa Frost et al., 268–72. México: El Colegio de México; Tucson: University of Arizona Press, 1979.

Pagden, Anthony. "Identity Formation in Spanish America." In *Identity Formation in the Atlantic World*, ed. Nicolas Cany and Anthony Pagden, 51–94. Princeton, N.J.: Princeton University Press, 1993.

Pajarón Parody, Concepción. "Antonio María Bucareli." In *Los virreyes de Nueva España en el reinado de Carlos III*, vol. 2, ed. José Antonio Calderón Quijano. Sevilla: Escuela de Estudios Hispano-Americanos, 1967.

———. *Gobierno en Filipinas de D. Fernando Manuel Bustamante y Bustillo (1717-1719)*. Vol. 155. Sevilla: Escuela de Estudios Hispano-Americanos, 1964.

Palmer, Colin. *Slaves of the White God: Blacks in Mexico, 1570–1650*. Cambridge, Mass.: Harvard University Press, 1976.

Pazos, Manuel R. "Un español ilustre en México colonial: Don Roque Yáñez, 1735–1787." In *Archivo Ibero-Americano*, Segunda Epoca, 31 (1971): 97–172.

Pérez Embid, Javier ed. *Huelva y su historia*. 3 vols. Huelva: Caja de Ahorros, Diputación de Huelva, 1986–94.

Pérez Galdós, Benito. *Trafalgar*. Buenos Aires: Espasa Calpe, 1968.

Pescador, Juan Javier. *De bautizados a fieles difuntos, familia y mentalidades en una parroquia urbana: Santa Catarina de México, 1568–1882*. México: El Colegio de México, 1992.

———. "The New World inside a Basque Village: The Oiartzun Valley and its Atlantic Exchanges, 1550–1800." Ph.D. diss, University of Michigan, 1998.

Ponsot, Pierre. "En Andalousie occidentale: Systemes de transports et developpement économique (XVIe-XIXe siècles)." *Annales, Economies, Sociétés* 31 (1976): 1195–1214.

Priestley, Herbert Ingram. *José de Gálvez, Visitor-General of New Spain (1765–71)*. Berkeley and Los Angeles: University of California Press, 1916.

Probert, Alan. "Episodes of Mining History." *Journal of the West* (Apr. 1975): 5–18.

———. "A Name in Spain-the Condes de Regla." *The Augustan: An International Journal of Things Historical, Heraldic, and Genealogical* 18 (1976): 52–56.

———. "The Pachuca Papers: The Real del Monte Partido Riots, 1766." *Journal of the West*, no. l (Jan. 1973): 85–125.

———. "Pedro Romero de Terreros: The Genius of the Vizcaína Vein." *Journal of the West* 14, no. 2 (Apr. 1975): 51–77.

———. *En pos de la plata*. Pachuca: Compañía Real del Monte y Pachuca, 1987.

Pullan, Brian. *Rich and Poor in Renaissance Venice: The Social Institutions of a Catholic State to 1620*. Cambridge, Mass.: Harvard University Press, 1971.

Ramírez Montes, Guillermina, y José Iturrate. *Un ilustre ayalés en México: Juan Antonio de Urrutia y Arana (1667–1743)*. Vitoria: Caja de Ahorros Municipal, 1980.

Ramos, Agustín. "La herencia de los Bustamante o el verdadero fundador del Monte de Piedad y genio genuino de la veta vizcaína (Una aportación historiográfica)." Ponencia del Congreso de Minería, 1987.

———. *Tu eres Pedro*. México: Joaquín Moritz, 1996.

Randall, Robert W. *Real del Monte: A British Mining Venture in Mexico*. Austin: University of Texas Press, 1972.

Real del Monte: El esplendor de ayer para siempre. México: Gobierno del Estado de Hidalgo,1997.

Reglas y condiciones bajo las quales se ha proyectado establecer la Compañía de Minas en este Nueva España. De Orden de el Escmo. Señor Virrey. México: Imprenta del Nuevo Rezado de Doña María de Ribera, 1749.

Reyes, Aurelio de los. *Los caminos de la plata*. México: Universidad Ibero-Americana, 1991.

Rico González, Victor, ed. *Documentos sobre la expulsión de los jesuitas y ocupaciones de sus temporalidades en Nueva España (1772–1783)*. México: 1949.

Riley, James Denson. *Hacendados jesuitas en México, El Colegio Máximo de San Pedro y San Pablo, 1685–1767*. México: SepSetentas, 1976.

Ringrose, David. *Transportation and Economic Stagnation in Spain*. Durham, N.C.: Duke University Press, 1970.

Riva Palacio, Vicente. *México através de los siglos*. 5 vols. Barcelona: Espasa, 1888–89.

Rivera Cambas, Manuel. *Los governantes de México*. Vol. 2. México: Aguilar Ortiz, 1872.

Robertson, William Parish. *A Visit to Mexico*. Vol. 2. London: Simpkin Marshall, 1853.

Rodriguez, Laura. "The Spanish Riots of 1766." *Past and Present* 59 (1973): 117–46.

Romero de Terreros y Vinent, Juan. *Apuntes biográficos del Sr. D. Pedro Romero de Terreros, primer conde de Regla*. Madrid: J. M. Ducazal, 1858.

Romero de Terreros, Manuel. "La casa del conde de Regla." *Boletín de la Sociedad Geografía y Estadística*, 5a época (1913): 424–31.

———. *Una casa del siglo XVIII en México, la del conde de San Bartolomé de Jala*. México: UNAM, 1957.

———. *El conde de Regla: Creso de Nueva España*. México: Ediciones Xochitl, 1943.

———. "La condesa escribe." *Historia Mexicana* 1 (1952): 456–67.

———. "Los hijos menores de los primeros condes de Regla." *Memorias de la Academia Mexicana de la historia* 3 (Apr.–June 1944): 189–200.

———. *Pedro de Terreros, el primer español que pisó el continente americano*. México: Porrua, 1941.

———. "El segundo conde de Regla." *Memorias de la Academia de la Historia* 1 (1942).

Romero de Terreros Castilla, Juan M. *San Sabá, misión para los Apaches: El plan Terreros para consolidar la frontera norte de Nueva España*. Madrid: Real Sociedad Bascongada de Amigos del País, 2000.

Rojas y Andrade, Francisco. *Elogio funebre del Señor Don Pedro Ramón Romero de Terreros y Trebuesto y Dávalos, 27 Nov. 1809*. México: Imprenta de Jáuregui, 1810.

Rubio, Dario. *El nacional Monte de Piedad*. México: Talleres Gráficos de la Cía Editora, 1949.

Rubio Mañé, Ignacio, ed. "Gente de España en la ciudad de México año 1689." *Boletín de AGN*, 2d series (Jan.-Mar. 1966): 5–545.

Ruiz Gomar, Rogelio. "La pintura del retrato en Nueva España." In *El retrato novohispano en el siglo XVIII*. Puebla: Museo poblano del arte virreinal, 1999–2000.

Ruiz y Villafranca y Cárdenas, José. *Sermón que en las exequias funerales celebradas el día 28 de mayo del año de 1782 en el Colegio Apostólico de San Francisco de Pachuca a su síndico el Señor Conde de Regla, Don Pedro Romero de Terreros Llanto de la religion derramado en la muerte del Señor Pedro Romero de Terreros*. México: Zúñiga y Ontiveros, 1796.

Rumeu de Armas, Antonio. *Historia de la previsión social en España: Cofradías, gremios, hermandades, montepíos*. Madrid: Editorial Revista de Derecho Privado, 1933.

Sarabia Viejo, María Justina. *Juego de gallos en Nueva España*. Sevilla: Escuela de Estudios Hispano-Americanos, 1972.

Sarrablo Aguareles, Eugenio. *El conde de Fuenclara: Embajador y virrey de Nueva España (1687–1752)*. Vol. 2. Sevilla: Escuela de Estudios Hispano-Americanos, 1955–66.

Schell, William, Jr. "Silver Symbiosis: Re-Orienting Mexican Economic History." *The Hispanic American Historical Review* 81, no. 1 (Feb. 2001): 89–134.

Serrera Contreras, Ramón. "La ciudad de Santiago de Querétaro a fines del siglo XVIII, Apuntes para su historia urbana." *Anuario de Estudios Americanos* 30 (1973): 439–555.

Simón Díaz, José. *Historia del Colegio Imperial de Madrid.* Madrid: Instituto de Estudios Madrileños, 1992.

Sloan, Dorothy. *Untitled Painting of the Franciscan Mission of San Sabá in the Province of Texas.* Austin, Texas: Wind River Press, 1989.

Socolow, Susan M. *The Merchants of Buenos Aires: 1778–1810.* Cambridge: Cambridge University Press, 1978.

Solano, Francisco de. *Antonio de Ulloa y la Nueva España.* México: UNAM, 1987.

Stein, Barbara. "Concepts and Realities of Spanish Economic Growth." *Historia Ibérica* 1 (1989).

Suárez, Modesto. "Mansión en la soledad." *Reforma* (Mexico City), Jan. 17, 2002.

Super, John. "Querétaro Obrajes: Industry and Society in Provincial Mexico, 1600–1810." *Hispanic American Historical Review* 56 (1976): 197–216.

———. *La vida en Querétaro durante la colonia 1531–1810.* México: Fondo de Cultura Económica, 1980.

Tandeter, Enrique. *Coercion and Market: Silver Mining in Colonial Potosí, 1692–1826.* Albuquerque: University of New Mexico Press, 1993.

Taylor, William B. *Drinking, Homicide, and Rebellion in Colonial Mexican Villages.* Stanford, Calif.: Stanford University Press, 1979.

Tenenbaum, Barbara, ed. *Encyclopedia of Latin American History and Culture.* 5 vols. New York: Scribners, 1996.

TePaske, John J., and Herbert S. Klein. *Ingresos y egresos de la real hacienda de Nueva España.* Colección Fuentes. 2 Vols. México: INAH, 1986.

Torales, Cristina. *La compañía de comercio de Francisco Ignacio de Yreata (1767–97)* II. México: Instituto Mexicano de Comercio Exterior, 1985.

———. "La familia Ireata, Yturbe e Icaza." In *Familias novohispanas: siglos XVI al XIX,* ed. Pilar Gonzalbo Aizpuru, 181–202. México: El Colegio de México, 1991.

———. "Del nacimiento a la muerte en las familias de la élite novohispana del siglo XVIII." In *Familia y vida privada en la historia de Iberamérica,* ed. Pilar Gonzalbo Aizpuru et al., 423–36. México: El Colegio de México and UNAM, 1996.

Tovar de Teresa, Guillermo. *Ciudad de palacios: Crónica de una herencia perdida.* 2 vols. México: Fundación Cultural Televisa, 1990.

Trabulse, Elias. " 'Comentario' on Roberto Moreno. 'Mineria y Metalurgia.' " In *Ciencia y tecnología en el Nuevo Mundo,* ed. E. Trabulse, 147–72. México: El Colegio de México, 1994.

———. "Los origenes de la tecnología mexicana: El desague de minas en la Nueva España." *Ciencia* 31 (1980): 69–78.

———. "Régimen de trabajo." In *El trabajo y los trabajadores en la historia de México,* ed. Elsa Frost et al., 272–76. México: El Colegio de México; Tucson: University of Arizona Press, 1979.

Ulloa, Antonio de. "Descripción de parte de Nueva España." BLAC, Colección Genero García, vol. 15; Piezas Sueltas, vol. 4. Published ed.: Francisco de Solano, *Antonio de Ulloa y la Nueva España.* México: UNAM, 1987.

Valdés, Dennis N. "The Decline of Slavery in Mexico." *The Americas* 44 (1987): 167–94.

Vargas-Lobsinger, María. "El ascenso social y económico de los imigrantes españoles: El caso de Francisco de Valdivielso (1683–1749)." *Historia Mexicana* 35 (1986): 601–19.

Velasco, Cuauhutmoc. "Los trabajadores mineros en la Nueva España, 1750–1810." In *La clase obrera en la historia de México: De la colonia al imperio,* ed. Pablo González Casanova, Enrique Florescano, et al. 239–98. México: Siglo Veintiuno, 1980.

Velasco Ceballos, Rómulo. "La administración de d. Frey Antonio María de Bucareli y Ursua." 2 vols. 1: *Publicaciones del Archivo General de la Nación*, XXV. México: Talleres Gráficos de la Nación, 1936.

Velázquez, María del Carmen. "José Alejandro Bustamante y Bustillo, minero de Pachuca." *Historia Mexicana* 25, no. 3 (1976): 335–62.

Vergara y Vergara, José. *El convento y colegio de San Francisco de Pachuca*. Pachuca: INAH, 1986.

Villamil, Antonio. *El Monte de Piedad: Memoria histórica del nacional Monte de Piedad que por orden del c. director Mariano Riva Palacios ha reformado el c. contador Antonio Villamil*. México: Ignacio Escalante, 1877.

Villaseñor y Sánchez, José Antonio. *Teatro americano: Descripción de la Nueva España*. 2 vols. Facsimile 1951. México: Hogal, 1746.

Viquiera Albán, Juan Pedro. *Relajados o reprimidos diversiones públicas y vida social en la ciudad de México durante el siglo de las luces*. México: Fondo de Cultura Ecnómica, 1987.

Ward, Henry. *Mexico in 1827*. Vol. 2. London: Colburn, 1829.

Weber, David J. *The Spanish Frontier in North America*. New Haven, Conn.: Yale University Press, 1992.

Weddle, Robert S. "Cross and Crown: The Spanish Missions in Texas." In *Hispanic Texas: A Historical Guide*, ed. Helen Simons and Cathryn A. Hoyt, 24–36. Austin: University of Texas Press, 1992.

———. *The San Sabá Mission: Spanish Pivot in Texas*. Austin: University of Texas Press, 1964.

White, Richard Scott. "The Painting: *The Destruction of the Mission San Sabá*, Document of Service to the King." Ph.D. diss., Texas Technical University, 2000.

Wolf, Eric R. "The Mexican Bajío in the Eighteenth Century: An Analysis of Cultural Integration." *Middle American Research Institute*, vol. 17. New Orleans: La.: Tulane University, 1955.

Wright, David. *Querétaro en el siglo xvi: Fuentes documentales primarias*. Querétaro: Gobierno del Estado de Querétaro, 1989.

———. "La vida cotidiana en Querétaro durante la época barroca." In *Querétaro: Ciudad barroca*, ed. Juan Antonio Isla Estrada, 13–44. México: Gobierno del Estado de Querétaro, 1988.

Zarate Toscano, Veronica. "La muerte de un noble novohispano: El conde de Regla." *Historia Moderna*, no. 5 (1996): 183–99.

———. *Los nobles ante la muerte en México: Actitudes, ceremonias, y memoria, 1750–1850*. México: Colegio de México and Instituto Mora, 2000.

Zavala, Silvio, and María Castelo. *Fuentes para la historia del trabajo en Nueva España*. 8 vols. México: Fondo de Cultura Económica, 1945.

Zelaa y Hidalgo, José María. *Las glorias de Querétaro*. Obra re-impresa por Mariano Velázquez. Querétaro: Tipografía del Editor, 1860.

Zorilla, Juan Fidel. *El poder colonial en Nuevo Santander*. México: Porrua, 1976.

Zúñiga y Ontiveros, Felipe. *Diario y calendario manual y guia de forasteros de México*. Ed. Angeles Rubio-Argüelles. Instituto de Estudios y Documentos Históricos, Serie Cuadernos, no. 14. México: Claustro de Sor Juana, 1991.

Index